Gael Force
A Century of Football at Queen's

Football at Queen's University has one of the richest, and certainly one of the longest, histories of any sport in Canada; the Golden Gaels have been a presence in Canadian football at both the amateur and professional level since 1882. *Gael Force* traces this history, chronicling the team's ups and downs and integrating them within the history of the university, the country, and the sport in general.

Gael Force provides a wealth of interesting facts and engaging anecdotes as well as profiles and photographs of the coaches, captains, and players. Daub takes the reader through a century of Queen's football, from the first "Dominion" championship in 1893 with Curtis and his boys, through three consecutive Grey Cup wins in the 1920s, the 1934–35 victory of the "Fearless Fourteen," the 1955 season when Gus Braccia, Ronnie Stewart, Gary Schreider, Lou Bruce, Al Kocman, "Jocko" Thompson, and the rest of that "band of merry men" brought Queen's back into the limelight, the golden years of the 1960s, to the 1978 and 1992 Vanier Cup championship seasons.

Gael Force is a tribute to the long-standing football legacy at Queen's and an important historical and sociological study of college sport in Canada.

MERV DAUB is a professor in the School of Business, Queen's University. He played football at Queen's in the 1960s and was co-captain in 1965. He coached the Golden Gaels in the 1970s and in 1991, and is a member of the Queen's Football Hall of Fame.

GAEL FORCE

A Century of Football at Queen's

MERV DAUB

McGill-Queen's University Press
Montreal & Kingston • London • Buffalo

© McGill-Queen's University Press 1996
ISBN 0-7735-1509-7 (cloth)
ISBN 0-7735-1519-4 (paper)

Legal deposit third quarter 1996
Bibliothèque nationale du Québec

Printed in Canada on acid-free paper

Canadian Cataloguing in Publication Data

Daub, Mervin, 1943–
Gael force : a century of football at Queen's
Includes bibliographical references and index.
ISBN 0-7735-1509-7 (bound) –
ISBN 0-7735-1519-4 (pbk.)
1. Golden Gaels (Football team) – History.
2. Queen's University (Kingston, Ont.) –
Football – History. I. Title.
GV958.Q43D39 1996   796.335′63′0971372   C96-900503-2

Typeset in Palatino 10/13
by Caractéra inc., Quebec City

This book is dedicated to all those who have played the game at Queen's or have been associated with it. It is also meant for those who faithfully followed the team down the years, and for those who played against the Gaels.

Its publication has been made possible by the following friends of Queen's Football:

The Alumni Association
Mr Ed Andrew
Mr Don Bayne
Dr George Carson
Dr Bob Climie
Dr Cal Connor
Mr Jim Courtwright
Ms Elaine Forshaw
Mr John Gordon
Dr John Gordon
Dr Jack Kerr
Mr Bob Latham
Mr Fred Leaman
Mr Heino Lilles
Mr Hal McCarney
Dr Jay McMahan
Mr Bill and Ms Susan Miklas
Mr Kent Plumley
Dr Terry Porter
Mr Guy Potvin
Queen's University
Mr Laird Rasmussen
Mr Bob Stevens
Dr Jocko Thompson
Mr Peter Thompson
Mr Jim Ware
Mr Bill Wright

Contents

APPENDICES

Tables

Illustrations

Preface

The desire to do a history of football at Queen's University is a natural one inasmuch as Queen's has perhaps the richest and certainly one of the longest such histories of any sport in Canada. As well, tradition and history are important to Queen's. Several attempts to write its football history have been made over the years, but all came to naught, usually because of the serious illness or death of the writers. Whether this was a form of Gaelic curse on the whole project was something about which I speculated with some interest as I pushed along through what follows. But it might also simply have been a result of the amount of work involved.

At a conservative estimate, more than two thousand men have worn the uniform of the senior football team during the 104 seasons the game has been played at Queen's (to the end of the 1994 season, and not counting the war years when nobody played any games at all). At least two thousand more have played for intermediate and junior teams or have practised but never dressed for games. Still thousands of others have been associated with the game at Queen's – as team doctors, managers, trainers, equipment people, cheerleaders, members of the band, radio broadcasters, newspaper reporters, photographers, and heaven knows what else. How to capture their collective story is not easily conceived. Nor is the ebb and flow of this history as it sits against that of the university, against that of the sport (and sports generally) elsewhere in Canada and the United States, and even against that of Canada itself (which at times – during wars, for example, becomes highly relevant, to say the least).

I have been driven in my attempt to draw all this together by the awareness that time marches on. In this respect, the death in 1993 of the well-known coach of the Gaels, Frank Tindall, was a particular catalyst. So too was the persistence of Hal McCarney, a longtime assistant coach and Gael booster, who had been encouraging me to take on the task (in his usually delicate manner) for some time before Frank's death. "Moose" became downright insistent after it, and for good reason. Besides Frank, many others with whom I could have talked had passed away before I started this project, and rich sources for the history were lost with them. It thus became clear that to delay any longer would be inexcusable.

I also owe a great deal of thanks to Doug Hargreaves, until recently the head coach of the team, for putting his work on the Hall of Fame at my disposal, for many talks, and for reading parts of the manuscript with his excellent critical eye. In this latter respect, I also wish to express my thanks to Bill Miklas, Sr, a longtime assistant coach and academic colleague of mine, to Hal McCarney himself, and to Jake Edwards, former Gael player, coach, and for years director of athletics at Queen's. Their many editorial suggestions have improved the text immeasurably. I am also indebted to the people at the Queen's Archives, particularly Paul Banfield, to the Queen's Alumni office, and to Bill Miklas, Jr, for their research help. Cheryl Gross, the sports information officer at Queen's, was a constant source of data and help in other ways, as were Ed Deans and Bill Sparrow, who had done that job for years before Ms Gross's arrival. Access to the huge collection of photographs by Queen's two main football photographers, Wally Berry and Art Martin, was willingly given. Their work, and that of George Innes of the Department of Geography's Media V lab, who copied many of the photographs for the book, have enhanced the product immeasurably. The support of Principal David Smith in the early stages made starting the work financially possible. Lilly Lloyd of the School of Business did yeoman service typing the entire manuscript from my often indecipherable scribblings. And finally, Elaine Forshaw, my partner, provided patience, understanding, and support throughout the several years the project has taken.

My thanks go also to all those ex-players and others associated with the team who graciously gave their time in interviews. Their recollections and anecdotes added a personal dimension to the work which is critical to any history of this sort. My sincere appreciation goes as well to those who answered my ad in the *Queen's Alumni Review* with letters full of stories which have further enriched the book. Lastly, I would like to thank Don Akenson and others at McGill-Queen's University Press (particularly three anonymous reviewers of the manuscript, whose suggestions for improving the book contributed importantly) for their continued support for this project. (Had Professor Akenson been less of a basketball player than he is, he would perhaps have had the good fortune to have played football!)

Clearly, many people have contributed to the book. Where identified, they are responsible for their opinions. Otherwise it is the author at work. While I have tried to be careful, it is inevitable that things have been left out and mistakes made. Certainly, the interpretation and emphasis is always open to debate. One can but try and, in the end, appeal to the reader's sense of fair play concerning what he or she finds objectionable. I hope that most of it will be enjoyable and informative. Cha gheill!

Merv Daub
Kingston, Ontario

Gael Force

"All these won fame in their own generation, and were the pride of their time"
Ecclesiasticus 44:7

Introduction

It is fall in Kingston, and the annual explosion of youthful energy that accompanies the students' return to the university is almost palpable. Everywhere, in the sun that nearly always characterizes this time of year, there is excited talk among small groups of students – organized and exuberant attempts by the incoming class of one faculty or another to outcry, outswear, and generally "outgross" (to use a modern term) all other incoming classes in other faculties, whether by dress, colour of hair, or otherwise. The limestone campus shimmers in the early fall heat, the trees are lush and green, and everything that seems right in God's heaven generally blesses the scene with a sense of life as it should be in all its innocence.

Through this sea of colour a young man in a heavy leather gold jacket will sometimes be seen making his way. It is altogether too hot for such outerwear, but no one seems to notice the fact. Rather, what is made known to the new by the old is that "he's a Gael; he plays football." Often, nothing more is said, or need be. The force of the tradition that is football at Queen's, built up over more than a century of play, has developed from a constellation of factors: parents and grandparents, stories of Queen's that inevitably revolve around football in their time, a knowledge of championships in recent years carried across Canada by television, and assorted other elements that shape or characterize what the total Queen's experience means. The identification of Queen's and football is really rather a remarkable occurrence and has been for quite some time.

Just why this should be so is unclear when one reflects on it. In the first place, it is not surprising that the game came to be played at Queen's, for it was taken up virtually everywhere in North America at the same time in the 1870s. And it should not be forgotten that Queen's was always open to new games, as the early history of hockey in Canada also illustrates. The real mystery is the importance of football to the university over such a long period.

As the preface indicated, except for the war years of 1915–18 and 1940–44, football has been played continually at the university since 1882. That is more than a century of seasons. During that time, Queen's has grown from a college of about two hundred students in two buildings to a large modern university, one of top rank in Canada; the nation has experienced wars, depression, rapid industrialization, immigration on a large scale, and the possibility in recent times of breakup; the world itself has survived the possibility of thermonuclear war, and humans have been to the moon. Through it all, year in and year out with only those two exceptions, Queen's has played football.

Its fortunes in those seasons have regularly attracted the attention not only of the student body but also of those farther afield. In certain periods this attention has been nationwide, as it was, for example, in 1893, 1922–24, 1934–35, 1955, 1968, 1978, and 1992. At other times the stands were full and the local media enthusiastic, but the results were so poor that only the players' mothers kept the programs as souvenirs. In still other times the team played before stands devoid of students, with only a few die-hard alumni and other loyal fans in attendance. Even then, the outcome was made known by the media, discussed and ruminated over by all and sundry, and then recalled when the good times returned.

The question that arises from all this is why. Why is Queen's known in Canada and elsewhere for its traditions, its Scottish heritage, its high standards, its alumni attachment, and its football? In a way, the central part that football plays in Queen's reputation and myth is more American than Canadian. Indeed, the closest parallel may well be the meaning football has had to the University of Notre Dame in the United States. There is certainly no parallel in the two Canadian football programs – at McGill and the University of Toronto – that have an equally long, indeed slightly longer, tradition.*

It seems likely that the explanation at both Queen's and Notre Dame is similar and that it lies in the peculiar social psychology which sport addresses in the two institutions. Both universities are situated in small communities, and in their early days they struggled for recognition and respectability as institutions of higher learning. Both grew out of religious traditions that provided essential organizational cohesion and a sense of "us against them," supported by a strong conviction that "God is on our side." Both could draw on a strong base of raw, immigrant or first-generation males from a working-class background, who were eager to get ahead in

---

* The University of Western Ontario and such Western universities as Alberta did not start playing football until nearly fifty years later, during the late 1920s. Since then, many of them have done very well indeed.

sport as well as life. These factors taken together – the need to prove something on the part of a tightly knit group in an out-of-the-way place, with plenty of raw energy – meant that there was fertile ground, not just at the outset but on a continuing basis, for some institution to represent or give voice to the collective's sense of itself, and to do so with a special fervour that would make those elsewhere take notice.

The sport of rugby football was suited to this need far more than the equally new games of hockey and baseball. The latter was too genteel and was a summer game, played when the colleges were empty; the former was a cold weather game of too few numbers – not only of players but, before indoor rinks, especially of spectators, an all-important requirement. As we shall see, soccer (or association football, as it was then called) was played at Queen's as elsewhere. Indeed, it was the primary focus of Queen's sporting activity (along with hockey and the annual track-and-field days) until rugby football came along; but in the short space of ten years, 1882–92, it was supplanted for reasons which the newspapers of the time allude to obliquely as relating to "manliness," "collective endeavour," "careful forethought and clever execution," and a host of other late-Victorian synonyms for an assertive, virile, male activity which all accepted as their ideal. Soccer simply did not measure up. But one suspects that "collective action," such as swift running and the kicking and handing around of the ball in the presence of tackling, hacking, blood, bruises, broken bones – and the various other manifestations of the organized mayhem that was the early rugby game – was just the ticket on a sunny fall day. This was especially true at a time when the new nation of Canada was growing at a phenomenal rate, building railroads from coast to coast; when, in the United States, Andrew Carnegie was constructing the great steel mills at Pittsburgh, and when Otto von Bismarck was forging the enlarged German nation that was to cause so much grief in the years to come.

But all of this is getting well ahead of the story. First, we should pause to reflect a little on the game itself. Where does rugby football come from? Why is it called "rugby" football? And is it really "foot" ball or might it be better known, at least in the modern context, as "hands" ball or "carrying an oblong disc" ball?

THE NATURE OF THE GAME[1]

The history of ball games that bear some resemblance to the North American football of today can be traced at least as far back as the Greeks. Wakefield and Marshall[2] report that a game was played in which a player could handle the ball when it was to be kicked (indeed, there is mention of such a game in the *Odyssey*).[3] Such a "handling" game was also played by the Romans.

Called harpastum, it took place on a rectangular space marked with base-lines at either end and divided into two halves by a centre line. Participants were allowed to tackle or wrestle in an effort to gain possession of the ball, which was small and filled with hair.[4] As the Roman Empire expanded, harpastum went with it, to Gaul (France) and, after the invasion of Britain, to England, Ireland, Scotland, and Wales.

Evidence indicates that from the collapse of the Roman Empire until near the end of the eighteenth century, a period of almost fifteen hundred years, people continued to play the game but under a chaotic variety of rules and often with considerable brutality, especially in the Dark and Middle Ages. Rural towns or villages played one another, often with much violence and serious injury. On occasion, thousands were involved, men and women both, kicking a skull from town to town, for example.[5] Tenants were pow-erless against the misuse of their property and stood little chance of recovery for damages. Because local rules abounded (as they did everywhere during this period, except in the Roman Catholic Church) and because little was written down, sometimes handling the ball was allowed and sometimes it was not. No doubt "tradition" was a flexible servant; if the opposition was known to have one or two good runners who handled the ball well, then, when one played at home, no ball handling would be allowed, only drib-bling. Little in human nature seems to have changed, in this respect at least.

By the end of the eighteenth century, the game, with all its inherent rowdiness, was considered a lower-class sport.[6] There was one place, how-ever, where the upper classes did come in contact with it, and that was in the public schools of Great Britain. There it was viewed by the schoolmasters as a necessary evil which allowed the young boys to blow off steam from their studies.* To prevent total mayhem, it became necessary to organize the game, and it was at this point that the first modern separation of soccer and rugby began to develop. The paving stones at Westminister School, for example, ruled out any tackling, and consequently the dribbling game became important there. At Rugby, on the other hand, with its abundance of grass, a tackling, contact game was safer and so developed. Bally has given a particularly good description of the game at this stage, which is worth quoting at length:

---

* Indeed, it has been argued by some that it is perhaps the game that young boys most naturally play – one of "keep away," combined with jostling, fight-ing for possession, and passing to a friend, with much running around and a lot of yelling. All that would be needed to make it a sport, rather than just a game, would be a few rules, some way to decide who wins, and the presence of an arbitrator or referee.

Prior to 1840, rugby-style football matches were played on grass fields which were suitable for severe body contact. The goals at either end of the field were composed of two uprights and a crossbar. One unusual feature was that the field itself did not have any real boundaries and hence stationary scrummages were often ringed by spectators. Matches often occurred between players from a single school House and players from the rest of the School. One report described an early game in which 300 boys engaged, as "legalized mayhem" (Reyburn 1971). The boys, under direction of the senior, were divided according to their size. The large, heavy boys became the "chargers, bulldogs or players up," and were the forwards in the scrummage (Marples 1954). The smaller players were the "light brigade, dodgers or quarters," whose task was to wait for the ball to emerge from the scrummage. Finally, the fags were placed in goal and represented the goalkeepers, a remnant of the old dribbling game.

The essence of the game during the 1830s was the scrummage, the boys strained against each other and attempted to kick the ball downfield. Needless to say, many kicks that were aimed at the ball ended up on some poor opponent's shin. The art of "hacking" or kicking an opponent was an effective means of moving the ball and the opponents in the desired direction. Very occasionally, the ball would emerge from the scrummage and the swift backs would kick the ball downfield in a manner resembling dribbling. Since the offside rule applied, the players were not able to pass the ball forward with the foot. Thus a column attack developed in which the players ran more or less behind the ball dribbler. Once the ball had been kicked into the opponent's goal, the ball could be touched down with the hands. This entitled the scoring team to try a kick-at-goal. The task of the fags was to prevent such a touchdown from occurring, either by falling on the ball or by knocking down the man dribbling the ball. The latter method could be considered as a very early form of tackling. The only other time that handling was permitted was in the execution of a free kick. At this time, running-in or running with the ball was not an accepted practice. However, in 1823 at Rugby School, a young boy by the name of William Webb Ellis picked up the ball and ran with it. Wakefield and Marshall (1930) have described this incident and its significance:

> In the latter half of 1823 originated, though without premeditation, that change in one of the rules which more than any other has since distinguished the Rugby School game from the Association rules. A boy of the name of Ellis while playing Bigside at football that year caught the ball in his arms. This being so, according to the then rule, he ought to have retired as far back as he pleased, without parting with the ball, for the combatants on the other side could only advance to the spot where he caught the ball, and were unable to rush further forward until he had either punted it or placed it for someone else to kick, for it was by means of these placed kicks that most of the goals in those days were scored. But the moment the ball touched the ground, the other side might rush on. Ellis, for the first time,

disregarded this rule and on catching the ball, instead of retiring backwards, rushed forward with the ball in his hands towards the opposite goal.

This action was viewed with disapproval by the other members of the school. The importance of his action was not realized until almost twenty years later, after such men as Jim Makie, a great runner-in, made running-in popular. Nevertheless, Ellis' action was responsible for giving rugby the characteristics which distinguished it from the other games of football in England. Although running-in was legalized in 1841–42, it did not become popular as a form of attack until the 1860s.

In 1846, a set of rules were formalized in an attempt to standardize some of the features of play. Some of the aspects of the style of play of the 1840s and 1850s can be derived from these rules. The most important new feature of the game resulted from the legalizing of running-in or running with the ball. Nevertheless, dribbling the ball with the foot was still the main form of attack. The scrummage remained the predominant feature of the game because of the numerous players. When the ball did occasionally emerge, dribbling was the only form of attack because the rules forbade the player from picking up the ball from the ground and running with it. The only time that running was allowed was if the ball was caught directly from a kick because passing the ball was not allowed. Furthermore, heeling the ball out of the scrummage was considered illegal, which effectively neutralize any attempts at organized backplay. Hacking still remained the most important part of the game even if the rules did stipulate that a player could not hack above the knee, or with a heel, or while holding the ball carrier and hacking at the same time! One rule which was rather humorous was that members of a team were forbidden from standing on the crossbar to prevent a goal from being scored.

Another obvious peculiarity of the game was the length of the matches. Since the main feature of the game was the long, exhausting scrummages, the ball emerged very seldom and few goals were scored by the backs. The forwards were seldom able to push their opponents into their own end zone and then touch the ball down for a touchdown. For these reasons, games often lasted several days before the match was decided. Finally in 1846, the rules declared that the game should be drawn if no goal had been scored after five consecutive afternoons of play.[7]

While the story of William Webb Ellis single-handedly starting the modern game of rugby football may well be true, as the excerpt from Bally implies, it is more likely that there was a gradual recognition of the fact that there really were two different games involved and that rules were needed to regulate both. Dr Thomas Arnold, the progressive headmaster of Rugby, was one of those who recognized this and did much to structure the play in the early nineteenth-century.[8] Thus it is that the game came to be known as Rugby football.

Certainly, its development appealed to a growing sense of Victorian brashness and self-importance. Moreover, the British influence was spreading

throughout the world during this period. As in Roman times, football went
with the growing empire. There seems little doubt that rugby football was
introduced to Canada by British immigrants who arrived after the War of
1812.[9] Britain heavily garrisoned its colonies of Upper and Lower Canada
for years after that war in an effort to prevent the Americans from expand-
ing north across the border. Canals, roads, and railroads were built, settlers
were given land, and universities were started. Many of the newcomers
were officers of the army or navy, engineers, or others who had acquired
their training in England and had attended a public school. They thus knew
about rugby football and no doubt found it just the thing to while away an
idyllic afternoon "on the frontier." The natural violence of the game would
have been nothing out of the ordinary to the environment in which they
found themselves or to the professions they practised. Some of these people
were garrisoned in Kingston.

It is worth noting here that the game in the United States obviously did
not have the same direct origins as it did in Canada. Danzig,[10] in his book
on the origins of football in the United States, has little to say on the period
leading up to the end of the Civil War in 1865. He simply reports that all
the American colleges (ergo, all players in the United States) played association football (soccer) until the time Princeton played Rutgers (1869) in a
form of rugby, which was arguably the first such formal game of its kind.
After that, rugby gradually caught on, with Harvard leading the way.[11]
Soccer would be dead as the American college game by the 1890s, just as it
was in Canada. One can suppose, however, that the Americans could hardly
have been unaware of rugby, because of their trading and other relationships
with both England and Canada. In time, of course, and particularly with
the arrival on the scene of Teddy Roosevelt as president, it came to mean
the same thing to young Americans as it did to the Victorian British and
the brash Canadian colonists.* And even later, in this century particularly,

---

* Indeed, Frank Cosentino uses a quotation from Roosevelt as the introduction
  to his book *Canadian Football*. It goes as follows (one finds many other such
  references in the accounts of rugby matches): "It is not the critic who counts,
  not the man who points out how the strong man stumbled, or where the doer
  of deeds could have done better. The credit belongs to the man who is actually
  in the arena; whose face is marred by dust and sweat and blood; who strives
  valiantly; who errs and comes short again and again; who knows the great
  enthusiasms and the great devotions and spends himself in a worthy cause;
  who knows best in the end the triumph of high achievement; and who at the
  worst, if he fails, at the least fails while daring greatly; so that his place shall
  never be with the cold and timid souls who know neither victory nor defeat."

it has become America's game. Certainly, at the college level it is almost identified with life itself.

For a host of reasons, then, it was natural that Queen's began to play rugby football in the late 1870s and early 1880s. McGill was playing it, and very soon thereafter so was Toronto. The garrisons were playing; the new military college in Kingston was playing; professors were coming from England and Scotland who knew the game; and even the Americans – particularly the Americans – were playing. It was a game that was in a state of radical change as far as the rules of play were concerned, and it would remain so until the First World War and beyond (indeed, until the forward pass was well established; at that point, in the 1930s, the modern game is almost totally recognizable). Because of the speed of its adoption, it arguably fulfilled an important need in society at large for a sporting game of a certain type, and especially a certain time.

PARALLEL HISTORIES

In tracing the history of the game at Queen's, we shall come to see certain themes, or parallel histories, that had an effect on it. In the first place, there was the university itself. For this we shall rely on the histories of Queen's written by Calvin, Neatby, and Gibson.[12] We shall see that the university was often occupied with other things – especially finances – as it grew and developed, that it was sometimes deliriously indulgent of the game, sometimes ambivalent, and on other occasions wished it would go away.

Then there is the perspective of larger events. In the early days of football at Queen's, the Boer War broke out. Then there was the First World War, when the game was not played – and in which some of the stars of the prewar period lost their lives. There was the Great Depression of the 1930s and then the Second World War. The succeeding years of peace saw the baby boom, which by the 1960s had resulted in more, bigger, and better-coached players coming to the university. Then there was a period in the 1970s when the game was in serious danger from American civil suits against helmet makers. Various other significant events will also be noted as we pass through the history of the game at the university.

Sociological and psychological issues will also demand attention. For example, what if any were the differences in the players, or in the game and how it was viewed, as a result of the atmosphere and circumstances of the Roaring Twenties as opposed to those of the Dirty Thirties? Were the players "more serious" in the latter era? Or consider what if any was the impact on football of the emergence of the hippies of the 1960s. The hair of the players was certainly longer, but did that mean anything? Does the transition of Queen's from a mainly working-class university to a more upper-class one in the 1980s, with a greater percentage of private or prep school graduates as students and players, have any implications? And what about increased academic standards for admission? Then again, how does feminism and the movement for gender equality in sport in recent times have an impact? And what is the effect of competing sports philosophies that emphasize breadth of participation and team sports over specialization in a few selected sports for competition at a superior level? What do these things mean for football at Queen's? Moving farther afield, what does the trend to increased globalization mean for the Canadian college football game? Or what is the effect on it of free trade with the United States and Mexico?

Again, the ideas spill forth.[13] There is always the question of "brutality" and of injuries in general. And what of the use of drugs, whether performance enhancing or otherwise, and of alcohol? The latter and its association with the game – not so much through the players as through the fans – has drawn attention in almost every decade. It has been argued, for example, that efforts to deal with it harshly have recently had the effect of reducing student attendance at regular games to a mere handful.[14] What is to be made of this argument? Does such a situation matter to the game? Has it occurred before?

There is thus much to consider besides the record of games won and lost, of points scored for and against, of championships won and lost. To be sure, these will be documented. But there is also the need to touch on the individuals involved, especially those who most made their mark, and also to discuss the many issues cited above. Together they will serve both to put a human face on the game and to place it in the larger context. Before beginning, however, and to provide an overall perspective to the story, we should see what the record actually was.

THE RECORD[15]

Queen's has been playing rugby football on a university team basis since its first season in the fall of 1882. In reporting the playing record of these years, one has several choices, the three most obvious being to cover the entire period, to report on the hundred or so years dating from Queen's first championship in 1893, or to begin with the formation of the first intercollegiate union (the Canadian Intercollegiate Rugby Football Union) in 1898. The first would have been the most complete, but the scores for a considerable number of games went unreported, and the opponents varied considerably from season to season, often including city teams, the military, and so on. And since neither the University of Toronto nor McGill (the principal basis of comparison over the entire period) is reported to have won the championship, such as it was, during these early years, it was decided not to include the statistics for the first eleven seasons.[16] Certainly, 1898 and the formation of the Intercollegiate Union would have made a suitable starting point, but since good data were available for the 1890s, it seemed logical to include Queen's first championship in the statistics. Finally, a "century of football" had a nice ring to it … so it was decided to give the statistics from 1893 to 1994.

Keeping in mind the general limitations of all such statistical exercises, it can be said that during the 102 (inclusive) years from 1893 to 1994 (not counting the war years, 1915–18 and 1940–44, not including exhibitions, and considering only league and playoff games), the senior rugby football team at Queen's played 612 games in 93 seasons.[17] Of these, it won 335 (or 55 per cent), lost 262 (43 per cent), and tied 15 (2 per cent). In 59 (or 63 per cent) of those 93 seasons, it won more games than it lost (47 seasons) or had a break-even record (12 seasons), and in 30 (33 per cent) of them it won a championship of one sort or another.[18] During that time it outscored the opposition 10,366 to 8,590.*

If one thinks in averages, this record suggests that Queen's won more games than it lost, by a decent margin. On average, it had a winning season every other year, a championship once every three years, and it outscored its opponents by about 17 to 14 in the average game. Typical of averages, this is somewhat misleading, because the record is highly variable by era or decade. For example, the team won more championships in the ten seasons of the 1920s than it had in all the years up to 1919 (33 seasons); there were no losing seasons in the 1960s, whereas in the stretch from 1946 to 1952 they were all losing seasons; and points for and against grow steadily with the decades rather than being evenly distributed.

---

* I have made a rough estimate of the number of people who might have watched Queen's play football over this period ("rough" being the operative word). Bearing in mind that Queen's regularly drew close to 10,000 spectators at home and in Montreal from the 1920s to the 1960s, and probably twice that number in Toronto; adding in attendance at Western from the 1930s and a reasonable television audience in recent years, and making liberal allowance for bad weather, as well as for the thin crowds before the First World War (and, on occasion, since the 1970s), an average of 3,000 "watchers" per game does not seem unreasonable. This suggests that something on the order of 2 million people would have seen Queen's play since 1882, a fact that perhaps accounts, along with the team's good playing record, for the university being well known for football – and being well known more generally too, though there obviously are other reasons why the university is so well known.

Regardless, the record speaks for itself. During this same period (1893–1994), the University of Toronto (Varsity) had 29 championship seasons, McGill only 12.[19] This suggests that Queen's played the game very well down all these years and was arguably the best, given the university's slight numerical advantage over Varsity in winning seasons (and bearing in mind its substantial disadvantage in size of student body). Before we turn to how this was accomplished, a brief word is necessary on the approach and organization of the material that follows.

METHODOLOGY AND ORGANIZATION

As indicated above, there is a large body of information to draw on and many aspects to consider. There are several obvious approaches that it would be tempting to take in a book such as this – for example, a dry recitation of the record, complete with a systematic recounting of the rules (just to liven things up!). Then again, there is always the possibility of a collection of anecdotes of the type, "I remember the time when we were on the 35-yard line late in the fourth quarter and …" or "… when old Jack Jones was at the Queen's Hotel in Montreal after the McGill game and …" or "… when Ted Reeve [or Frank Tindall or …] looked down the bench at me before the game and said …"; or all of the above. These collections are often humorous but usually only to the individuals directly involved. In addition, they are unable to carry the narrative very far. Yet both approaches are necessary to a certain extent, as is some attempt to draw in the larger issues of life surrounding the game.

In this latter respect, historians are always plagued with the decision of whether to organize a work along thematic lines or chronologically. The choice seems to depend on the subject. Here, chronology has won out principally because it felt more comfortable than a book on Queen's football organized in chapters with titles such as "War and Football at Queen's," "Booze and Drugs and Football at Queen's," and so on.

So one starts at the beginning (indeed, before the beginning) and moves forward to the present, breaking the historical line where it seems natural to do so. Thus, chapter 1 covers the period from 1882 to 1914, the last season before the First World War, while chapter 2 looks at the years 1919–29, the Roaring Twenties more generally, and Queen's football in particular (Grey Cups were won and the university went football mad). In chapter 3 the 1930s are considered, and in chapter 4 the period 1945–59 (which begins badly but gets better by the mid-1950s). Chapter 5 looks at the Golden Sixties, chapter 6 at the 1970s (when the coaching torch was passed from Tindall to Hargreaves), and in chapter 7 the record is brought up to 1994. A conclusion then rounds off the story.

As to sources, I relied heavily on the student newspaper, the *Queen's Journal* (found in the university library) and the Kingston *Whig-Standard* (in Queen's archives) for accounts of individual games; on interviews with selected former players (see appendix c);[20] on various histories – of the game, the university, and general events (see bibliography); and on a variety of other sources, such as personal correspondence, articles in the *Queen's Alumni Review*, and so on. The illustrations are from Queen's University Archives and other sources, particularly two photographers long associated with the game at Queen's, Wallace R. Berry and Art Martin. All these ingredients have been stirred together to make the stew that follows (perhaps the metaphor is not exactly the right one … but it will do).

1

The Early Days
1882–1914

"This year has seen the inauguration of a new venture, the organization of a Rugby football club at Queen's. With only a week's practice the Rugby team met and closely contested a match with the RMC cadets, confessedly one of the finest, if not the finest, of our Canadian clubs." *Queen's Journal*, 10 January 1883

As the above review of the inaugural season suggests, the first formal rugby football game between a Queen's University team and an outside opponent (informal games had been played at the university throughout the preceding ten or so years) was played on Wednesday, 11 October 1882. It was described by the *Queen's Journal* as follows:

On the afternoon of Wednesday, Oct. 11th, a very interesting and exciting match was played in the cricket ground between the Queen's, and Royal Military College, Rugby teams. The day was a splendid one for the game, but was rather cool for the spectators, many of whom were ladies. At about 3:45 the cadets arrived on the ground and at 4 o'clock the opposing teams took their positions. They were represented as follows:

Royal Military College – Forwards: A. Jolly, H. Strange, W. Van Straubenzie, W. Warner, E.J. Duffus, M.W. Neyland and J.T. Lang. Backs: W. Von Iffland and P.G. Twying. Halfbacks: W.B. Carruthers, captain of the team and D.C. Campbell. Quarterbacks: R. Davidson and M. Von Hugel and centre back: J. Woodman.

Queen's College – Forwards: T.G. Marquis, J. Renton, R.M. Dennistoun, F. Strange, E.W. Rathbun, H. Young, G.F. Henderson, A. Ferguson and D. Ferguson. Backs: J. Booth and H. Rathbun. Quarterbacks: W. Coy and J. Foxton. Halfbacks: A. Gordon, captain of the team, and M. Hamilton.

The cadets, as usual, looked remarkably well on the field in their neat recreation uniforms, while the students were for the most part dressed in blue jerseys and knickerbockers. As regards the weight, the cadets certainly had the advantage, and they soon showed the students that there is more in Rugby football than can be mastered in a week, for although the latter, all things being considered, played a good defence game, their playing as a team was not nearly as good as that of several individual members.

For the first half the "gowns" played with a wind blowing strongly from the northeast, but in spite of this advantage the game was one of defence throughout. Now and then, however, a good run would be made at the cadets' goal by either Hamilton or Gordon, who had they been more closely pushed by their own forwards, would have come dangerously near the goal-line of the cadets. Another redeeming feature was the drop-kicking of Booth, which without doubt, prevented the cadets from obtaining several touchdowns that they otherwise would have taken. Neyland, Carruthers, and Jolly did some good service for their team although the playing of the last named gentleman was at times a little rough. Play had been going on for half an hour, when Neyland, having made a good run, and well-earned his success, scored a touchdown, and the goal was finally taken by Duffus by a place-kick. Play was immediately resumed, and some stubborn play shown by praiseworthy attempts to rush the ball up the field, while Woodman and Carruthers were particularly anxious to move it in the opposite direction. Half-time was then called, after which the cadets had the wind to back them.

Lang took the first kick and sent the ball clear over the students goal, but it didn't count. Neyland now secured it under his left arm and after having passed everything in the field, he rounded to behind the College goal, and touched it down. Davidson was this time given the privilege of kicking for the goal, but his attempt was futile, and Hamilton was not long in grabbing the ball and rushing it down to the cadets' goal. But Weller was there, and he having tucked it under his arm, proceeded to bring it back up the field only to be repulsed by College forces. The cadets, however, once more rushed the ball up the field, and Campbell having secured a good chance, kicked the second game for the cadets at 5:20.

After three cheers had been given by the members of each team for the others, the spectators and players dispersed.[1]

In the following issue, the *Journal* reported in a self-satisfied manner:

We are more than pleased, in the interest of College pastime to note the vigorous stride that has been taken since the close of the last session in the direction of fostering the only game, perhaps, which is peculiarly suited to our Canadian Colleges, where the only time for outdoor sport is the few weeks of open weather after the opening of the College session in October.

The want of organized effort to excite an interest in football and to place it upon such a footing as it rightly deserves, has been long felt, and to supply this want the JOURNAL was earnest in its efforts both last session and in previous years in advocating the formation of a football association.[2]

In the same issue, a description is given of the second game played in that first year, an away outing to Brockville. Anyone who has ever been associated with Queen's football, whether as a player or spectator, will hear echoes of his or her own experience in this first detailed description of the travelling aspects of an away game:

On Saturday morning about 5 a.m. a van containing the Rugby team from the College drove out to the G.T.R. depot. Although the air was bitterly cold and the comet in full bloom, the party was a jolly one and in the best of spirits. The heavy man of the team was the last to appear on the scene, but he arrived all right at a 2:40 gait, and explained that he had overslept himself. The day promised to be a fine one for the game, and when the train was boarded and the party fairly off, everyone determined to enjoy himself as much as possible. Accordingly, to start with some of the familiar College songs were sung with a will and a gusto that made the uninitiated passenger stare. It was soon seen that some hours would elapse before the "dashing mixed" reached Brockville, and the speeches and songs were employed to while away the time, and the prospects of victory or defeat were eagerly discussed. At every way-station a general stampede was made for the platform, and there was always plenty of time to see everything before the train moved on again. At Brockville, Mr. J. Hutcheson, B.A., an old Queen's boy, was found waiting to welcome the team, with the captain of the B Brockville Club, Mr. Wanklyn, both of whom did all in their power to make the Kingston boys' visit a pleasant one. After the team had been registered at the Revere House, and some of the anxious inquiries made about the dinner hour, the party separated and each one amused himself as best he could until the welcome stroke of twelve sounded, when a very good dinner was partaken of at the hotel. After dinner the jerseys and the knickerbockers were donned and a few of the vainer members of the team got tin-types taken which were a source of great admiration to themselves.[3]

As can be seen from the photo (p. 18), the "College boys" did indeed wear jerseys (blue), knickerbockers (white), and black stockings. Most of the team played in ordinary walking shoes (though a few wore canvas shoes) "with three pieces of narrow leather, about an eighth of an inch thick, nailed across the soles,"[4] presumably to increase the traction on the grass or a wet field.

That first team went on to play two more games after the Brockville match (which they won), losing again to the Royal Military College but winning against a Kingston city team. Thus, the first season ended with two wins and two losses. But by the end of the second season, in 1883, in which the team went two and one, the *Journal* felt confident enough to editorialize:

It is a matter of congratulations that we have a football club that plays the old game under the Rugby Union rules. Although it was not until last session that efforts were put forward to form a Rugby football club at Queen's, yet since it has been in existence, a large number of our students have been tempted to indulge in the wild and exhilarating sport. To those who are not conversant with the nature of the game

The first Tricolour football team, 1882. *Left to right, top row:* A.D. Cartwright, Fred Strange, Ramsay Duff, J.F. Booth, Joseph Foxton, Thomas Marquis, C.J. Booth, Aeneas Macdonnell. *Middle row:* R.M. Dennistoun, R.A. Gordon, Herbert Rathbun. *Bottom row:* Fred Young, A. Montgomery, R.M. Hamilton, William Coy (Queen's University Archives [QUA])

of Rugby, and to those who have never indulged in the delightful excitement of a "scrimmage," a match game between opposing teams appears to be little less dangerous than a free fight or a railway collision; but once the players enter into a contest and recognize the fact that it is their duty to get the ball over their opponents' crossbar, all feelings of danger and fear, if ever they existed, are banished.

This year our club defeated the Cadets of the Royal Military College, a team which is respected from Montreal to Toronto. Brockville also fell prey to our ambition. Yet although a gratifying measure of success has greeted our team, its members must not forget that they are still some distance from the top of the heap, and until they reach the top (which they can, and we hope they will, do) they should bear their successes with equanimity and always keep in mind the well-known maxim that "practice makes perfect." In this respect we must say that we fear want of practice brought about the one defeat which forms the dark side of our club's otherwise glowing picture. This is to be regretted … It is to be hoped that next session when the campus is in good shape for football and every other manly sport, that the Rugby boys … will not neglect to keep themselves in trim so that they may achieve victories even greater than those which have already fallen to their lot … and the grand old game of Rugby will find a home at Queen's from which it will never be dislodged.[5]

The same issue included a wonderful spoof on the nature of the game, a sure sign in those days (when spoofs and doggerel were featured in virtually every issue of the *Journal*) that the activity was a centre of student life. Thus, the allusions would have been understood by everyone. Part of the spoof went as follows:

I haint never seen no prize fite nor a battle, but I seen a game of Rugby. It's lots uv fun. My brother Bill, he sez its a bully game. I think so too – a bully game to stay out uv. Bill he paid Rugby the other day and Snooksy – that's my sister, Snooksy is – Snooksy, she said she guessed he wuz a konterfeit Bill when he got dun, fur nobody would hav took him fur the same Bill that commenced playin he loked that bad. To start, a lot uv 'em stan' on a line an' put their han's on their nees an' look at a ball … Then won fellar sez, in loud an' sonorous tones, "warnin'" an tries to kick the stuffin' out uv the ball. Purty soon won feller grabs it, an' about the time he haz gone six feet, some big fellar jumps on his back and noks him down. Then six or ate more pile on till the fust man is clean hid from site. They sit on him ekal to a korner's jury. All the time the fellar has bin hollerin "down" in a voice choked with emosion and dead grass, tho' what he wants to make that statement fur, I can't see. Ennybody with haf a eye cud see that he wuz down, and the bettin wuz even that he woodn't git up again. They all stood in a line, facin' each other, an' somebody grabbed the ball an' throwed it to nother fellar. Then the two lines had a fite, an' the fellar with the ball started to run, an' somebody jumped on to his kote-dollar, an' when the gang got dun with him, he was sent home fur repares … Then they got a supe in this fellar's place an' the game went merrily on.[6]

THE ORIGINS OF THE GAME AT QUEEN'S

What are the origins of this rugby at Queen's? Who, if anyone, could be said to have been instrumental in starting up the game? What became of these people? What game did they play? What was the situation at Queen's at the time? And what was happening in the country?

To answer the last question first, in the 1870s and early 1880s we find ourselves in a world in which the American Civil War (1861–65), Canadian Confederation (1867), and the Franco-Prussian War in Europe (1870–71) are

relatively recent events. In the Canadian case, John A. Macdonald (of Kingston), our first prime minister, was turned out of office over a railroad
scandal in 1874, but has been re-elected in 1878 after the failure of the
railroad policy of his successor, Alexander Mackenzie. Canada's population
is around 4 million, with only Montreal and Toronto having more than
100,000 people. It is a time of vigorous economic activity throughout Quebec
and Ontario, fuelled by immigration, agriculture, Macdonald's National
Policy (of tariff protection, railroad construction, and so on), exports to
Britain (under continuing preferential treatment), and a booming American
economy next door. Kingston and London are the two major centres in
Ontario, apart from Toronto, which share in this growth. In Kingston's case,
it is because of the institutional benefits that flow from having Macdonald
as prime minister – the prisons and military bases maintained in the city –
and especially because of its geographical advantage, situated as it is at the
head of the river astride the most important inland transportation links.

Queen's at this time was a small eastern Ontario university, strongly
associated with the Scottish church and operating under a charter from
Queen Victoria. In that first football season of 1882, the "total attendance at
the university was about 275 with 165 in Arts, 86 in Medicine, 20 in Theology and 2 in Law. The teaching staff numbered 30. The university included
the present residence of the Principal [Summerhill] and the adjacent houses,
which were partly used for classrooms, the old Medical building, and the
Old Arts Building [now Theological Hall], which had been erected a year
or two before."[7]

Queen's existence as an institution had always been precarious, and the
1870s proved no exception. William Snodgrass, the principal from 1864 to
1877, had had to deal with a series of "shocks" throughout his tenure: loss
of financial support (the government had withdrawn its grant, and a sizable
portion of the endowment was lost in a bank failure); schisms in the church;
disciplinary problems; and ongoing difficulties with the Faculty of Medicine.[8] Indeed at one point, in 1870–71, the university was down to twenty-
five students in arts and four in theology, and was on the point of vanishing.
But Snodgrass persevered, and by 1877, when he retired rather suddenly to
a parish in Scotland, he had built the university back up to eighty students,
the largest registration since 1864.

He was followed by the dynamic George Monro Grant, the first Canadian-
born principal of the university, who was to remain principal throughout
the first twenty years of football at Queen's (until 1902) and to support it
actively.[9] That football, or "the game," was consistent with Grant's larger
image of the university and its role in Canadian life cannot be doubted. In
particular, Grant was strongly opposed to the oft-mooted suggestion that
there should be but one large university in Ontario, centred in Toronto. He

considered that competition was healthy for universities as for other institutions, and he probably viewed a Queen's rugby football team that was
capable of challenging Toronto and others as yet another manifestation of
such competition. Grant set out to obtain enough money to ensure that
Queen's could support itself in this independent stance. A campaign was
started to raise funds for a new building, an extension to the library, and
chairs in theology and science. By July 1878 Grant had the money, and by
mid-1874 the new building was ready. People were impressed. More importantly, this achievement strengthened Grant's hand with the provincial
government in Toronto, so much so that in April 1885 Queen's definitively
rejected a proposed union (into a larger, single university) and decided to
go it alone.[10]

So both the institutional and the larger environment were very supportive
of the establishment of a team to represent the university. The university
did have an association football (soccer) team; but as the *Journal* reported,
association football had not enjoyed much success, and it was clearly not
something with which the students and their developing sense of Grant's
dynamism could identify: "Football is played this session in the spiritless
and shiftless way which has characterized the game here for the last three
or four years. Of course, there is as good material in the college as there
was a few years ago; but the sporting spirit necessary to develop it seems
lacking. We sigh for the times when we could turn out one of the best
fifteens in Canada."[11]

Far better in this respect was the new game of rugby, about which there
was undoubtedly an awareness. As well, it could not have escaped the
notice of Queen's students and faculty alike that McGill had been playing
rugby since the late 1860s, indeed had played Harvard in 1874, and that the
first rugby football unions in Canada were being proposed for 1882.
Quebec's was organized in February 1882 and included five teams, and the
Ontario Rugby Football Union was formed in January 1883. Together they
made up the Canadian Rugby Union in 1883.[12] What was more, the University of Toronto had been involved in the game for some time – it had played
Michigan in 1879 – so, of course, Ontario education politics demanded that
there be a Queen's presence.

To this situation was added the inevitable catalyst in the form of "a group
of enthusiastic freshmen, headed by C. Jackson Booth."[13] Booth, his brother
Fred, and R.A. Gordon, all of whom had played rugby at Ottawa Collegiate,
arrived at Queen's in the fall of 1882 and began to talk up the game and
the possibility of fielding a team as a "fine advertisement for the university."
They argued that "by competing with teams from larger cities, it would
unify the undergraduates around a theme, promote a national outlook, and
thus further the interests of the university"[14] – all interests of Grant,

McGill vs Harvard, 1874 (William Notman, McCord Museum of Canadian History, Notman Photographic Archives)

incidentally. They were successful in short order, for the first game was played on 11 October 1882 and included the Booths, Gordon, some disaffected soccer players, and others (as detailed at the beginning of this chapter).

Booth, in a letter to W. Garvock fifty-five years later, described the team and game in the 1882–83 inaugural season as follows:

The first team to represent Queen's was light but husky, and could have held its own with many a squad that later wore the Tricolour. The next year it was heavier and averaged about one hundred and seventy pounds. The forwards were strong and hard tacklers. The backfield was fast, and could kick as well as catch and run. Hamilton, Kennedy and Dennistoun stood over six feet. Logie was also tall. Coy, the quarterback, was the smallest man …

The team was made up of fifteen men, a fullback, three halves, one quarter, three scrummage and seven forwards, and the playing time for a game was two three-quarter-hour periods. No time was taken off when the ball went into touch. There were no huddles and conferences to consider the next play – a play that in modern football most likely has been worked out by the coach, reviewed in a chalk-talk on a blackboard, and then tried out in practice. Strategy was evolved as the game went on. There was no coach or trainer …

C. Jackson Booth (QUA)

If a player was disabled and it was impossible to keep him playing – and there was plenty of give and take in those days – the captain of the opposing team would decide whether a fresh player would be allowed to take his place. Sometimes, in the first period, a new man would be allowed to come in, but it depended on the skill of the substitute and that of the injured player. In the second period, fresh men would seldom be allowed to enter the game …

There was much more kicking than now. One misses the long kicks that were an important part of the game in our time. Forward passing has replaced the kicking to a large extent … There is an element of surprise in the forward pass, and when it is completed gives the spectators a great thrill – but it does not take the place of kicking … How did the players run and tackle? The first team soon learned to tackle low, although we did not have the advantage of any tackling dummy …

When the ball was kicked into touch, there was a tussle for it. It gave a team the advantage to get the ball when it went into touch. Both teams lined up at right-angles to the touch-line, and a player would throw it in, if possible, to one of his own side. That would give some of those six footers like Saul an advantage in grabbing it and it was an advantage to have a tall player like Kennedy or Hamilton throw the ball in too …

The main object was to kick a goal … It was more important to kick a field goal or score a goal by a place-kick than to secure a touchdown. The team that kicked the most goals won. After a touchdown, the ball would be brought out immediately in front of the spot where the touchdown was made, and a place kick attempted. If that kick was successful, it counted more than if the team scored two touchdowns but did not kick a goal … Kicks to the dead-line were not allowed, but rouges and safety-touchs were.[15]

The game described here is not yet the modern one (as noted earlier, it would not be the modern game until the 1930s), but there are recognizable elements.[16] As well, the game was to change quickly. By the late 1880s, for example, under the influence of Harvard, Walter Camp at Yale, and others involved with the American game (particularly Yost of Michigan and Stagg of Chicago)[17] the Canadian game abandoned the scrum in favour of the "snapping back" of the ball to put it in play; and by 1897 the system of downs was introduced to ensure turnover of possession. Meanwhile, especially in those first seasons, the rules of play remained highly variable. They only settled down over time – after about twenty-five years.

What became of that first team? In 1937 Garvock reported on the players as follows:

A.D. Cartwright, son of the late Sir Richard Cartwright, the doughty opponent of Sir John A. Macdonald, was for many years the secretary of the Board of Railway Commissioners. Recently superannuated, he resides in Ottawa. He was wiry and hard to tackle. Fred Strange was a fast runner and ball-carrier. He went to Portland, Oregon after playing with Queen's. He was not an undergraduate,[18] but in the early days of rugby a certain number of city players were allowed on the team …

Joseph Foxton was a tower of strength as a scrimmage man. It is believed that he is now dead. T.G. Marquis was a well-known journalist. For a time he was the editor of the Ottawa Free Press and later a notable contributor to the Toronto Star. He was a powerful plunger and a terror to his opponents. He died a year or so ago …

Aeneas Macdonnell was a fast forward, always on the ball. His whereabouts are not known. R.N. Dennistoun, who with Marquis and Foxton made up a strong scrimmage, is now a distinguished member of the Manitoba Court of Appeal. William Coy practised medicine for many years in Vancouver and passed on in 1936.

J. Fred Booth, who was associated with his brother in J.R. Booth Ltd. until his death in 1930, shared the kicking honour on the first team. He was also a hockey player of note and introduced this sport to Queen's when he cut an india-rubber lacrosse ball into an octagonal-shaped disc, from which evolved the modern puck.

R.A. Gordon, a good kicker and runner, learned the game in Ottawa. He was elected captain because of his natural qualifications as a leader, and he could uphold his end in any argument or dispute. He died in New York. Ramsey Duff eventually became a colonel in the permanent force of Canada, and was stationed at Kingston until his death in Egypt during the Great War.

Herbert Rathbun, who is also dead, came from Deseronto, where his family was well-known in the lumber business. Fred Young, a county judge in Prince Rupert, B.C., died last May. R.M. Hamilton, an excellent kicker, now resides in Peterboro.

C. Jackson Booth, who in his time had few equals as a punter and drop-kicker, has not lost his early enthusiasm for rugby since that first game was played at Queen's fifty-five years ago. He rarely misses seeing the team play every year. A benefactor of the university and a member of its Board of Trustees, he is keenly interested in the welfare of Queen's, and his counsel is highly valued by his associates on the Board.[19]

This pattern of subsequent success was to repeat itself with later Queen's football players. It suggests, at the very least, that the modern stereotype of the dumb football player was never accurate at Queen's. How it came to develop will be examined later.

THE FIRST CHAMPIONSHIP: 1893

The first decade of rugby football at Queen's passed with considerable interest but without any outstanding success. The team played in the Ontario Rugby Football Union (ORFU) against various university and city clubs. Meanwhile, attempts were made to improve the facilities. In 1884 a fee of one dollar per student was levied from each of the three hundred in residence, and one-twentieth of this sum, along with a loan of $500, went to a new football field (with cinder track). Before this, the team had played on the old Kingston cricket grounds (in front of the present courthouse in Macdonald Park). That same year the Tricolour was adopted after many years of discussion, the red, gold, and blue coming from the gules, or, and azure of the university's coat of arms, which itself was an adaptation of the coat of arms of the University of Edinburgh, on which Queen's had modelled itself in 1841.[20] Then, on 24 October 1891, after an official committee had researched the issue at length, a Queen's yell was officially adopted:

> Queen's, Queen's, Queen's!
> Oil Thigh no Banrighinn gu Brath!
> Cha gheill! Cha gheill! Cha gheill!

As all good Queen's people know, the direct translation from the Gaelic goes:

> Queen's, Queen's, Queen's!
> Queen's forever!
> No surrender!*

In his history of Queen's first century, Calvin commented as follows on this period of the game:

The informality (of plays and rules) of these early days contrasts vividly with the seriousness of the game to-day. The *Journal* gives an account of a game with McGill, 3 November 1888. The team went to Montreal on Friday afternoon and spent Saturday morning sightseeing. "In the afternoon the secretary telephoned to McGill – the telephone was a new toy in 1888 – to ask when the game would be. Three o'clock he was told. The two captains chose a referee just before the game; then removed all superfluous clothing, took their places on the field." Presently Queen's scored a touchdown. The referee allowed the goal following it, but immediately afterwards he "consulted some of the spectators, and through their advice changed his decision." Fortunately for good feeling, Queen's won the game 5–4. On Monday they defeated Montreal 2 to 1, and the *Journal* calls them "Champions of Quebec" by virtue of this double win.

The 2 to 1 victory … is interesting because a year or two earlier it would have been a draw … because four points had to be scored before a game could be declared.

[Also] down to fairly recent times a Canadian rugby football team numbered fifteen players but (especially) in the early games played by Queen's the positions varied enormously … (e.g., in 1883, in only two games, four different line-ups were used). [Today things have come full circle because such a variety of line-ups, or formations, in modern terminology, are not strange at all but an important part of the strategy of the game] …

For many years each team, besides its fifteen players, had a non-playing "Field-Captain." They are not often mentioned in the accounts of the games … [and] early in 1891 were abolished. Their chief duty had been, according to the *Journal*, "to confuse and coerce the referee, and to get a decision for his side" – the good old days.[21]

Despite a strong interest and plenty of intramural play, the team enjoyed no championship success during this period, and the *Journal* often complained of the turnover in players, which was largely the result of the

---

* Hamilton reports that these words, along with others, were set to the music of the "Battle Hymn of the Republic" to give the college its song – that most North American of traditions – in 1898. It appears more or less in its modern form in the 1903 Queen's song book. It had numerous verses, but by 1908 the *Journal* had already observed that "hardly anybody could get beyond the first verse" (Hamilton, *Queen's, Queen's, Queens*, 11).

constant changes in the nonstudent players, who were regularly used along with students. Ottawa won the championship, such as it was, from 1884 to 1889; Hamilton, from 1890 to 1892.

In 1893 all this changed. After an opening loss to Ottawa (23–13), Queen's won the return match 25–3, thereby winning the total points series with Ottawa 38–26. After beating Hamilton 27–13, Queen's returned to play a home-and-home with Varsity for the Ontario championship. It won both games by a combined score of 55–4. There was little left but to try for the "Championship of Canada," which in effect meant a game against the Quebec champions of that year, the Montreal Athletic Association team. The game was played on Thanksgiving Day in Montreal, and Queen's won 29–11.

There are numerous accounts of this game and of the ensuing pandemonium at the university and throughout Kingston. Thousands met the victorious team at the train station, and there was a parade to City Hall, as well as numerous speeches.[22] Perhaps the best description of the whole experience is given in the following letter, which the captain of the team, the legendary Guy Curtis, wrote to his mother several days after the game. It is in the university's archives and was printed in the *Queen's Review*[23] after its donation to the university in 1930, following Curtis's death:

Dear Mother –

Received your register all OK on my return from Montreal. As you know after we beat Toronto and won the Ontario Championship Cup nothing would do but that we must try to win the Championship of Canada, so we arranged a match for Thanksgiving Day. The Canadian Union guaranteed us our expenses so we took a parlour car and travelled in style. We got there on the evening before and got a good night's rest and beat the Montrealers, the Champions of Quebec, and gained the proud title of Champions of Canada. I will send you a couple of the Montreal papers, and you will see how we beat them with our heads as well as our feet, how the Queen's Captain was a thorough general and how his men obeyed him. How the telegrams came in after the game and congratulations from all quarters. I cannot get the space to describe it all.

The Montreal team gave us a banquet that night and treated us nobly. We stayed over until Friday and were met at the station by all the boys and had a procession headed by the band. As the train came in the band played "See the Conquering Heroes Come." After the procession they made a few of us speak. Capt. Curtis the 1st of the team of course. Although my maiden effort, they say that the dignified Capt. did well. The enthusiasm was great, and if I do say so myself I think we deserved it; we had to play 8 hard battles to win it, and deserved to have our position recognized. After you get through with the papers I send, let some of the folks read them, but get them back if possible. I did not get hurt at all in Montreal. We were a queer looking combination going on the field in Montreal all covered with pads, bandages, etc. but the old veterans swept everything before them and gained a glorious victory. While I was dressing before the game, I received a telegram from H.B. Rathbun of Deseronto which read as follows: "The eyes of Queen's old veterans are upon you and look for a glorious victory." After the game I think the best telegram I got was from Prof. Jas. Williamson, Vice-Principal of the College, an old man, 51 years a Prof. in the College. It was: "Victors from start to finish, congratulations."

The streets were crowded here during the game waiting for the news of the game. The half-time score was read out at the Opera House between the Acts, and the best joke of all it was read out at every stage of the game at some theological conference that was being held in one of the churches here. Tonight in Chalmers Church Rev. MacGillivray is to preach from the subject: "Valuable Lessons from Queen's Championship team on the Football field." I have a photo taken with my nose guard on; will I send it to you? I guess I will not need my heavy overcoat until Christmas. I know what you will write, but no lectures remember.

Yours,

GUY

The Champions of Canada were photographed yesterday.

G.C.

Curtis was, of course, the key. Without doubt, the longest serving of all Queen's football players (the next closest are a series of individuals over the years at six or seven seasons), he came to the university from Delta, east of Smiths Falls, in 1886 and played until 1898, a total of twelve seasons. He also played hockey during these years and for three more, until he left the university in 1901 at the age of thirty-two.[24] By the 1893 season he was effectively the playing coach, diagramming plays and generally indicating what should be done as well as helping to effect it on the field. The *Queen's Review*, in his obituary, described him thus:

A difficult man to analyze. Physically a perfect specimen of manhood; strong vigorous, adroit and agile, and yet gentle and considerate. Ambitious to win, but not at any price; modest, even bashful, but on the campus or ice lost in the concentration of the contest. In sport his was an unusually acute and resourceful mind, keen in the contemplation of what could be planned to be done, or what had to be done, but apparently untouched by the studious life of Queen's.[25]

The last sentence is apt. Curtis was simply not interested in the academic side of university life, as a recent article on him has noted:

His academic record was something of an embarrassment. Between 1886 and 1892 he failed junior courses in philosophy, physics, and math four times each, and in senior English a grand total of five times.

He certainly wasn't slow. He was famous for his complex blackboard diagrams of rugby strategy and for his encyclopedic knowledge of the rule books.

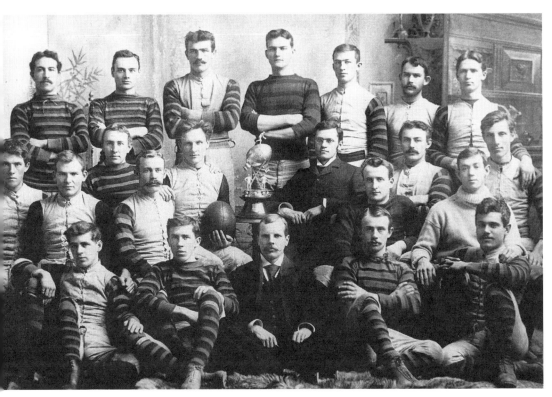

Champions of Canada, 1893. *Left to right, top row:* F. Moore, W. Moffatt,
G.F. Kennedy, R. Laird, T.S. Scott, J.M. Farrell, T. Mooney. *Middle rows:*
J.S. Rayside, A.E. Ross, H.H. Horsey, T.H. Farrell, Guy Curtis, Prof. S.W. Dyde,
F. McCammon, J. Cranston, C.E. Wilson, C.R. Webster. *Bottom row:* C.B. Fox,
D.R. Maclennan, A.B. Ford, A.H.S. McRae, W.C. Baker (QUA)

But even the fierce Principal George Grant – who hauled him into his office on
more than one occasion – couldn't get him to take academics seriously.

Between 1893 and 1901 Curtis registered simply as an "extramural student in regular attendance" – meaning that he had an excuse to show up for sports.[26]

It should be stressed that Curtis was not in any way an anomaly for his
time. One suspects that if he had been, Queen's would soon have prevented
his playing (as in fact it did when eligibility rules were introduced in 1898).
But it was common practice in those days to use nonstudents, or "loosely
interpreted" students, on university teams. As Curtis's obituary noted,
"There was then no Intercollegiate Union with stringent regulations as to
eligibility. Town and gown teams contended together; the rules were elastic,
and elastically interpreted to determine who was a bona fide student at a
seat of learning."[27]

So the memory of Curtis is in no way shameful to Queen's football or to the university, despite his academic record, and Curtis should lie easy in his grave (not that it is reported that it ever bothered him!).[28]

UP TO THE FIRST WAR

Needless to say, this first championship sent the campus into a state of football frenzy during the fall that followed. Hear the *Journal* of 7 November 1896:

> The football man is now the craze,
>   With his long and shaggy hair;
> With his padded suit in the dirt to root,
>   With blood to spill and spare.
>
> He has guards on his legs and muffs on his ears,
>   And a covering for his nose,
> And he dives in the game for glory and fame,
>   And slaughters his college foes.
>
> Then here's to the lad who's the latest fad,
>   Who's out for blood and gore;
> May he vanquish his foes by kicks and blows,
>   For that's what he's living for.[29]

The team's success did not hurt the fund raising either. In December 1894 the *Journal* reported: "The impetus given to college athletics by winning the Rugby Championship of Canada last year bore immediate fruit in efforts towards obtaining a new campus. That these efforts were well-directed was evident to everyone on their return to school this fall."[30] But the euphoria generated by the 1893 championship did not lead to the successes that Curtis and no doubt others had anticipated. In 1894 the team won the Ontario championship but lost to Ottawa for the Dominion championship. This was as close as Queen's would get for the next five years, which were mediocre seasons at best (see table 1).* It would be 1900 before Queen's

---

* Queen's also developed quite a reputation for being "kickers" (playing dirty), one it seems to have retained, however unfairly, down all the years to the present. The *Journal* of 1 December 1894 reported that Marshall of Hamilton told Arthur Ross (one of the early stars of Queen's): "I won't play with you anymore. I don't like you anymore." One can almost hear two little boys talking after a particularly bad dust up.

Table 1
Queen's football record, 1893–1914[1]

Year	Won	Lost	Tied	For	Against
1893c[2]N[3]	6	2	0	182	79
1894cN	2	1	0	41	19
1895N	3	3	0	64	44
1896	0	3	0	17	31
1897N	1	1	0	12	22
1898	1	3	0	15	17
1899N	2	2	0	20	21
1900cN	2	2	1	43	26
1901	1	3	0	30	43
1902	1	2	1	13	27
1903	0	3	1	28	58
1904cN	4	1	0	77	31
1905	1	4	1	75	105
1906	2	3	0	77	63
1907	2	3	1	53	71
1908N	5	1	0	90	50
1909N	3	3	0	84	63
1910N	3	3	0	67	53
1911	0	6	0	59	124
1912	2	4	0	42	74
1913	2	4	0	46	121
1914	0	4	0	46	93
Total	43	61	5	1,181	1,232

Source: Queen's University, 75 Years of Football + 10, and newspaper reports for the years 1893–97
[1] League and playoff games only
[2] c indicates championship year
[3] N indicates non-losing (i.e., winning or tied) season

again won a championship. During those years Varsity was winning with considerable regularity.[31]

Perhaps the two most important occurrences directly involving the game at Queen's took place in the 1897–98 period with the formation of the Canadian Intercollegiate Rugby Football Union (CIRFU) in 1898 and (linked with but certainly more important than the formation of CIRFU) the declaration that anyone who was not a student in good standing was ineligible for play.[32] This pronouncement by the Senate of the university, after growing dissatisfaction with situations such as that of Curtis and others, came very suddenly just before the 1897 season, and no doubt it explains the relatively few games played that year (as everyone scrambled to field an eligible team). It no doubt also explains the formation, with like-minded universities, of the CIRFU the following year. It must regrettably be reported that Varsity won the first CIRFU championship in 1898.

Outside the university, the economy was growing in leaps and bounds, fuelled by raw materials, quick economic development based on foreign investment, and trade. Thousands of farmers were flooding into Manitoba and into what would become Saskatchewan and Alberta. Thanks to all this activity, Canada had become one of the richest nations in the world.[33] Not surprisingly, with the resurgence of British imperialism, Canada was called on to supply money and men in emergencies – for example, to relieve General Gordon at Khartoum in 1884.

Principal Grant was one of the strong pro-imperialist voices in the debate that developed between the pro- and anti-imperialism camps in Canada. J.M. Bumsted notes:

The prevailing philosophy of Canadian and British universities in the last quarter of the nineteenth century, Idealism, was the perfect philosophical underpinning for a generation of paternalistic imperialists. It exalted British civilization and political progress into the perfect Idealist State, fully worthy of its Empire, and insisted that every member of the Empire had a duty to promote its principles. "The Empire to which we belong," wrote Principal George Monro Grant of Queen's University in 1890, "is admittedly the greatest the world has ever seen. In it, the rights of all men are sacred and the rights of great men are also sacred. It is world-wide and therefore offers most opportunities for all kinds of noblest service to humanity, through the serving of fellow citizens in every quarter of the globe ... Of the few great nations of the future, the English-speaking people is destined, if we are only true to ourselves, to be the greatest, simply because it represents most fully the highest political and spiritual life that humanity has yet realized."[34]

Consequently, when Britain requested troops for the Boer War in July 1899, the question exercised students at Queen's particularly, though others in Canada were also concerned. Wilfrid Laurier, who had become prime minister in 1896), at first sent one thousand men, all volunteers; then six thousand more; and before the war ended in 1902, another thousand – again, all volunteers – had been sent. As far as one can tell, this did not directly affect the team in terms of players lost to active service, though some Queen's men certainly served in the war; the *Journal* makes reference to the departure and return of officers throughout the war years. Whether they might have been interested in playing football is not known.

It could not have been a critical lack, for in 1900 and again in 1904, Queen's struck gold, winning the intercollegiate championship (which was rightly but with some puffery referred to as the Intercollegiate Championship *of Canada*). The 1900 season was a tightly run thing, with Queen's winning the total points, home-and-home against McGill by 17–13 and against Varsity by 26–13, so that despite only two wins, a tie, and a loss, it

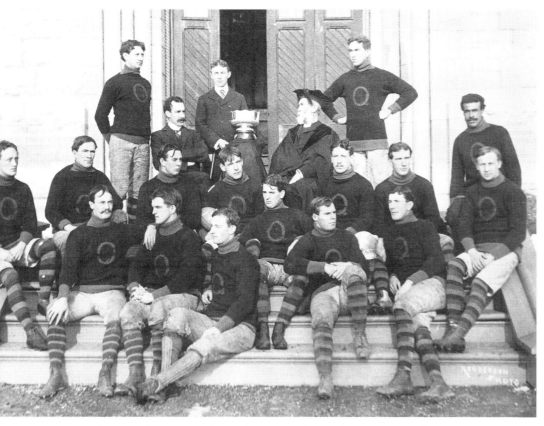

Intercollegiate Champions of Canada, 1900. *Left to right, top row:* F. Etherington, M. Ferguson, G.F. Dalton, Principal Grant, A.H. Britton. *Middle row:* E.J.F. Williams, Ac. McDonald, C. Clarke, Forrest Weatherhead, Knox Walkem, B.L. Simpson, Alfie Pearce. *Bottom row:* H. Devitt, H.E. Paul, P.F. Carr-Harris, E. Richardson, W.T. Shirreff, I.T. Hill, J.M. Young (QUA)

still won the championship. In 1904 a playoff was needed, Queen's and McGill both having handled Varsity easily but being tied in the home-and-home with a victory each and being tied in points. Queen's won the playoff 6–0.

The photograph of the 1900 team (see above) is significant in several respects. First, Principal Grant is present in academic dress, signifying the team's importance to the school. It has been some years now since the principal of the university has appeared in the team photo. Second, at the extreme right can be seen one of the earliest appearances of Mr Alfie Pearce (eventually to be spelt Pierce), a Queen's institution in later years. Of the players, Etherington, the flying wing, went on to become Canada's first

Teddy Etherington (1898–1901). From Gananoque, he was named to Alfie Pierce's all-star team as "the best flying wing" Alfie ever saw. Etherington was a star all four years, serving as team vice-president in 1900 and team captain in 1901. This Queen's class valedictorian later became Canada's first professor of anatomy (at Queen's) and served as Queen's dean of medicine for five years (Queen's Football Hall of Fame [QFHF]).

professor of anatomy and the dean of medicine at Queen's, and ultimately to have a building on campus named in his memory. Williams was to have a relation, Jack Williams, on the 1904 championship team who later served as sergeant-at-arms in the House of Commons for many years. There is a Richardson here and a Carr-Harris. Both are well-known names at Queen's. George Taylor Richardson, who played before the First World War, in which he was killed on active service, had the university's new stadium named in his memory in 1921 (and the existing one in 1971). McDonald ultimately found his way into the Queen's Football Hall of Fame, as did Etherington. There is a J. Young. Years later, in the 1960s, another J. Young, sometimes playing the same position, was to have an outstanding career not only at Queen's but in the Canadian (professional) Football League with the B.C. Lions. At Queen's it seems that there are always these echoes from the past that can be found in the present.

After the 1900 season, with that one exception of 1904, fate was not kind to Queen's. Ten of the fourteen seasons to 1914 were losing ones; in six of

Jack Williams (1904–05, 1908). A teammate of George T. Richardson, he was one of the work-horse ball carriers and first punters of the great Queen's Tricolour teams of the early 1900s. He went on to play professionally with the Ottawa Rough Riders and later served many years as the sergeant-at-arms in the House of Commons (QFHF)

them the team lost every game or won only once (see table 1). Since the Intercollegiate Union had withdrawn from the overall Canadian Rugby Union in 1900, there had not been any playing for Dominion championships. But the Intercollegiate Union returned to the Canadian Rugby Union in 1905 to compete for the national championship. A new trophy for football supremacy in Canada was donated by Governor General Earl Grey, and the first championship game for it was played in 1909 between the Ottawa team (coached by Tom "King" Clancy), as champion of the city-based league (the "Big Four" of Ottawa, Hamilton, Toronto, and Montreal), and the University of Toronto, which was the intercollegiate champion. Varsity beat Ottawa handily, 31–7, to win the first Grey Cup. The universities were to win seven of the first nine Grey Cups.

Nevertheless, the situation at Queen's became particularly grave after 1910, as would be remembered after the war when Queen's set out to rebuild its former reputation for football excellence. There is no single factor to which one can point to explain the decline. It could not have been facilities, for in Grant's time the number of buildings had doubled, and by 1912 the university had its own new sports and gymnasium building, as well as new athletic grounds adjoining it.[35] Certainly, luck had something to do with it: the 1911 team, which went 0–6, lost three games by a total of four points. The *Journal* mentions a sense of complacency because of the earlier championships, and in fact Queen's came very close to being champion again in 1908, losing in a final playoff game to Varsity after having easily beaten the team during the season. In view of the poor record, there was much discussion about whether Queen's needed a professional coach.[36] But there was another factor too: there is little doubt that the approaching clouds of war began to have an impact.

Historian Hilda Neatby observed that "from 1909, the question of Canadian defence, the Canadian obligation, if any, to contribute to Britain's naval expenditures [to pay for its costly arms race with the Germans], and the manner in which this might be done, were matters of lively, and even acrimonious, discussion."[37] Despite some local opposition, it can fairly be said that Queen's strongly supported the war, from the principal on down. Principal Grant had died suddenly in May 1902, and Daniel M. Gordon, his successor, supported universal military training for men. Partly because of this, Queen's had a corps of engineers from 1910 onwards under the command of a professor of civil engineering, Alexander Macphail. Within three weeks of the declaration of war in early August 1914, Macphail left with the corps – 120 men, soon to be followed by others – to set up the large processing camps at Valcartier, Quebec, for those going overseas. By February 1915, 300 of Queen's male undergraduates had volunteered, as well as a considerable number of the university's staff and graduates.

From September 1914, five hours of drill per week were compulsory for men; women worked for the Red Cross. Two groups of engineers went overseas in 1914 and early 1915. At one point, three of the nine companies of engineers in France were commanded by professors from the School of Mining; two field batteries went. Etherington of the 1900 team headed the

Norman "Tout" Leckie (1908–10). One
of the greats of the early Queen's teams,
he went on to play professionally with
the Hamilton Tigers and served with dis-
tinction in the Canadian armed forces in
Europe. He was killed at the Battle of
Ypres in 1915 (QFHF)

military hospital in Cairo and, after 1916, the hospital in France. And so the
story continued. By 1916, the university was down to 600 students and in
severe straits.

It is surprising that the 1914 season was actually played; by the fall of
1915, it would have been impossible to field a team if the season had gone
ahead. What is not surprising is that many of the players from the immediate prewar teams found their way into battle and that some died. There
was Norman "Tout" Leckie, for instance, who played for the 1908 team that
almost won it all, and also played in 1909 and 1910. After several seasons
with Hamilton, he volunteered for service and was killed at Ypres in 1915.
Then there was Ernie Sliter, who seemed to have no luck. After a good career
at Queen's and a year with the Argos, he went overseas in 1914, had an
aircraft shot out from under him over Germany, and lost a leg. Invalided

Ernie Sliter (1910, 1912). Following a distinguished intercollegiate football career
and one year with the "Big Four" Toronto Argos, he went overseas with the
Canadian armed forces. His aircraft was
shot down over Germany and he lost a
leg. Later, when homeward bound, his
ship was torpedoed (QFHF)

home, his ship was torpedoed off the English coast. Fortunately, Ernie was
a good swimmer! He survived once again and returned home to a long and
rewarding career in education at Kingston Collegiate. The photographs of
Leckie and Sliter, together with their Hall of Fame citations, are included
here to represent the memory of all those players who fought, were
wounded, or killed in that terrible war.

CONCLUSION

The war was the end of an era in Queen's football, just as it was the end in
many other respects. By the time the game was resumed in 1919, it was

quite literally a different world. No longer was there mention of "manly courage, spirit, and muscle" or the virtues of the game's brutality or collective action. The innocence of the late-nineteenth and early-twentieth centuries was gone.

It had been a wonderful period, the time from 1882 to the fall of 1914. Danzig has captured the feeling well in the title of his book: *Oh How They Played the Game*. One thinks of the Booths, of Curtis, Ross, Etherington, Jack Williams, Art Turner, and Tout Leckie. While Queen's may have lost more than it won (43 wins, 61 losses, and 5 ties in 109 games), and while it may have been marginally outscored by its opponents (1,181 for, 1,232 against – about 10.9 vs 11.4 points per game), it did win those celebrated early championships in 1893, 1900, and 1904. In doing so, as well as always playing tough ("mean" or "dirty" would be the judgment of the opposition, of course), the players established the foundation for Queen's football that would carry it forward over the years, providing the memories against which subsequent teams would judge themselves. It is not too strong to suggest that they also gave the university a focal point for its collective myth, establishing Queen's as a name and a place in the minds of virtually all Canadians in a way that excellence in the classics or medicine would possibly not have done.

2

Days of Glory
The 1920s

The First World War ended at the eleventh hour of the eleventh day of the eleventh month of 1918. By any standard, it had been the largest and worst armed conflict in human history.[1] It was known as the Great War, "the war to end all wars." Patriotic fervour had swept Canadians into it, and 620,000 had served (out of a population of around 8 million), nearly all of them volunteers. Of that total, about 61,000 were killed and another 172,000 wounded – in other words, about 30 per cent of those serving were killed or wounded. Canada's contribution was thus substantial, though by 1917 it was not without controversy – that relating to conscription.[2] Because of the large losses of men relative to the population, certain segments of Canadian society would take years to recover; Newfoundland, which was later to join Confederation, is a prime example. The same was true everywhere in Europe, where an entire generation of men had been virtually wiped out. Whether they were aristocrats, poets, or common men, few had survived.*

The university was not immune from the sacrifice, especially in view of the avowed imperialism of Grant, Gordon, and others; 179 Queen's graduates lost their lives in the war. Students and staff members had poured overseas throughout the early years of the conflict, and by the spring of

---

* In the chapter on the Battle of the Somme (July 1916) in his book *The Face of Battle*, Keegan makes clear why this happened and how it felt to be part of that futile savagery. Poets such as Rupert Brooke have done so as well. As will be noted below in connection with the Second World War (and it is still possible to talk with Queen's footballers from before that war who survived it), despite the analogy that coaches and others in the game often draw between football and war, those who have been in both allow no such analogy. Football is a game. War is unspeakable. This was especially true of the trench warfare of the First World War.

1917 almost a thousand Queen's men were on military service, as well as thirty-four professors. The loss in registrations and revenues, combined with a policy of maintaining all staff on half-pay while on service (a practice abandoned by late 1916 except on a selective basis), meant that Queen's found itself in serious financial trouble.[3] To alleviate this condition, the university turned part of the campus (Grant, Nicol, and the old arts halls) into a convalescent hospital for 600 Canadian soldiers who were being invalided home. As well, it went on a desperate fund-raising campaign in 1917 which provided a much-needed $1 million, a large sum in those days, from various sources including the Carnegie Foundation, Chancellor Douglas himself, and many alumni across Canada.

Following the war, in the spring of 1919, the new principal, Robert B. Taylor, who had taken over from Gordon in late 1917, was reported to be "full of hope."[4] There was a burst of activity everywhere. People were anxious to put the war behind them, to get back to lives set aside five years earlier. Plans were drawn up to revitalize the medical faculty, to push into new areas such as business education, to provide education for returning veterans, to build new library facilities, and so on.

Unfortunately, the immediate postwar period was not the best of times for pushing ahead either in Canada or abroad. During the demobilization period of 1918–19, one of the most serious epidemics ever to hit Canada broke out. More than 50,000 Canadians died of Spanish influenza, only 10,000 less than had been killed in the entire war. Inflation was a serious problem until 1922 as pent-up demand and the slow transition from military to civilian production drove up prices. Strikes and other industrial unrest were prevalent in 1919 and 1920.[5] Then in 1921 the international wheat market collapsed and bad droughts devastated the prairies. Many of these problems were also being manifested internationally, indeed to a much greater extent in countries such as France and Britain. The latter was still a large market for Canadian goods, and as a result, Canadian trade suffered. However, Ontario suffered less than some other parts of Canada. Because of strong markets for pulp and paper, mining, hydroelectricity, and cars, it was among the first areas to experience the boom conditions that were to become what people characteristically recall about the 1920s. Meanwhile, the farming community in Ontario, being far less dependent on wheat than the prairies, did very well with dairy products, tobacco, and other produce.

While all this was taking place, Queen's, as part of its "return to normalcy," decided, along with McGill and the University of Toronto, to resume playing football in the fall of 1919. That this was an unsettled time is an understatement. Those interested in playing no doubt trickled in as they were demobilized, but they would find it hard to take playing seriously after what they had just been through. Some might even be physically undernourished. In any event, they would mainly be concerned with taking their studies seriously and getting out and into a job as quickly as possible. To exacerbate the situation, there was a full-blown epidemic on, and getting sick from playing football on a wet and cold fall day might have seemed akin to near suicide, something especially not to be risked after surviving the hell of war and rain in the mud of the trenches in Europe. All things considered, it is a wonder that anybody showed up at all.

The reminiscences of Professor McLeod, who was a student in the 1920s, bear this out: "Jack Williams, a former player, was the coach, training was sporadic, and the team did poorly. It lost every game by a considerable score."[6] In fact, the team played four games (McGill and Varsity twice each, home-and-home), scoring a total of 9 points during the entire season while having 126 scored against it (see table 2 below). Thus, "a considerable score" seems rather an understatement – it was a total disaster!

The next year, the first of the new decade, was only marginally better. This time, despite a new coach (Professor Lindsay Malcolm of the Faculty of Science) and better training, the team scored a total of only 13 points, had 108 scored against, and again lost all four games by "handsome margins."[7] However, Queen's fortunes were about to change dramatically. But before turning to those exciting events, it is worth taking a moment to update the game as it was being played at the beginning of the 1920s. The last time we looked, in the 1880s and 1990s, it had been quite close to sanctioned brawling. By 1920 a lot had changed.

THE GAME ITSELF, C. 1920

At the beginning of the 1920s the game bore little resemblance to the one Queen's had played in the early 1880s. Forty years of experience and of exposure to different styles of play had resulted in many changes in rules and procedures. Sports historian Frank Cosentino has described these changes:

By 1921 ... the new rules committee of the CRU [the Canadian Rugby Union, to which all teams in Canada belonged] had moved farther from the British game and closer to the American. The main features were:

1 Twelve men to a side.
2 Snap back instead of scrimmage.
3 Quarterback may carry the ball beyond the line of scrimmage.
4 At least five men on the line of scrimmage when ball is put in play.

5 Substitution at any time; no more than 18 players of one team shall take part in any game.
6 Only ten men allowed on a buck into the line, until the play is past the line of scrimmage.
7 Scoring: 5 for a try, 1 for a convert, rouge or a touch in goal, and 2 for a safety touch.[8]

Cosentino goes on to describe the Grey Cup of 1921, the second after the war and the first involving a western team, the Edmonton Eskimos, who played the Toronto Argonauts:

The game was an interesting contrast in styles. The Argonauts played the traditional "single-wing" alignment, featuring extension plays and end-runs: the Westerners, with their "American tactics," played an early version of the T-formation, the quarterback handing the ball to one of his running backs who would plunge directly into the line of scrimmage in an effort to gain yardage or a touchdown. It was the Argonauts who prevailed, as much because of Harry "Red" Batstone and Lionel Conacher as their style of play.[9]

Games in the bigger centres were regularly played before large crowds; for instance, the 1920 Grey Cup between Varsity and the Argonauts drew 15,000 to Varsity Stadium (note that college teams still played against city teams during this period). Teams had distinctive uniforms and other accoutrements: rudimentary helmets made of leather, though these were not mandatory and were without face or mouth guard of any kind; some thigh, shoulder, and other padding; and special shoes (or "cleats"). In certain circumstances, deriving from the war perhaps, a small band of musicians might be present to play and practise manœuvres before the game and when the teams rested at the halfway point.[10]

This, then, was the football milieu in which Queen's found itself at the end of the First World War. Although the university had had a strong tradition of the game before the war and had made steps to resume playing after the war, it very quickly found itself overmatched and outspent (having no large stadium and getting no gate receipt splits when it played in the large Montreal and Toronto stadiums). Some fundamental decisions about Queen's continued commitment to the game had to be made. As we shall see, it did not hesitate. A new stadium was built in the summer of 1921; a full-time coach and athletic director was hired, along with a trainer; and a few important players, especially Harry Batstone – one of the heroes of the Grey Cup for Toronto in 1921 – were "encouraged" to attend Queen's. As a result, the fortunes of the team improved dramatically.

THE DAYS OF GLORY: 1921–1925

It is difficult to know where to begin, for much happened in the two years immediately following the 1919 season – roughly from December 1919 to November 1921. Sufficiently embarrassed by that first postwar season and under pressure from students, alumni, and others, and particularly from Professor Malcolm of the Faculty of Science, the university decided to act.[11] In quick succession (though there was some secrecy surrounding the actions, which were announced as a package in March 1920), Queen's reorganized the administrative and financial control of athletics into a new Athletic Board of Control; it obtained $50,000 from the Richardson family for a new stadium, to be built in honour of George Richardson, who had played before the war and been killed in it; built another practice field, the existing Tindall Field, beside the stadium; and moved to hire a full-time coach and trainer for the team as soon as possible.

The stadium was planned for completion in time for the 1921 season. When it became clear that a new coach could not be obtained for the 1920 season, Professor Malcolm took on the job. Although he knew little about the game except what he had picked up from playing briefly before the war, he nonetheless brought a greater rigour to the training by insisting on regular practices and by hiring the first full-time trainer the university had ever had.* No doubt he also wrote the part of Principal Taylor's welcoming address to the students in October of that year in which the principal urged all able-bodied men to turn out for football and for the student body to support the team actively by attending all the games.

This did not bear immediate fruit. As noted above, the 1920 season was again a disaster. But faint glimmerings of what was to come did appear. It was recorded that the intermediate team "did quite well, but lost out in the final game to Toronto," thereby providing a base for the 1921 season.[12] Work

---

*   This was Billy Hughes, a professional boxer (Canadian bantam and feather-weight champion) from Sault Ste Marie. Like Malcolm, he was a force in his own right. Head boxing coach as well football trainer (and also coach and trainer of the 1924 Canadian boxing team for the Paris Olympics), he brought Queen's one of its lasting traditions, for it was Hughes who brought with him to Queen's in the fall of 1920 his pet bear Boo Hoo. The bear was the first of a succession of bears who lived at the arena, appeared at the games, and created more or less general mayhem down through the 1950s until, after a hiatus of a decade or so, Boo Hoo was resurrected as the figurative bear of today, a prac-tice much more in keeping with the mascots of professional sporting teams, to say nothing of modern ideas of animal rights.

on the stadium went ahead, and with the hiring of the new coach for the 1921 season, things began to fall into place.* George Awrey, an insurance executive from Hamilton and Toronto, had played for Hamilton before the war, had extensive coaching experience there, and brought to the university an up-to-date knowledge of administration and coaching.[13] He was appointed director of athletics and secretary-treasurer of the new Athletic Board of Control.

The first game in the new stadium was played on 8 October 1921 before a crowd of 3,500 spectators, along with various dignitaries and an army band. A training table had been set up for the team, catered by the infamous local bootlegger Dollar Bill. The players had slept the night together in the new arena and had been working out together for weeks; and some new players had been added to the team, notably Frank "Pep" Leadlay. The team was ready for Varsity, and it won 9–5, with Bill Campbell scoring the first touchdown in the new stadium. It then lost badly to McGill – apparently, everyone on the team was ill with flu[14] – but beat McGill in the return match. Because of a subsequent loss to Varsity by one point and because of Varsity's twin victories over McGill, Varsity won the championship. But the season had been a substantial improvement over 1919 and 1920.

By the fall of 1922 there was a strong sense of optimism and resolve in the air around the campus:

There is a snap and a confidence in the voice and the movements of George Awrey as he jollies and cajoles the rugby players through the hard, tiresome dummy practises and conditioning which seems to say, "We can and shall bring the Cup home this year!" … Among the players every man realizes that a win this year means not only a championship, but the crowning of a long struggle, the retrieving of the misfortunes of the last few lean years, and the restoration of Queen's to the proud position which she once held in rugby and should never have lost. Last but not least there are the fans who crowd the stand and bleachers every afternoon to watch the practices and who, having tasted the fruits of last year's near victory, will back the team to the finish. We have the team, the coach, the trainer, we have the backing both of the alumni and the student body, and barring the unconscious carelessness

---

* McLeod reports that the stadium was built under Malcolm's supervision with the help of student labour. He also reports that when some of the walls were repaired in the 1960s, many bags of cement were found in the walls with the paper intact. He observed: "Possibly the students became tired and just dumped the bags there. This may have contributed to the cost … which was just about double the original estimate" ("Reminiscences," 14).

Intercollegiate and Dominion champions, 1923. *Left to right:* Coach W. Hughes,
"Doc" Campbell, "Red" McKelvey, Harry Batstone, "Pep" Leadlay, Johnny Evans,
Roy Reynolds, "Chick" Mundell, Hank Brown, T. Bond, "Curly" Lewis, "Liz"

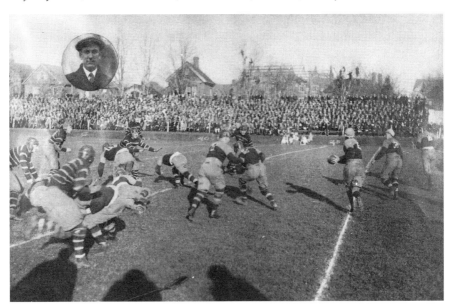

The boys in action: 27 October 1923 (QUA)

of over-confidence, it will take a wonderful team to wrest the championship from
Queen's this year.[15]

In his reminiscences, Professor McLeod disingenuously noted that "it was
the same team with one or two additions to the team that played in 1921."[16]

Walker, "Unk" Muirhead, "Ken" McNeil, "Tiny" Adams, "Babe" Grondin,
"Baldy" Baldwin, "Gib" McKelvey, John Delahaye, Pres. McLeod, "Bud" Thomas,
M.F. Badgley (QUA)

But one of those "additions" was Harry "Red" Batstone, also known as Bat,
who had been a star of the Grey Cup for the Argonauts the previous year.
   Queen's opened against McGill (which was well coached throughout this
period by the famous Frank Shaughnessy) with a 12–1 victory. Queen's next
beat Varsity and then McGill again before losing a shocker against Varsity
to force a playoff. This the team won, thereby gaining the intercollegiate
championship. This result led to the Eastern Canadian championship game
against the Argonauts, which Queen's won 12–11. All that remained now
was to play the western champions, the Edmonton Elks, who both formerly
and later were known as the Eskimos. Once again, the university did not
hesitate. Money was collected to support the travelling expenses of the
westerners, and on 2 December 1922, on frozen ground after a snowfall,
Queen's beat the Elks 13–1 to capture the Grey Cup. Awrey and his players
had delivered.[17] The campus and the city reacted in ways reminiscent of
that first Dominion championship in 1893. Parades were organized, trains
were met, speeches given. The Kingston *Whig* was full of front-page copy
on the story, and short biographies of the coach, trainer, and each of the
players filled successive issues of the *Queen's Journal*.
   The names are familiar to almost everyone who knows Queen's football,
and they can be recalled at the slightest prompting by most older Queen's
grads these many years later. Since the team was to remain virtually intact
for the next three years, it is worth commenting briefly on who some of
them were. Johnny Evans, a Kingston boy in Meds, was the quarterback

Table 2
Queen's football record, 1919–1929[1]

Year	Won	Lost	Tied	For	Against
1919	0	4	0	9	126
1920	0	4	0	13	108
1921N[2]	2	2	0	28	46
1922c[3]N	6	1	0	85	66
1923CN	6	0	0	137	19
1924CN	6	0	0	73	37
1925CN	5	1	0	70	27
1926	2	3	0	34	33
1927CN	3	2	0	42	43
1928N	2	2	0	29	24
1929CN	6	2	0	110	33
Total	38	21	0	630	562

Source: Queen's University, 75 Years of Football + 10
[1] League and playoff games only
[2] N indicates non-losing (i.e., winning or tied) season
[3] c indicates championship year

and a unanimous choice for Canadian all-star at that position. The other four making up the backfield were Pep Leadlay (Science '25), who was from Hamilton and had played three years of city ball; Harry Batstone (Commerce '26, Meds '32), who also was from Hamilton and had played for the Argonauts; Doc Campbell (also Meds) from Kingston; and Dave Harding, the best secondary defensive player in Canada that year). Bud Thomas and Liz Walker, both perennial all-stars who were captains in the years to come, played on the outsides; and the group known as the doctors (since virtually all of them later graduated in medicine) – Art "Curly" Lewis, Orvin Carson, and John "Red" McKelvey – along with Chick Mundell and Bill Muirhead, played along the line.[18]

The shocker loss to Varsity before the run-up to the championship in 1922 was the last time Queen's was to lose a football game until it lost to the Ottawa Rough Riders in the Eastern Canadian finals in 1925. The historical record indicates that this was to be the longest winning streak in Queen's football history; it ran for eighteen league and playoff games (or for twenty-six games if one includes exhibitions.[19] In 1923 the team defeated the Rough Riders and the Argos in exhibition games; it trounced McGill and Varsity twice each in the regular season, the Hamilton Tigers at Kingston at the end of November for the Eastern Canadian championship, and the Regina Roughriders on 1 December in Varsity Stadium for the Grey Cup. In only one game was the score even remotely close, a game against Varsity early on, which Queen's won 9–3; and the Grey Cup was an embarrassment.

Regina was beaten 54–0![20] The team thus won six games and lost or tied none. It scored 137 points and had only 19 scored against. This was the best points for-and-against season's record in the history of Queen's football from 1893 to 1994 (see table 2).

The team rolled on through 1924 virtually unchanged in personnel and certainly untouched by the opposition. The only close call was against Varsity on 8 November, when Queen's won by just 14–13. That year Hamilton and Balmy Beach were defeated in post-season play. After considerable dispute over transportation subsidization, the West finally decided not to challenge for the Grey Cup, so the Tricolour was once more the Grey Cup champion – for the third year in succession.[21] Queen's had again won six games and lost or tied none, scoring 73 points for, against the opposition's 37.

Then came 1925 which gave every indication of repeating the 1922–24 season results. Queen's won all its season games (again only one, the opener against Varsity, was close, 8–5) and it beat Balmy Beach in the Eastern Canadian final by 21–9. But the winning streak came to an end with a loss to the Ottawa Rough Riders in Ottawa under appalling conditions at the end of November.* Ottawa went on to win the Grey Cup, one that Queen's would always figure might rightfully have been its own in better circumstances. Still, the Tricolour was intercollegiate champion for a fourth straight time.

HOW DID THEY DO IT?

The reader may well wonder how this small school in a provincial city was able over the four years 1922–25 to produce a team that won twenty-three of twenty-five games, four intercollegiate championships, and three Grey Cups. How had it become "the best football team in the country"? The

---

* Years later, Carl Voss, the famous NHL hockey player and referee, who was a member of that 1925 team, wrote: "I will never forget my 1925 experience with Queen's when we played the Rough Riders in Ottawa. We went to Ottawa from Kingston by bus on the day before the game. The snow was more than a foot deep and on one occasion the bus went off the road and into the ditch. Some 30 of us practically lifted it back on the road. The day of the game they had cleaned the field as best they could but it was necessary to paint the field markings red to show against the white base" (*Ottawa Journal*, 29 November 1967). The *Queen's Journal* reported that the field was "as hard as a rock, with footing slippery" but that "Ottawa deserved the win on the play of the day even though they could not likely defeat Queen's one game out of three in normal conditions."

Toronto Star also wanted to know! It sent a newshound, one Gregory Clark, to discover the secret of Queen's success. Clark reported as follows:

The secret of this success in the rugby field [lies] not in the science of rugby [but] you will find [it is] a romantic and dramatic and human thing …

First because it's a team, no quarrelling or jealousy. Second because the men on the Queen's team are intellectually above the average. They are without exception good students. [Principal Taylor reports that] Leadley is a brilliant man … He prepared a plan of a system of waterworks for Kingston which is a beautiful piece of drafting and a well-schemed piece of engineering as ever was seen around here … I could review the whole team. They are all men of first-class rating intellectually … this is a very considerable factor … [Third] back of the team is the essential goodwill and interest of a body of students. "We are all a team, a unit, all pulling together … in all activities of this small university" [Taylor].[22]

[Also] determination is a mighty big factor in sport. Dr. Taylor spoke of Queen's as a poor man's university [where] a man without means could enter to the full in the life of the university, and get an education with the minimum of means … This factor intensified the team spirit in the university.[23]

While all very nice, and no doubt a part of the explanation, there was a bit more to it than this – a lot of hard work, for instance, and good coaching:

The team lives together in a small building very like an army hut for the period of its rugby play … They live a hard and rigorous life. Up at six, over to the stadium for a run, a toss and kick of the ball. Back for a rub and breakfast, off to lectures all day, back to the stadium at four o'clock until dark in rugby togs … practising formations, working on this scientific angle of modern rugby or that … until the movement becomes as automatic as the soldier's response to command. Here the Queen's team … achieves the miracle of coordination and muscle that permits them to reach the top of that narrow ladder, the Dominion Championship … They play cards for recreation after evening meal and professors will drop in and tutor in subjects in which they are handicapped by the demands of modern rugby …

This coach [Hughes] is part of the Queen's success. He knows this science of rugby. He thinks formations all day and dreams new plays all night. He is intense, and keen … He speaks loudly and emphatically. None of the lily coach about Hughes.[24]

As one reflects on Clark's explanation of how the team functioned, it comes to have an uncanny resemblance to the way large American college football programs could be characterized as operating today. What is not mentioned is that, like today's American programs, such an operation could not have been carried out without the benefit of considerable monetary expenditure, not only for meals, housing, travel, and equipment but also for recruiting, publicity, and the actual support of the players. The former group of expenses is perhaps understandable, and it may well have been just as Clark reported it – namely, that "the players pay their own board." But he does not report where they got the money to do so, nor does he describe the economics of the football operation more generally. He may well not have known, or may not have thought to ask, or perhaps he was too "gentlemanly" to do so! Since this question of money resurfaces at several points in later times, it is worth commenting on here at some length.

To begin with, it is important to note that much of what is obtainable is by inference or anecdote, for hardly any records of the financing of football exist from this period at Queen's. However, it is clear from the writings of Cosentino and McLeod that both of them accept what was popularly believed at the time – that Queen's bought the services of at least some of these players and that it invested considerable money in its football program to ensure its success. This certainly makes sense. It is simply stretching credulity to believe, for example, that Pep Leadlay came to Queen's from the Hamilton Tigers city team in 1921 to enrol in the Faculty of Science because he "loved to design waterworks systems in Kingston"; or that Red Batstone, also from Hamilton and the hero of the 1921 Grey Cup for the Argonauts, should come to Queen's in 1922, be admitted to the university (without having finished high school) to study commerce and then medicine because the university recognized a "first-rate intellect" in the raw and because it told Batstone this and encouraged him to apply – while expecting him to pay his own way.* Among other expenses, Billy Hughes the trainer had to be paid, and his assistant Alf Pierce had to be maintained. Hughes, a former city team coach, had come on short notice at the end of the 1922 season and had stayed on.

It is much easier to believe that George Awrey was appointed director of athletics and, importantly, secretary-treasurer of the Athletic Board of Control because of his connections to Big Four football, his Hamilton links, and his understanding that football was a business like any other. He was given overall operational control to run the program as he saw fit, and no doubt he would have negotiated for this much as one would today at Michigan,

---

* This should not be taken as a comment on the abilities of either man or any of the others of this period. As is noted below, they all graduated, and many became considerable successes later on. It is rather to "call a spade a spade" as the situation existed in 1920–25 and to acknowledge "that while 'official amateurism' was the stated rule, it was ignored 'below the line' in almost all leagues" (Cosentino, personal correspondence).

Notre Dame, or Florida.[25] That he should have set up an operation resembling today's American college football operation without the one key ingredient of today, namely, money for the players (via scholarships or whatever one chooses to call the payment), is to misunderstand Awrey and his times. Athletic scholarships did not exist in U.S. college circles until later; instead, the players in American colleges were paid directly.[26] Awrey therefore copied the U.S. system, as he understood it, for Queen's; and he enjoyed the same success that such a focused effort usually brings.

So it is rather disingenuous for Clark or anyone else to suggest that the wonderful success of the 1920s was due to something special in the water or air of Kingston and of Queen's. Local spirit was certainly a factor. But so were money and hard work. It should be stressed that there is little doubt that McGill and Varsity also were active in this regard. While their greater size (there were 4,000 students at Toronto) and their proportionately greater gate receipts would have helped in any bidding war for players, the fact that both universities competed for players with professional teams in their respective cities worked to their disadvantage (witness Batstone). It is likely that Leadlay, Batstone, and the others were unique in that they were intellectually oriented, as Principal Taylor mentioned to Clark. Certainly, their subsequent success indicates this. And it may have been the opportunity to go to a small university in a small town where they would get their chance (Leadlay, for example, was a notoriously shy man) that tipped the scales for Queen's, given that the money on offer was reasonable and that they knew Awrey from his Hamilton reputation.

It is equally certain that the solid core of excellent Kingston-raised players such as Evans, Campbell, and the others – who may have come to Queen's of their own accord or may, in certain cases, have been "encouraged" by money to "stay around" – came together with Batstone and Leadlay to make up a team which, because of their hard work, basic intelligence, and special tutoring, stayed together for several years, so much so that after a while it truly did become as "automatic" as Clark observed that it had.

So all of these factors must be taken together to explain what happened in the 1920s. No one of them is sufficient by itself to do the trick. As for the monetary aspect, some may be tempted to judge the university harshly for its actions. But the practice was widespread, and it was necessary if one was to compete at all. And given the milieu of Queen's at the time, it was simply unthinkable that the university would stop playing football completely.[27] Having decided to play, there was really only one possible course of action if one wanted to become competitive, and that was to spend money. So an attitude of "sober realism," rather than a value judgment based on standards viewed down the lens of time (or, equally questionably, complete blindness to the practices of the day), is the best way to view what

— RUNNING THEM DOWN —

QUEEN'S! QUEEN'S!! QUEEN'S!!!

DON'T COUNT YOUR CHICKENS

BEFORE THEY'RE SQUASHED.

Rhymes of A Rugby Rooter

Who is the Captain of the van,
A very gallant gentleman,
The idol of many a rugby fan—
        "Doc." Campbell.

Who boots 'em high and boots 'em low,
Sure that straight as a die they'll go
Between the goal posts—Hurrah! just so!
        "Pep" Leadley.

Who is half of the famous combination
Who caused the Argos consternation,
Who in spite of rumours will stay at his station—
        Harry "Red" Batstone.

Who paws up the ground and tears his hair,
And cries aloud in his despair:
"For the love of H . . . . is no one there !"
        Bill Muirhead.

Who is it crouching, ready to spring
Watching the chance for an opening
Razzed by the crowd, but as cool as a king—
        "Red" McKelvey.

Who is it plunges with many a whack.
Always answers the Referee back,
Hurdles opponents who block his track—
        "Chicks" Mundell.

Who is this figure, stocky and stout,
"The brainest ever," the newspapers shout,
Whose tactics put rival teams to rout,
        "Johnny" Evans.

Who is the man who gets "down under,"
Who tackles low without a blunder
Who for his age is a perfect wonder !
        "Bud" Thomas.

Another who hurdles through the air,
Tackling low, and tackling fair,
Wing with "Bud"—A wondrous pair,
        "Liz." Walker.

A flavour of the 1920s! (*Queen's Journal*, November/December 1923)

transpired. The fact that the amounts of money given directly to the players were probably quite small, and that virtually all of those involved graduated and had successful careers, also weighs heavily in judging the acceptability of what went on.

In moving on from this period, though, it is better to leave with the impression of what a wonderful time it must have been. By 1924 the economy had at last turned strongly upwards, the war and the flu were behind everyone, the university had built several new facilities, and the football team was winning every game it played, as well as the Grey Cup, year after year. Life in the fall must have been good, the weekends particularly so, with the new stadium bursting with people, a new pipe band in place, Boo Hoo the bear running mad, and Bill "Hairpin" Holdcroft – a First War vet, tall, gangly, and awkward – leading the cheers with his crazy series of energetic, jerky motions that ended in a trademark hop. There were big weekend trips to Toronto and McGill; Queen's on the sports pages of the big city dailies on a regular basis; and the team having dinner with the mayor of Toronto at Hart House. There must have been something truly special about those times. Gibson, in his official history of the university, noted: "For a few years of triumphant innocence, football was king at Queen's. 'Red' McKelvey was elected President of the AMS, and the *Queen's Journal* happily converted itself into a continuous sports column interspersed now and then with a highly sentimental account of the most recent dance."[28] Gibson went on to report that Principal Taylor was of the opinion that "this fine football team did the university much good and created a new corporate spirit."

AND THEN MORE SUCCESS

The loss to the Ottawa Rough Riders at the end of the 1925 season brought a halt to these marvellous times. However, this setback was to prove temporary in one respect, though it was permanent in another. By 1927 Queen's was back winning the intercollegiate championship, and it did so again in 1929. But it never again won a Grey Cup or dominated Canadian football as it had in the 1922–25 period.

Perhaps it was inevitable that the run of success would come to an end, since the players could be expected to graduate and leave. Batstone, Leadlay, McKelvey, Lewis, and Norrie – indeed, all the big names from 1922–25 except Liz Walker, who was named captain for the 1926 season – graduated in 1926. Thus, 1925 was their last season. Nevertheless, the *Journal* was confident about the 1926 season: "Don't worry about Queen's next year. Hughes has a wealth of material in his youngsters, and he'll have a team."

The *Journal* was right in a sense, for Carl Voss, Gib McKelvey (Red McKelvey's younger brother), Bubs Britton, Irish Monaghan, and some of the younger players stepped in to play well. But the principal reason Queen's did as well as it did was that Batstone returned to the university just after the first game of the season (which Queen's lost) and enrolled in medicine, his short experience of selling insurance in Hamilton not having been to his liking. Batstone's presence made a big difference, though it could get Queen's only as far as a playoff game with Varsity for the championship, which was lost 8–0.

The 1927 season looked as if it had all the potential for a total debacle on the scale of the 1919 and 1920 experiences. Hughes resigned both as coach and as athletics director in mid-1927. No doubt his discretion to run things as he saw fit had been severely circumscribed by the financial reforms which the Athletic Board of Control had introduced.[29] Hughes went on to coach Ottawa in the city league. Not only did his departure cause considerable confusion, but several of the players were declared ineligible for play on academic grounds. Orrin Carson, a former player, agreed to coach, and several players were "found" to help bolster the team (there are clear references in both the Varsity and McGill student papers to Queen's being up to its old tricks of buying players).* Batstone was still capable of making a difference, and it was largely thanks to him and Freddy Warren that the team, after a close opening loss to McGill, won the rest of its intercollegiate games that season and also the championship, though by very close scores; the total points for and against were 36–22. The championship earned Queen's the right to compete for the Eastern Canadian title against the Hamilton Tigers, who were coached by sportswriter Mike Rodden, who had been a prewar Queen's footballer. Queen's lost 21–6, with Pep Leadlay, who was now playing for the Tigers, almost single-handedly accounting for all the points against his former teammates.[30] It did not help that Batstone was injured and could not play.

---

* For example: "Another of the wandering minstrels of Rugby, the first of which was 'Irish' Monaghan, has gone wandering. 'Ga' Mungovan, who played for the Argonauts against Queen's last weekend has wandered to Queen's (no doubt suddenly lonesome for the friends he made in the Limestone City) and will line up against McGill here Saturday." This extract is from the McGill student newspaper as reported in the *Queen's Journal* (15 October 1927), which severely chastised the McGill paper for drawing totally false conclusions from Mungovan's behaviour.

In 1928 the team lost the opener to Varsity in a close game but came back to win against McGill and Varsity, only to lose to McGill in a muddy game late in the season in Montreal. It was not a particularly successful year. No doubt part of the explanation was that Gib McKelvey and three others had been declared ineligible for play for three years because of an off-season fight at a basketball game in the spring of 1928. Also, the spring of 1928 saw the first student strike at Queen's, a strike over who controlled student activities off campus (it involved the scheduling of a dance). Although it was only a one-day affair, it drew national attention and led to the resignation of Principal Taylor in the spring of 1929; the trustees were fed up with what they viewed as his too light-hearted control of the students. It is likely that the fallout from the spring's occurrences meant that the customary full-blown antics around the football season were somewhat subdued in the fall of 1928, and the fortunes of the football team were reduced accordingly.

However, in 1929 Queen's was back on track, with Ike Sutton as captain and Batstone as coach. Batstone's injuries, studies, and no doubt age had at last caused him to retire after the 1927 season, though he had helped with the team in 1928. In 1929 he was pressed into service as coach only three weeks before the start of the season, when Carson was unable to continue. It was clear from the early games that Queen's was once again strong. There were sizable early victories against McGill and Varsity, with Bubs Britton, Bob Elliott (from Kingston), Howie Carter and Red Gilmour leading the way. Queen's then won 25–2 against the University of Western Ontario (which was playing for the first time) in the first intercollegiate game ever played in London. Queen's would have gone undefeated had it not been for a last-minute loss to Varsity in a kicking duel in Toronto, 7–6. This necessitated a playoff against Varsity the following weekend. Queen's won the toss to hold the game. It put in extra seats at Richardson Stadium and the next weekend won 15–5.

It had been a season like those of the early 1920s, with six wins and one narrow defeat; 109 points for, 19 against. There was talk of another Grey Cup and, of course, a desire for revenge on Rodden and the Tigers, who once again were the city-league champions and who would be coming to Kingston as Queen's opponent for the Eastern Canadian title in the fall of 1929.

A huge pre-game parade, complete with floats and a pep rally, was held on campus, all organized by Gib McKelvey (who, it will be recalled, had time on his hands in the fall!). But it was all to no avail. Pep Leadlay did it to Queen's again. This time he gained 11 of Hamilton's 14 points, against 3 for Queen's, to take Hamilton to the Grey Cup, which Hamilton won handily against Regina the following week. The *Journal* was not amused by Rodden's use of his other position – sports editor of the Toronto *Globe* – to

Frank "Pep" Leadlay (1921–25). From Hamilton, he was one of the most prolific scorers of his time (123 points in five seasons). He led the team to three Grey Cup championships (1922–24) and still holds two Grey Cup records, for most touchdowns (9) and converts (7) in a single game. He played with the Hamilton Tigers and is a charter member of the Canadian Football Hall of Fame (QFHF)

describe the game's outcome from his perspective as the winning coach.* He wrote that "Queen's University proved no match for the Jungle Kings ... the score was 14–3 and on the play might easily have been more." He

_____

* A certain conflict of interest was apparently not of concern to the *Globe*'s owners. Not to fear, for Queen's was to gain its revenge in this respect during the 1930s, as we shall see. It is ironic that Rodden eventually became sports editor of the Kingston *Whig-Standard* and wrote many columns covering Queen's games and singing the glories of Queen's. He was in many ways the dean of Canadian sportswriters. He is in both the Queen's Football Hall of Fame and the Canadian Football Hall of Fame, and his papers are in Queen's University Archives.

Harry "Red" Batstone (1922–27).
A great all-round athlete, one day
in 1921 he played in a Toronto
Argonauts game, left early to play
in an Ontario baseball final, and
that night played senior hockey in
Aurora. He played in five Grey
Cup games and later coached the
Gaels for three years. He was a
charter member of the Canadian
Football Hall of Fame (QFHF)

went on, as the *Journal* put it, "to tell the sport-loving public of Ontario, just
what a wretched bunch of howlers inhabited the Limestone City, and what
an unsportsmanlike mob local officials are." Needless to say, Rodden's
comments were dispatched as so much big-city vanity and as yet another
demonstration, if one were needed, of "how not to accept victory
modestly."[31]

CONCLUSION

Although the decade after the war had begun disastrously, it had seen the
finest hour of Queen's football since the university began playing nearly
fifty years earlier. Counting 1919, Queen's had won 38 games out of a total
of 59; it had had 8 winning seasons out of 11, had gone undefeated for
18 league and playoff games (26 in all), an all-time record at Queen's, and
in the process had won six intercollegiate championships and three Grey

J.L. "Red" McKelvey (1919, 1921–25).
From Kingston, he came to Queen's at
the age of fifteen. Coach Hargreaves
called him "one of the most gifted individuals ever to wear the Tricolour." He
played with Leadlay and Batstone in
one of the most explosive backfields in
Canadian football history. He later
served as the first full-time head of
obstetrics at the University of Minnesota (QFHF)

Cups. It is little wonder that Principal Taylor was moved to observe "that
the football team had done the university much good" for it had single-
handedly kept the university's name before the eye of the general public
throughout the entire period and indeed had helped "create a new corporate
spirit" at Queen's.

   In many ways it was a time at Queen's that would never be recaptured.
Rodden, writing much later in life, would say that the 1960s were the closest
he could recall to the 1920s. These were the Roaring Twenties: collegiate life
was fast, loose, and fun, and "booze" was a large part of the scene as were
liberated women. It was the age of the Flapper, the Charleston, Dusenbergs,
Prohibition, and the Mob, with fabulous wealth and few questions asked.
Clearly it couldn't last. Indeed, the first signs of the coming darkness were
already on the horizon in the fall of 1929. On 29 October, just two weeks

James "Bubs" Britton (1925–29). An outstanding athlete from Toronto, he was the 1928 team captain. He excelled as a flying wing, was twice named an all-Canadian, and later played for the Argonauts. He was also hockey team captain, was elected Alma Mater Society president and was also elected to the Tricolour Society. Canada's first ambassador to Thailand, he was a member of the foreign service for nearly forty years (QFHF)

before that final game against Hamilton, the stock market crashed, signalling the beginning of the end of the boom in stock and real estate. In Wall Street, men jumped out of windows. So, it is said, did some on Toronto's Bay Street.

The university, too, was in transition and somewhat lacking in direction. Taylor was a lame duck as the search for a new principal went forward. Meanwhile, there was considerable in-fighting among the trustees over who would get the job.[32] A suitable Canadian could not be found – several, including O.S. Skelton, having turned it down – and not until September 1930 did the new principal, William Fyfe, an Englishman, take up his post. By then the downturn in the business cycle had become pronounced.

Before moving on to look at the 1930s, it is worth noting what happened to some of the football greats of the 1920s. What became of Batstone and Leadlay? And what of "Red" McKelvey, Bubs Britton, Honey Reynolds,

Chick Mundell, Sprout Shaw, Bozo Norrie, Doc Campbell, and the others in that era of the nicknamed hero? A sampling is surely enough.

As we know, Leadlay, who had probably been the best of this very good group at Queen's (for among other attributes he could drop-kick so well on the fly), graduated and played on with the Tigers while working as an engineer for SISCO. He helped design several of the rail tunnels in Hamilton for Canadian Pacific before returning to Queen's in 1948 as one of the engineers in the campus engineering department. He retired in 1972 after contributing to the huge building boom on campus in the fifties and sixties. Batstone graduated as a doctor in the early thirties and went on to a successful practice at the psychiatric hospital in Kingston. Red McKelvey, one of the Kingston boys, also graduated in medicine and later became the first head of obstetrics at the University of Minnesota. Finally, Bubs Britton, captain of the 1928 team and Alma Mater Society president,[33] was in the foreign service for nearly forty years, at one point being Canada's first ambassador to Thailand. Their photographs and their Queen's Football Hall of Fame citations have been included here to represent all who played in those teams, and to serve as a reminder of the days of glory for the Tricolour – the 1920s.

3
The Dirty Thirties
But Triumphs Nonetheless

Everything grew worse for the country and the university soon after that championship season of 1929. As the economic collapse spread through the larger economies of Europe and the United States, the resource trade of exporting countries such as Canada began to suffer from a loss of markets as others stopped buying or could not pay existing debts. The situation was compounded by a general increase in the level of tariffs in many countries in an effort to preserve domestic production and thereby protect domestic employment. Since everyone began acting in a similar way, all trade suffered and, counter productively, so did employment, thus making the situation worse. Finally, inappropriate monetary policy, especially in the United States, led to the restriction of liquidity in the economic system and successive banking failures, which rippled through the system touching every aspect of commercial life.

Unemployment in Canada grew dramatically, from 116,000 in 1929 to 741,000 in 1932, and to 826,000 in 1933. "Non-agricultural unemployment was something over 27% in 1933, in the depths of the recession; and when underemployment and the lack of work for women seeking to re-enter the workforce is added, it was probably closer to 50%."[1] Farmers suffered throughout the decade not only from falling grain prices but from continued drought. Many lost their farms as a result. All this led to long lines of people seeking "relief" through "the dole," which in Canada customarily came from private charity and municipalities.[2] They were overwhelmed by the size of the problems and by a lack of financial support from either the federal government or the provincial governments, which struggled to maintain balanced budgets until 1935.

In addition to great personal hardship, the situation brought considerable political and social turmoil. Mackenzie King, for example, lost the federal election of 1930 to R.B. Bennett, the Conservative leader; Social Credit under "Bible Bill" Aberhart and Ernest Manning became a force in Alberta politics; the Co-operative Commonwealth Federation (CCF) became a power in the

West under the leadership of J.S. Woodsworth; and in Quebec, Maurice Duplessis came to the fore as leader of the Union Nationale.[3] Meanwhile, many of the unemployed went into relief camps, rode the rails, or lived in shanty towns. Some marched on Ottawa and held demonstrations, and on several occasions clashed with the authorities. Speaking very generally, the Depression grew worse until 1933, stayed relatively bad through 1935, and then gradually improved, with another slight slump in 1939.

No university could hope to remain immune from all this turmoil for long, least of all Queen's, which, it will be recalled, prided itself on being "the poor man's university." Its revenues were bound to suffer on all fronts: from reduced student fees; from endowment investments, many of which were in the form of mortgages or other interest-bearing financial instruments whose performance could be expected to deteriorate as the Depression increased; and from the hard-pressed provincial government's annual grant, which would perforce have to stabilize or fall as tax revenues to the province began to deteriorate from the fall in economic activity.

The fall in earnings on the endowment and the reduction in government grants pretty much materialized as one would expect, but the revenue from student fees held up, principally because of gradual fee increases through 1935, despite a slight fall in enrolment.[4] The university also ruthlessly cut costs. The moving force in this area was a tough Scot, William E. McNeill (he of McNeill House), who as vice-principal and treasurer reduced costs everywhere possible, except by laying off faculty or cutting salaries. (They were frozen but never cut, a remarkable achievement and one that is still remembered around the university.) Temperatures in all the buildings were reduced in order to use less coal; maintenance was delayed; great care was taken in the letting of all contracts; part-time faculty and staff hirings were cut to nearly zero; and so on. All this was not pretty, but the university survived. Indeed, it was considered a model among Canadian universities for its fiscal ingenuity and the propriety of its books.[5]

Adding to the difficulties of the university was the arrival in 1930 of the new principal, William Hamilton Fyfe. Having come from England, Fyfe did not know Queen's well. He thus had difficulty dealing with the various factions among the staff, some of whom had clearly opposed his appointment in the first place, and he generally failed to live up to expectations. It should also be said he had the misfortune to be principal in the worst part of the worst depression to hit the world since the mid-nineteenth century. He left in 1935 to head the University of Aberdeen.*

---

* More directly relevant to the subject at hand, Fyfe detested football. In a scathing general report to the university when he left, he devoted a special section, entitled "Gladitorial Games," to the subject. "Fyfe deplored the football fever

BUT THERE WAS FOOTBALL

This was not exactly a pleasant environment in which to play football, though the game did provide a kind of relief from all of life's little miseries, at least in the fall. Even so, Queen's started the decade well, repeating as champions in 1930, again under Batstone as coach (see table 3). The scores were much lower and generally quite close; for example, 3–0 over Western, 6–0 over McGill). The losses were to Varsity in mid-season (6–1) and to Hamilton in the interprovincial/intercollegiate championship game leading to the Grey Cup. Queen's was ahead 2–1 going into the last quarter, but it lost 8–3 on a late touchdown – Leadlay still causing the damage! Despite the departure of Ike Sutton, who in June 1930 had graduated in medicine, the 1930 team had a solid base of good veteran ballplayers in the form of the "wandering minstrel" Ga Mungovan, Bob Elliott, Howard Carter, Red Gilmour, Gib McKelvey (back from his suspension), Howard Hamlin, Bud Gorman, and others. And, of course, Batstone was by now establishing a reputation as an excellent coach.

The 1930 season was notable in one other respect, for it was the last season in which the forward pass was formally banned from the eastern game.[6] The West had been experimenting with it for some time, but the East had remained loyal to the more traditional single-wing, extension, kicking game. But in February 1931, at the annual meeting of the Canadian Rugby Union (CRU), the governing body for all football in Canada, the forward pass was formally adapted throughout the union for the 1931 season.[7] Despite this apparently radical change in the nature of the game,[8] it had no dramatic impact. Only gradually did it come to change the game, especially at Queen's, where the forward pass did not really become an important part of the offence until after the Second World War.

In 1931 Batstone was back as coach for the last time, for he was to graduate in medicine in 1932. The season began well enough, with three close victories (3–2 over Varsity, 5–4 over McGill, 8–3 over Western) and a tie (9–9 with McGill). However, a narrow loss to Western (3–2) early in November on a muddy field turned the good luck Queen's had been having in the close games, and the team lost the following week 17–0 to Varsity in

which, thanks to 'press propaganda and the infantile enthusiasm of the middle-aged' swept the campus every autumn and prevented 'all but the most sensible of students' from getting down to work. No other distraction, not even drinking or dancing, rivalled 'this baneful influence'" (Gibson, *To Serve and Yet Be Free*, 129). It is possible to understand from this quotation why Fyfe had some difficulties at Queen's.

Table 3
Queen's football record, 1930–1939[1]

Year	Won	Lost	Tied	For	Against
1930c[2]n[3]	5	2	0	42	20
1931n	3	2	1	27	38
1932	1	3	2	45	69
1933n	4	3	0	40	45
1934cn	5	2	0	37	31
1935cn	4	3	1	73	93
1936n	4	3	0	42	32
1937cn	5	2	0	42	32
1938	0	6	0	30	70
1939n	3	3	0	57	67
Total	35	29	4	435	497

Source: Queen's University, 75 Years of Football + 10

[1] League and playoff games only

[2] c indicates championship season

[3] n indicates non-losing (i.e., winning or tied) season

what the *Journal* called "a severe upset." Western went on to win its first intercollegiate championship that year. It is interesting to note that the forward pass was actually tried by most teams; Queen's tried five "forwards" against Varsity in the last game. It was tried particularly by McGill, which had an American graduate student named Warren Stevens instruct the players – until he switched to the Winged Wheelers, where he threw the first touchdown pass in the East in the game against Ottawa on 10 October 1931.[9]

The fall of 1932 brought fundamental changes to the program. Replacing Batstone as head coach was Milton Burt, an Argonaut player of the 1920s. Before coming to Queen's, he had been coach of the Sarnia Imperials, champions of the Ontario Rugby Football Union in 1931. Graduations and exam failures had taken twelve of the eighteen players from the 1931 championship team, so Burt had his hands full. He and the team were unable to deliver. They won only one game that year, lost three, and tied two others for the worst season Queen's had had since 1921. Varsity, now coached by Warren Stevens who had left the professional game to become athletic director and head coach (much as Awrey had done at Queen's ten years earlier), won the championship.

By the fall of 1933 Burt was gone, replaced by the Ring Lardner-like Ted Reeve.[10] Known as Old Lantern Jaw, the Moaner, and various other sobriquets (based on his appearance, his many broken bones, and the imaginary characters in his newspaper columns), Reeve had been a star player with the Balmy Beach Hurricanes of the 1920s and was a popular Toronto *Telegram*

sports columnist both before and during the time he coached the Tricolour.*
He was to coach for six seasons (1933–38) and win three championships
(losing two others in playoff games) all without a contract, working year to
year "on his honour." And he was to prove a more than adequate revenge
on the *Globe*'s Rodden, writing his column each Saturday evening after the
game and reflecting his clear liking for the university.

Years later, Reeve wrote in the *Telegram*: "Yes, there were a lot of happy
days at Queen's when the trees were turning gold and red against the
background of the old stone buildings, the smell of burning leaves hung in
the autumn air, and the Galloping Gaels were whooping it up through
practise at Richardson Stadium. Coaching was all right, like that." Reeve
was clearly a romantic of the first order. He was also a man who loved his
drink. There is a story that in later years, in the Maple Leaf Gardens press
room, someone pointed out that he was wearing only one foot rubber
instead of two. Reeve responded that he had done it on purpose in case he
got drunk and wanted to walk home with one foot in the gutter. He was a
man who was a larger-than-life Pied Piper to the many young men he met
not only at Queen's but during the war and after.[11]

Reeve made a difference immediately, even though he had no senior
coaching experience; but he had had success at the high school level in
Toronto. Like Awrey in the 1920s, his mere presence at Queen's began to
attract good ballplayers, for instance, Abe Zvonkin of the Tigers. And as
with Awrey, it was a combination of deliberate policy and money that made
it happen. The head of the Athletic Board of Control in those days was a
local businessman and road builder, T.A. "Tom" McGinnis, who "was
responsible for attracting experienced footballers to Queen's [including
Reeve] and for gathering financial support from other men interested in
football."[12] Summer jobs for players were found on road and survey crews
by Bill Norman and others in the Department of Highways. Meanwhile,
medical faculty, including Blimey Austin, contributed both directly and with
their medical expertise. Others made similar contributions.

Without this direct and indirect aid the program would have collapsed.
The Depression had reached its worst point by the fall of 1933, and people

---

* Reeve was described years later (in a tribute column by Bob Hanley of the
  Hamilton *Spectator*) as "long, angular, slouched, his prominent features are the
  prominent beak and jutting jaw, the appearance is shaggy dog and much of the
  humour is dead-pan." Several of Reeve's favourite imaginary characters were
  Moaner McGuffey, Alice Wippersnapper, Nutsey Fagan, and Bozo the Airedale,
  all of whom hung out in Bowles A.C., a restaurant full of cronies something
  like the bar in the old TV series "Cheers."

were desperate for any kind of work.[13] Young men of any athletic ability were attracted to whatever source could offer them remuneration for their football skills, for it was the only salable thing they seemed to possess. American footballers flowed into Canada in response to the money being offered, especially the younger players. They included Lew Hayman, Andy Mullan, and two who would eventually have a large impact on Canadian college football: Frank Tindall and John Metras. Queen's recognized that it had to compete in this respect or football would die, and this would have been intolerable in view of Queen's glories in the 1920s. So the university once again acted.[14]

Despite little being expected of him and despite having a still inexperienced team, Reeve almost won the championship in 1933, his players losing in a playoff to Varsity (10–3) after beating Varsity twice during the regular season. The intermediate team that year also had been good. Losses due to graduation were small. And with Reeve and McGinnis hard at work recruiting potential newcomers, the 1934 season began to look as if it had serious championship potential.

"THE FEARLESS FOURTEEN"

The season began precariously enough, with a 2–1 win over Western in the rain* and a last-minute 5–4 squeaker against McGill. Because Reeve stressed defence, his teams scored very few points. Of the forty-two games he coached between 1933 and 1938, nineteen were decided by less than three points either way; as table 3 demonstrates, the points for Queen's in those seasons were 40, 37, 73, 32, 42, and 30, noticeably less than 10 per game. Fortunately, the opposition usually scored even fewer, although overall in those six years Reeve's teams were outscored 304–234.

---

* Edwards reports that it was "so wet that before the game a student rowed a boat in one low corner of the field where a sign read 'Don't feed the ducks'" ("the Fearless Fourteen," 8). Drainage was a problem in the old Richardson Stadium for years. This was because the field was highly crowned in the middle and had a quarter-mile cinder track around the outside which sat on a raised embankment three feet above the field. One can think that such an arrangement would better suit reservoir construction, unless there were a lot of conduits for the water to run off, which obviously there were not. The track and embankment were removed in later years. Edwards reports that injuries occurred when players were tackled into the embankment, which was just out of bounds along the side lines – not a pretty situation.

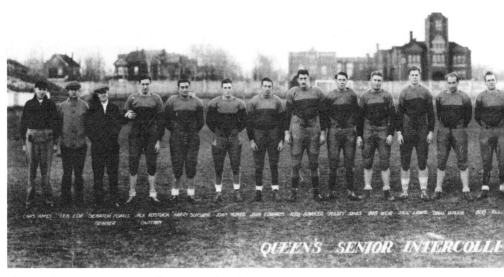

The Fearless Fourteen, 1934 champions (QUA)

As Herb Hamilton has noted, "The unlikely source of inspiration for this team was the loss of five players on the eve of the [next] crucial game against Varsity".[15] They had been banned from athletics for the rest of the year by the Alma Mater Society (AMS) court because they belonged to a fraternity. Gibson notes that "debate on the fraternity question was recurrent through the 1920s, but it was left to the 1930s to provide the drama."[16] Starting in 1930–31, student opinion, as represented by the AMS, fluctuated from being for fraternities to being against them, reversing its stand in March 1933 and then reversing again in February 1934 to ban all fraternities. The existing fraternities sought a compromise to keep all fraternities local and under the supervision of a joint committee of the AMS and the Senate. But in the fall of 1934 the medical fraternity associated itself with an international one, thereby breaking the compromise. The Senate, Board of Trustees, and Athletic Board of Control agreed to uphold the verdict of the AMS court when it suspended all twenty-four members of the fraternity from student activities for a year. Four of the twenty-four were members of the eighteen-man senior football team, and three of the four were of particular note: Hub Hamlin, Billy Glass, and Frank Earle. Reeve, in keeping with the spirit of the ruling, refused to call up members of the intermediate team and played the rest of the season with only fourteen men, thereby creating a football legend at Queen's, for he won the championship with just those fourteen – the Fearless Fourteen.[17]

Learning of the suspension before the Varsity game, the team (twelve going both ways, with only two substitutes) stiffened for the overflow homecoming crowd of 10,000 and won 4–3. The following week, on a sunny

RUGBY "CHAMPIONS" 1934

and dry end-of-October day at Varsity Stadium, this time before 21,000, Varsity turned the tables, winning 7–6 on the last play of the game. (Munro punted, and his kick was kicked back into the Queen's end zone. All points in the game came on punts.) Then it was McGill at home: Queen's 8–4, based on a blocked kick recovery and return for a touchdown by Abe Zvonkin, the only touchdown Queen's scored that entire year. The final league game of the year, at London, was merely a prelude to the playoff game against Varsity, which by this time was required, given the records of both teams and the split in season games. Held in Toronto, the playoff was as near run a thing as the entire season, the final score being 8–7 in Queen's favour. "The Tricolour had won the Yates Trophy against all odds, and with only fourteen players."[18]

When one considers modern football's multiple-man "platooning" systems, it seems incredible that a team could play seven games with only fourteen men dressed for each game, score only one touchdown in the entire season, stress defence with hard and tight tackling, which was bound to cause some injury, and still win. The Lost Battalion, as they were sometimes called, must indeed have been otherworldly as they kept coming at the opposition, never cracking, kicking and chasing, tackling like demons, and in many cases winning by only one point (2–1, 5–4, 4–3, 8–7). It would have been enough to give even the strong men of Varsity nightmares. How did they do it?

The players are easily listed: Reg Barker (former Hamilton Tiger from Pickering), John Kostuik (captain, Timmins), Doug Waugh (Kingston), Abe Zvonkin (Hamilton), Bob Weir (Ottawa), Bob Elliott (Kingston), Johnny

Wing (Gananoque), Harry Sonshine (Toronto, still playing without a helmet), Ed Barnabe ("Barnapple," drop kicker and passer from Ottawa U), Johnny Munro (punter and back from Jarvis Collegiate in Toronto), Curly Krug (Peterborough), and Jake Edwards (Ottawa Rough Riders), with Kirkland and Jones as substitutes (both from Reeve's earlier club, Balmy Beach).[19] Zvonkin scored the one touchdown, Barnabe and Munro did all the kicking for scores, and the rest played tenacious defence.

So how did they do it? It was just possible if no one was seriously hurt, if the team was cohesive, if the opposition was not overwhelmingly superior, and if they were lucky. Each of these was a factor. Edwards and Munro both report that although injuries did occur, none were major.[20] The trainer, who was as legendary in his time as Billy Hughes of the 1920s, was John "Senator Jake" Powell. A salty-mouthed but kind-hearted man, Powell used a combination of threats, embarrassment, careful attention to warm-ups and rub-downs, and various medical skills to keep the team going through the sprains, twists, bruises, and other minor aches and pains that were inevitable in such a situation.* While he had ready access to the best medical advice possible (as we have seen, doctors were always around the team), Powell himself was no small part of the reason the team was able to keep going as it did.

Secondly, the team had a purpose: to show that it could win in spite of the suspensions. Also, the players were close personally, principally because of Reeve's personality. They ate at a common training table each day in the old Student Union building, and in the evenings they often joined Reeve in his room at the union to help him with his column for the *Telegram*. There they would talk about the day's events, "have a beer or two," and sometimes even study. Since there were so few of them, it is easy to understand how they came to think of themselves as a gang with a mission (in modern terminology, "the Dirty Dozen plus two"), and that they did not want to let down their buddies or their friendly mentor and father figure, Reeve. It should also be remembered that the economic situation off the campus "wonderfully focused the mind."[21] Playing well and being successful academically were important because they ensured a good summer job and

---

* For example, Powell would not tolerate any malingering ("Get the hell off that training table! It's for real men"). He had a colourful vocabulary. All such players were "pisterines," the worst being "the hearn head of pisterines." He had a "loon list" of the craziest players (Johnny Wing was inevitably a member, as was Harry Sonshine, who was a personality in his own right). While these tactics may seem almost silly, they worked for young men full of themselves but welcoming of the male company and rank thereby conferred on them.

another year of decent circumstances. The alternative was unemployment; or, if one was extremely lucky, joining the pros, but this was by no means easy with the number of Americans coming north to play and when anyone with any athletic talent was willing to sell it for subsistent wages. There was also the fact that the team's average age was somewhat older than that of the student body as a whole.

Third, it is clear in retrospect that none of the other three schools were overwhelmingly superior to Queen's even when using all eighteen men, though Varsity came close in the opinion of Edwards, because of its outstanding kickers. Fourth, luck did play a role: several kicks bounced off goalposts in Queen's favour. In those one-point games, they made all the difference.[22] But all these facts should take nothing away from the achievement. To have taken the principled position after the first two games, a position that meant playing with only fourteen men (when few would have faulted Reeve if he had substituted from the intermediates), and then to win it all still seems the type of supremely ironic achievement that someone of Reeve's character would want to pull off. It gave the players a sense of themselves and their place in the history of football at Queen's – which still is unique.

LIGHTNING STRIKES AGAIN: 1935 AND 1937

By the fall of 1935 events outside football had started to make a difference to the severity of the Depression and, as a result, to the atmosphere surrounding the game. In the United States, President Roosevelt's New Deal program was beginning to make itself felt, dragging the American economy up from the bottom of the trough. This provided some export stimulation for the Canadian economy, which was also aided by the signing of a most-favoured-nation trade treaty between the two countries in 1935. As well, R.B. Bennett had announced his own version of the New Deal in January 1935, after years of opposing any such approach. Unfortunately, he lost the election that year to Mackenzie King, who received much of the political credit for the implementation of what were basically Bennett's policies. Internationally, 1935 was the year when the democracies began to pay some attention to rise of fascism. Although Hitler had become chancellor of Germany in 1933, it was only in 1935 that fascism really attracted attention, for it was in that year that Mussolini's Italy invaded Ethiopia. A year later, Canada began a modest program of rearmament.

As noted earlier, the university was thrown into uncertainty in the fall of 1935 by the rather sudden resignation of Principal Fyfe and the need, for the second time in six years, to find a new principal. After much early favouring of Vice-Principal McNeill, the balance swung towards Robert C.

Wallace, then head of the University of Alberta, a Scot (Orkneyman) who had lived in Canada for over twenty-five years and was the first scientist to be principal of Queen's. His appointment took effect on 1 September 1936 and lasted until 1951.

So the fall of 1935 was a time when change was in the air around football. Fortunately, the same was not true of the season. Back came Reeve's one-point wonders, who were once again at full strength, the suspensions having been served. After opening with a 9–7 loss to McGill, the team tied Varsity 2–2 and beat Western 4–1 before the games began to open up a little. The forward pass was beginning to have some impact on the games, with Munro passing to Bernie Thornton, George Sprague and other receivers. While defeating Western and McGill by relatively large scores (18–10 and 18–1, respectively), Queen's lost the return match against Varsity 19–14, forcing a playoff between the two. Queen's won it 6–4, having returned to the tough defensive game Reeve so favoured and thanks to the kicking of Barnabe and Munro.

Unable to resist one last try against the now heavily financed and strongly Americanized city teams, Queen's went up against Hamilton once again for the Eastern Canadian championship on 23 November – against the express wishes of the CRU and despite the official withdrawal of the Intercollegiate Union from Grey Cup play in 1934 (precisely because of the amount of money the city teams were paying their players in spite of their professedly amateur status). Queen's lost 44–4, and playing for the Grey Cup by Queen's teams passed forever into the history books. But the team was the intercollegiate champion.

The 1936 season was another close-run affair, marked by the infamous McGill riot in the opening game early in October. At the end of the game, with the result well in hand for Queen's (10–0),

a mass of Queen's freshmen, pyjama-clad and devilment-bent, poured across the playing field into the visitors' stands in pursuit of a number of McGill supporters who in the small hours of the morning [outwitting heavy Queen's security] had repainted in red the goal posts and various other fixtures in the stadium. In the general confusion, a number of guests were jostled and bruised including one McGill faculty member and his wife who wrote to [the] Principal ... conveying their utmost disgust at the behaviour of the Queen's "hoodlums" and pledging themselves in future "to shun Richardson Stadium like a plague."[23]

The principal was Wallace. The riot occurred the day after his installation, and it was his first Queen's game. He was not amused, especially as one of his mandates from the Board of Trustees on taking up the job was "to elevate the tone of student life."[24] So while operating within the established practices of student government at Queen's, he gradually tightened the disciplinary procedures.[25] He was never a strong supporter of football after that first exposure, and he came to see it as symptomatic of many of the aspects of student life that he was trying hard to control. He did retain an interest in individual football players, however, and was instrumental in bringing Jake Edwards back to Queen's in the fall of 1938 as the university's first director of physical education.[26] Edwards had been in Toronto doing graduate work and then playing for a year with the Argos.

Following the McGill game, the team lost the next two, to Varsity and Western, before rallying to defeat both of them in the return matches. A late-season return victory over McGill in Montreal set up a fourth straight yearly playoff against Varsity for the championship, which Queen's lost 11–3.

With Wallace having taken a steady hold, and the economy improving somewhat, 1937 brought a greater sense of optimism to the university. Reeve, in his usual preview of the season for the *Queen's Review*, wrote: "The outlook for the football season at Queen's this year would seem to point towards a sturdy, hard-hitting team … They will be underdogs on the dope sheets but they will be a fighting team. You may lay to that. And with a couple of reinforcements who may turn up (we usually find one dark horse or so), and a fair break on the hospital list, we may be in there again. Even if we have to brush up the goalpost play once more."[27] But it did not start well. Indeed, at one point Queen's was just a play away from total elimination from any chance of a championship. Having lost the first two games of the season (again by close scores, 5–3 to Varsity and 5–4 to Western), it was down 4–3 to McGill when, on the last play of the game, Bernie Thornton kicked a field goal to give Queen's the win 6–4. The team then won the return matches against McGill and Western, needing a win against Varsity on 13 November in Kingston to force a playoff for the championship two weeks later.

It rained: "The rain came down in bucketfuls; the field looked like a miniature lake, and not so miniature as that."[28] Signs appeared saying "Don't Feed the Swans," and students rowed around the field in a boat. The Varsity coach Warren Stevens told Reeve, "We can't play – my backfielders can't swim." It was to be known ever afterwards as the "Mud Bowl of '37." They played anyway, "ploughing through the boggy sections, wading through the smaller puddles, and swimming where the water was deep enough."[29] Queen's won 3–0 on the strength of Munro's punting of the wet ball.

This forced a playoff between the same two teams for the fifth consecutive year, this time in Toronto. The game has long been remembered both by those who took part in it and those who watched. Spotting Varsity an early lead, Queen's tied the game 5–5 with five minutes left. Then, playing two

The Mud Bowl, 13 November 1934 (Wally Berry Photo Collection, QUA)

scheduled overtime periods of ten minutes each, Queen's went up 7–5 on two singles by Thornton and Munro. Varsity marched back to the Queen's 16-yard line, only to have its attempted field goal on the last play of the game go wide by inches. Munro conceded the single point, and Queen's won the intercollegiate championship with its 7–6 victory.[30]

With its fourth title of the 1930s in the bag, only five players graduating, and several excellent prospects available from the intermediate team, things looked good for the 1938 season as well. Spirits were high at the university, despite a slowing of the economic recovery during 1938 and a financial crisis of sorts in the 1937–38 academic year (which was caused by Wallace's attempt to move too quickly with reform and was resolved by raising more money). The American President Franklin D. Roosevelt had visited Queen's in mid-August, just before the season started, to receive an honorary degree and to deliver what is now remembered as the definitive statement of American commitment to the defence of Canada in the event of war; it was the first public indication to the fascists that American neutrality should not be taken for granted.[31] Queen's was thus at the very centre of international attention, and it was justifiably pleased with itself.

But the football gods chose to look the other way. The 1938 season turned out to be a total disaster of the kind not seen since the 1919 and 1920 seasons. In a complete reversal of form, the team lost all of its six games, only one of which was even close. There had been far more losses to graduation than expected, and with Munro and the others gone, the players simply could not generate any offence. They had several early leads in games but ended up scoring only 30 points all season while allowing 70 to the opposition, who were now starting to pass with far greater success. As a result, the 1937 championship proved to be the last one Queen's would win in the 1930s. Indeed, it was the last one for nearly twenty years – until 1955 – the longest football championship dry spell in the school's history.

The 1939 season must have been a curious time. The country had been officially at war as of 10 September, just over a week after Germany struck against Poland and three weeks before the first game against Western. Nevertheless, the university, following the prime minister's lead in announcing that Canada would not repeat the war hysteria of 1914 by rushing men overseas, strove "to carry on as far as possible in a normal way."[32] It was able to do this largely because of the "phony war," the period between Germany's defeat of Poland and its expansion westward in the spring of 1940. This period, effectively the academic year 1939–40, was an anxious interlude of supposed normality while everyone faced the fact that sooner or later the time would come to fight.[33]

It was thus not an easy period for the football team or for any young man anywhere in Canada. Things at Queen's were made worse by the departure of Ted Reeve after the 1938 season* and by the need to adapt to the new coach, Frank Tindall, an American from Syracuse. As noted above, Tindall had arrived, along with the flood of American players moving north during the 1930s, to play for the Argonauts.[34] Many of the big-name players from the middle part of the decade, such as Munro, Barnabe, and Thornton, were gone. Tindall tried to open up the traditional Queen's game with passing, but his lack of experienced players showed. Several of the games were close affairs, most of which were won by Queen's. But the team could not contain

---

* Reeve coached professionally during the fall season of 1939. He then tried to enlist but was turned down because of his age (he was thirty-eight at the time) and numerous broken bones. He prevailed on his friend Conn Smythe (by then a major) who was commanding an artillery company in the militia to take him, and Reeve spent the war in Europe as Gunner Reeve. Munro (personal interview) reports that it was always amusing to meet up with Reeve during the war, in particular "to see this ordinary enlisted old guy in the artillery leading around a whole host of young majors, captains, and higher ups like some kind of Pied Piper – they were all enthralled by him." Reeve survived the war to return to his job as a sports columnist for the *Telegram*. He died in 1983, a strong supporter of Queen's to the end.

Western, which rolled over the rest of the league with a wide-open passing attack to win the championship in the last year of the decade.

CONCLUSION

Not only was the 1939 season the final one of the decade, but it was the last one for five years, since the universities (unlike the city leagues, which carried on throughout the war on a reduced basis) elected not to play the 1940 season or to play again until 1945.[35] Thus it is natural to think of the 1930s as a period complete in itself, one in which the team did well, winning thirty-five games while losing twenty-nine (table 3), taking four championships (and narrowly missing two others in playoffs), and having only two losing seasons out of ten.[36] It was not quite up to the results of the 1920s but was certainly an excellent showing by any standard.

It had been achieved by a combination of factors: the efforts of the players; the coaching of Ted Reeve, with considerable input from Batstone, who throughout the decade practised medicine in Kingston and helped with the team; and the financial guidance of men such as T.A. McGinnis and "the doctors," led by Blimey Austin but including Doc Campbell and others.

In this latter respect, the financial records of the Athletic Board of Control (chaired by McGinnis) show that, throughout the decade, football supported the other sports, aided by revenues from renting the rink to various teams and organizations. Table 4, which reports on the 1936 season as an example, shows that taking into account all sources of revenues and expenses, the football program ran a profit of $4,116.42. In 1995 dollars, this would be about $53,000 on gate receipts of about $178,000 (excluding student fees in lieu of admission, which contributed another $42,000 or so in 1995 dollars). What is not evident from this is how much of that profit was used to pay players, either directly or indirectly through "the doctors," who were often used as the vehicle, versus how much they would have received by having jobs in those very difficult times. In any event, the university never reported these transactions on any of its books, including those of the Athletic Board of Control.* This should not be taken as an indictment of Queen's football.

_____

* Indeed, there is evidence to indicate that it had absolutely no wish to do so. The registrar, in a letter replying to a Toronto alumnus whose cheque had arrived on her desk (for "scholarships" to be given to three named football players), told him to send the cheque to Mr McGinnis because such expenditures "do not appear on the books of the university"! See Queen's University Archives, "Minutes of the Athletic Board of Control, Files 1930–39," series 1, box 5, file 2.

Table 4
Athletic Board of Control: Statement of revenue and expenses for the year ending 15 April 1937:
Football

EXPENDITURE			REVENUE		
Travelling expenses			Senior games:		
Seniors:			26 Sept., Ottawa ex.	$439.15	
26 Sept., Ottawa	$223.25		30 Sept., Balmy Beach	389.62	
30 Sept., Balmy Beach	374.50		10 Oct., McGill	1,893.25	
17 Oct., Varsity	517.16		24 Oct., Western	1,563.00	
31 Oct., Western	477.55		7 Nov., Varsity	5,245.15	
14 Nov., McGill	393.08		21 Nov., Playoff	4,374.79	
21 Nov.,					$13,904.96
Toronto Playoff	564.70				($171,500.00)
		$2,550.24	Intermediate & junior games:		
Intermediates: 31 Oct., Ottawa		156.65	3 Oct., Ottawa	92.50	
Honoraria:			12 Oct., RMC	·208.10	
Doctor	300.00		17 Oct., RMC home game	62.50	
Ass't trainers	260.00		21 Oct., RMC	165.45	
		560.00	31 Oct., Kingston grads	54.00	
Coach: salary		1,500.00			582.55
Trainer: salary		522.50			
Equipment		1,303.46	Sale of programs		100.00
Wages: repairman		284.00	Proportion of special $4 fee		3,150.00
Advertising & printing		198.95			($38,732.00)
Travelling expenses: general		91.65			
Training table expense		732.75			
RMC share of gate		81.03			
Kingston grads share of gate		43.30			
Stadium rentals		2,170.72			
Amusement tax		1,164.29			
Trophy expense		414.38			
Ticket sellers, etc.		70.00			
Police		125.00			
Referees Senior	403.96				
Int. and junior	120.00				
		523.96			
Sundries		48.71			
Hospital & drugs		892.55			
Laundry		186.95			
Profit on football		4,116.42			
		($50,611.00)			
		$17,737.51			$17,737.51
		($218,095.00)			($218,095.00)

Source: Queen's University Archives, "Minutes of the Athletic Board of Control, Files 1930–39," 1/5/2.
Figures in brackets are 1995 dollar equivalents, obtained using the Consumer Price Index series (8–18)
from the *Historical Statistics of Canada*, 2nd edn., updated with the *Canadian Statistical Review*

Johnny Munro (1934–37). This multi-talented athlete and Queen's football great of the 1930s went on to play professionally with the Argos, and until 1960 officiated in the CFL Eastern Conference. He also had a distinguished business career, rising to become a senior executive at Canada Life (QFHF)

It was the way things were done in those days. All of those interviewed for this book suggested that it was necessary "not just to compete, but to keep a coat on one's back in those times." The fact that McGinnis, Austin, and the others did their job so well should be a cause of satisfaction, not denigration.

This is especially the case, given the clear record of graduation and the subsequent contributions of the footballers of the 1930s. In the first place, they went off to war, starting in that spring and fall of 1940, "not with the optimistic idealism of 1914 … but more with 'courage of a different kind' … the kind that recognizes all the dangers it is going to meet and yet resolves to meet them, with little enthusiasm and no heroics it is true, but

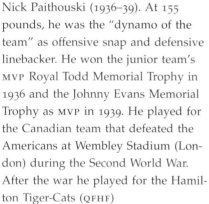

Nick Paithouski (1936–39). At 155 pounds, he was the "dynamo of the team" as offensive snap and defensive linebacker. He won the junior team's MVP Royal Todd Memorial Trophy in 1936 and the Johnny Evans Memorial Trophy as MVP in 1939. He played for the Canadian team that defeated the Americans at Wembley Stadium (London) during the Second World War. After the war he played for the Hamilton Tiger-Cats (QFHF)

Bob Elliott (1929–31, 1934). A native Kingston, he excelled in football, baseball, hockey, and curling. He both played for and coaches the Tricolour, serving as head coach in 1947 and as assistant to Frank Tindall in 1948. He was best known locally for developing top-calibre baseball teams during the 1940s and 1950s and as one of the foremost curling skips in Ontario (QFHF)

with steadfastness and determination."[37] Reg Barker of the early 1930s teams and a Queen's Football Hall of Famer went, and he died shortly after D-Day; Wimpy Byers won the Military Cross; Johnny Munro started as a foot soldier in the Royal Canadian Regiment and ended up commanding a squadron of twenty tanks in the Grenadier Guards; Colin Dafoe of the 1935 team was parachuted into the nasty partisan war in Yugoslavia and survived; George Carson was in the medical corps attached to Bomber and Fighter Command in England; John Brewster and others were in the air force; the list goes on.

Of those who did not go to war, many played professional ball after their Queen's days – for instance, Sonshine and Thornton. Others returned from the war to take part in the game: Zvonkin and Paithouski played for the Tigers; Munro became an official in the CFL; Elliott was head coach at

Ed Barnabe (1934–36). A native of Ottawa and a member of Ted Reeve's Fearless Fourteen, he was the 1934 Johnny Evans Memorial Trophy (MVP) winner and team captain (in 1936). He played quarterback and outside wing on offence and was an outstanding tackler on defence. A fine passer and kicker, his punts and drop kicks were responsible for many of Queen's close wins (QFHF)

Queen's for a season in 1947 and helped Tindall, off and on, for several years afterwards; Edwards coached the intermediate team at Queen's until it folded in the late 1950s.

As one might imagine, their subsequent careers were varied. Edwards, who is still remarkably active and fit in his mid-eighties, was at the centre of athletics at Queen's after the war and did not retire until 1977; Munro had a very successful career in the insurance business; Carson practised medicine for years in Kingston; others became lawyers, some rising to become senior partners in certain Bay Street law firms; still others taught school and became principals.

Compared with the 1920s, it is difficult to point to any really outstanding figures of the stature of Leadlay or Batstone. This may well be a consequence of Reeve's philosophy of the game, which stressed defence, low scoring, and teamwork. But mention should certainly be made of Munro, Barnabe, and Thornton, who did most of what little scoring there was in the middle of the decade, as well as Elliott, Carter, and Hamlin from the early part of

Bernie Thornton (1936–37). Bernie was an outside wing
and place kicker. Voted the 1937 team MVP winner of the
Johnny Evans Memorial Trophy, he was considered "a
great player and a clean sportsman." Bernie was named
to nearly every all-star team in the country, including
Liberty's all-Canadian selection. A 1937 arts graduate,
Bernie was a three-time all-star with the Argos. He also
played for the Blue Bombers (QFHF)

the decade and Stollery, Paithouski, and Curly Krug from later 1930s teams.
Photos of several of these players, with their Hall of Fame citations, have
been included here to represent the footballers of the 1930s.

   In summary, they gave Queen's one of its most successful decades of
football, they provided entertainment and a sense of pride for a student and
city population that was struggling to survive the worst economic depression in modern times, and they went on to fulfil their responsibilities both
in the war and during the long peace that followed. That is just about as
fine a legacy as one could hope for, especially from a time that will long be
remembered as the Dirty Thirties.

4
The Long Climb
1945–1959

As noted in the preceding chapter, all interuniversity competition was cancelled between 1940 and 1944 during the Second World War. But unlike the situation in the First World War, when many left the university to enlist, the cancellation was because of the need to accelerate academic work and because of the time required for military training on campus; there was little time to spare for athletics. As the war continued, initiation was cut back, dances were curtailed, and the mood grew steadily more serious.[1] Medical studies and then engineering were compressed into shorter periods to meet war needs; physics, economics, and mathematics professors, among others, were deeply involved in war-driven research, training, and management activities.

At the level of the country as a whole, the Second World War had a dramatic impact on the Canadian economy. For more than two years, from the fall of France in 1940 until well into the period of direct American participation in the war, Britain relied heavily on Canadian material support, not only directly but indirectly because of Canadian transshipment of American supplies. This support carried through to the end of the war, with the result that Canada's gross national product more than doubled in the six years from 1939 to 1945, with well over half of the war output going to those outside Canada. From its population of 12 million, Canada maintained a total military complement of one million men and fifty thousand women (in uniform), and it did this so well that by the end of the war it had the third-largest navy in the world, the fourth-largest air force, and an army of five divisions in the field. Canada's contribution in the Italian campaign, at Normandy and beyond, in the convoy and air wars, and in other theatres of war are well known and are proudly remembered a half-century later.[2]

By the end of 1943 it had become clear that the war would be won, and both the government and the university began postwar planning. The federal government was particularly concerned to avoid a postwar depression like that following the First World War. This, together with strong political pressure from western Canada, especially from grass-roots political parties such as the CCF, which were calling for social program reforms to ensure that the difficulties of the 1930s would not recur, led the wartime government of King to introduce social security and veterans' allowances legislation in the latter years of the war.[3] Veterans allowances were to have particularly important short-term consequences for the universities, while the social security changes would have more long-term effects in the country as a whole.

At Queen's, Vice-Principal McNeill, ever the thrifty treasurer of the university, had quietly been setting aside funds – even through the depths of the Depression – realizing that eventually the university would have to upgrade its facilities and build new ones. Beginning in 1945, his prudence and foresight, along with some hard-driving fundraising by Chancellor Dunning and others in the latter years of the war, began to pay off: a flood of students applied to Queen's. Indeed, large numbers were enrolling at all universities; by 1948, undergraduate enrolment at Canadian universities was twice what it had been ten years earlier. As the armed forces were demobilized, many of the more than one million veterans sought either to start at university or to continue their postponed university studies. In the first academic year after the war (1945–46), more than 60 per cent of the 3,000 students at Queen's were veterans. Their inclination to take up studies was strongly encouraged by generous government assistance programs for education, which were part of the veterans' allowance program.

One can imagine the pandemonium that ensued as students flooded in, as professors returned to take up their interrupted careers, and as administrators scrambled to find classroom space as well as to arrange a sensible scheduling of courses. These problems were small, however, compared with the need to find housing for everyone. People slept in bunk beds in the gymnasium; some even ended up in the wartime quonset huts on Alcan's properties; and people throughout the city opened their houses to student boarders for the first time. As Gibson remarked, "the university was flabbergasted" and struggled to cope with it all.[4] Into this maelstrom of activity, the university added the revival of intercollegiate sports. The war in Europe had ended in May 1945, and the war in the Pacific was over by August. Two months later, on 20 October, Queen's was once again in action, opening the football season of 1945 against Varsity.

THE IMMEDIATE POSTWAR YEARS: 1945–1947

The 1945 restart season was an understandably abbreviated one given the circumstances. Only four games were played, with Queen's going two and two under coach Bob Elliott, and with Western winning the championship. (A Kingston sportsman of considerable repute, Elliott had been one of the stars of the 1930s). What was not "abbreviated" was the outburst of emotion around the game and all the other activities that inevitably went with its resumption – initiation, dances, and, most importantly, football weekends. Gibson notes that "exuberances of student behavior ... [led] Queen's supporters, in their first two experiences of 'away games' in the autumn of 1945 ... fully equipped with paint, brushes, and refreshment ... to vandalize almost every standing structure at the University of Toronto and McGill. Their attentions were not well received."[5] The bills were paid by the levy of a fine of $500 on the entire student body.

As Gibson also notes, "the wartime suspension had left the university with no experienced players of intercollegiate calibre,"[6] and it took a while for the rebuilding to develop. As Queen's had done in the early 1920s when appointing Awrey, it hired someone from outside the university with coaching experience, in this case an American, Doug Munsson, who was taken on as coach and head of athletics for the 1946 season. It was Munsson's intention to develop Queen's football along the lines of the big American college programs. Accordingly, he began to recruit heavily, especially in the professional and ex-military team ranks.[7]

Unfortunately, Munsson had a style which several at the university found offensive – he became known as "the Big Monsoon," the big wind, because of his manner.[8] It is clear that Munsson seriously misjudged Queen's, and it him. So despite his heavy recruiting and despite running the then popular Notre Dame single-wing offence, the team went one and five in 1946, being outscored 138 to 41. By the 1947 season Munsson was gone, replaced by the ever-faithful local man, Bob Elliott, while the university searched anew for a head coach.

Elliott could manage little better. Although returning to the tight T in 1947 and with Lenard at quarterback, the team did even worse: no wins, five losses, and a tie. The situation was clearly becoming desperate, the team having won only three games in three years. This was unacceptable for a school that had enjoyed such outstanding success in the 1920s and 1930s. For the 1948 season, Orrin Carson and the other "doctors," veterans of the 1920s and 1930s and keepers of the Queen's football flame, convinced Frank Tindall, the 1939 coach, who was by this time working in the county clerk's office in Syracuse, to return to Queen's. It was not an easy sell because Tindall wanted assurances that the job would be somewhat permanent – not an unreasonable demand in view of the turnover from 1945 onwards and the fact that Tindall had a wife and young family to support.[9] It is likely that he got as much as he could have hoped for in that way. He stayed on until his retirement in 1975 and in due course had a major playing field at the university named after him, as well as the Coach of the Year Trophy in Canadian university football. He became a legend among Canadian college football coaches. Nevertheless, it was not any easier for him at the outset than it had been for Elliott or Munsson.

THE "CHARACTER-BUILDING" YEARS: 1948–1954

In 1948, Tindall's first year back at Queen's, he reverted to the single wing with Lenard at tailback and managed to improve things a bit, with two wins and four losses. But in 1949 it was two and three with a tie.* In 1950 it was two and four, in 1951 no wins and six losses, and so on (see table 5). Seven postwar seasons were to pass before the team had a non-losing season, and ten were to pass before it once again won a championship (in 1955). During that period, 1945–54, Queen's won only eighteen games. It lost forty, had two ties, and was badly outscored throughout. Gibson reports that during this time Tindall "cheerfully informed audiences of anxious alumni that at Queen's 'as everyone knows, we are less interested in winning than in building character among our players,' and adding, after a distinct pause, 'and in the last few years we've built an awful lot of character around here.'"[10]

Despite this wit, which was to become a Tindall trademark, he almost did not survive those difficult first years. There was a strong movement among some players and alumni to have him fired early on. It was alleged that he had been away from the game too long, was poorly organized, had no real offensive strategy (a most interesting fact considering his later, justified reputation as a master offensive football theorist), and that he therefore could not win. Fortunately, he managed to survive this early challenge, and with two championships in the mid-1950s he solidified his position. The 1960s would, of course, make his reputation.

There is considerable speculation about why this period was such a particularly bad one for Queen's football. After all, Queen's was recruiting as much as the other schools in the league, and it enjoyed some success at attracting several players of considerable quality and later fame.[11] Hal

---

* The tie game in 1949 was the source of another well-known Tindall *bon mot*. With the game tied, Tindall substituted at quarterback with three minutes left and the ball on Western's 15-yard line. His explicit instructions were to punt for the one point and the win. Instead, the substitute ran a handoff into the line, the back fumbled, the game ended up tied. Every sports writer in the country, as well as the conductor on the train home, asked Tindall why he hadn't punted. His reply to the conductor: "I didn't think of it."

Table 5
Queen's football record, 1945–1959[1]

Year	Won	Lost	Tied	For	Against
1945N[2]	2	2	0	35	61
1946	1	5	0	41	138
1947	0	5	1	33	146
1948	2	4	0	51	79
1949	2	3	1	75	73
1950	2	4	0	53	99
1951	0	6	0	43	118
1952	2	5	0	54	105
1953N	3	3	0	90	73
1954N	4	3	0	132	80
1955c[3]N	6	1	0	114	59
1956cN	5	1	1	106	55
1957	0	6	0	30	137
1958	2	4	0	67	150
1959	2	4	0	49	102
Total	33	56	3	973	1,475

Source: Queen's University, 75 Years of Football + 10
[1] League and playoff games only
[2] N indicates non-losing (i.e., winning or tied) season
[3] c indicates championship season

McCarney, for example, who arrived in 1948 from Loyola (and remained attached to Queen's football for many years) could have played pro with Ottawa but chose Queen's instead; Jim Charters (the "Doctor Jim" of later Hamilton Tiger-Cats fame and a major recruiter for Queen's in the 1960s) had an important career after leaving the university, as did Harry Lampman, Tip Logan, Bob Stevens, and several others. And this is not to ignore the outstanding careers of players such as Lenard and McKelvey while at Queen's. They were regularly named to the league all-star team.[12]

Evidently they were not enough, for the teams somehow never gelled, even though the records indicate that the score was close in many games (only to have the team inevitably find a way to lose). With time, a kind of defeatist attitude developed "where close losses came to be viewed as moral victories."[13]

What is likely is that there was simply not enough breadth of talent, let alone depth, at all the positions to make the team a contender. Lenard said that in one year in the late 1940s, he, at tailback, was the heaviest man on the team at 190 lbs., the line averaging 165 lbs.! He contends that Queen's drew from a much narrower recruiting base than the other three schools, an important factor in the postwar period when a lot of vets, having already been away for years, wanted to stay close to home for their schooling. There

Queen's vs Western, late 1940s (K. Carey)

was much less population mobility, and consequently the higher density of people in the Montreal, Toronto, and London areas made recruiting easier than in the less populous Kingston area.

   In spite of the dismal record, the team continued to draw capacity crowds, year in and year out, home and away. As in the 1920s and 1930s, football was still the centre of social life on campus in the fall if the amount of space devoted to it in the *Journal* and *Whig-Standard* is any gauge. The players were known to professors and townspeople alike. Harv Milne, a Kingston native, local entrepreneur, and one-time employee of the athletic department attached to football, remembers with considerable warmth playing against Queen's on a city-league hockey team in the late 1940s ("a bunch of thugs with a coach who had a monkey for a pet"). Many of the football players also played hockey. As might be expected, in more than one game a fight or two erupted. Milne fondly remembers "coldcocking" McCarney in one such melee, it being the same game in which the monkey, showing arguably good judgment, bit the referee's finger quite badly (the referee being none other than Mike Rodden, the columnist for the Toronto *Globe*). Fred Leaman, a local insurance agent, worked at the United Cigar Store in town and remembers the players coming in regularly for food, cigarettes, and other things. He too confirms the importance of football to Kingston in the fall during these years.[14]

The players also remember it as a good time, in spite of the poor record. They roomed together in the gym during the pre-season period and ate their evening meals as a group at Sugerman's Restaurant. Then there were the trips by train with the excitement of staying in big-city hotels. Most of the team were working-class boys to whom much of this was new. As always, several were "less than serious students" whose capacity for mischief showed their true intelligence much better than their grades did. The *Journal* reports on several incidents involving football players and more generally on student activities involving stink bombs, goalpost raids and defences, street parades, and various other practices that resulted in more levies being made on the student body to pay the damages.

Much of the hoopla that had long been part of the American college scene but had been somewhat missing in Canada came into full flower. A female section of the cheerleading corps appeared, and the pipe and brass bands were greatly expanded. Around 1950 a second bear mascot (again named Boo Hoo) appeared, and the team uniforms were changed from the old tricolour to a new, predominantly gold, colour.*

Meanwhile, innovations were being made in the game, one or two of which Queen's had an important hand in introducing. The practice of taking films of a game is a case in point, Queen's being the first university in Canada to do so by a considerable number of years, and well in advance of most professional clubs too. For this the university had to thank the initiative of Wallace Berry (Arts '42).

After his wartime service with the navy and some work with a film news company in Montreal, Berry decided to return to Kingston to make educational movies, and he set up his own photography studio. Having been interested in athletics as a student, he naturally gravitated to them on his

---

* McCarney was instrumental in both, getting the bear from the Moose Head Lodge in Mattawa (with Rodden's help). It was kept in a small building beside the old arena. McCarney helped supply bears at various intervals up to 1960, when the practice finally died out. An alligator also appeared for a while at one point! Fed on guppies, it died on a road trip to McGill when the heat in the stadium was turned off overnight before the game. The uniforms evolved from the 1930s older style through an interim stage of red pants and gold jerseys with red shoulder and arm slashes (1945–49) to the more modern "all gold" (by 1950).

Street parade, late 1940s or early 1950s (QUA)

return. As fate would have it, he ran into one of the "doctors" (George
Carson, chairman of the Athletic Board of Control), explained to him how
photography could be used in football, and, most importantly, said that his
old Montreal film company was about to import some state-of-the-art cameras from the United States. If Queen's acted quickly to come up with the
money, Berry felt sure that he could talk his old boss (Ben Novish, himself
a Queen's graduate) into letting Queen's have one. Carson seized the
moment, and in 1948–49 Queen's became the proud owner of one of the first
Arriflex cameras to be used in Canada, complete with one of the first zoom
lenses in Canada (a necessity for filming football from a distance). When the
National Film Board complained that it had ordered six cameras, it was

politely told that it had been possible to obtain only five. The Arriflex had a huge magazine (it could hold 1,600 feet of film – two magazines for a game) and was virtually indestructible, remaining in use until it was replaced by the video camera, with its instant picture availability, in the 1970s.

For years, Berry would climb a ladder to his perch under the roof of Richardson Stadium, shoot the game, ship the film to Montreal on the Saturday evening train, have it developed on Sunday by his old company in Montreal, and put it in the hands of Coach Tindall on Sunday evening or early Monday morning.[15] This added immeasurably to Tindall's ability to analyse what had gone wrong during the game and to prepare for the following week. Also of critical importance was "Popeye," as it came to be known (for the one eye of the camera), the 8 mm film of Queen's opponents' away games, which was shot by a Queen's fan who stayed one week ahead of the team. Before it became common practice to exchange films of games to allow for better preparation, this was Queen's special weapon for quite some time – until the other universities were able to catch up. Without it, things would have been much worse than they were.

The late 1940s and early 1950s were also a time of substantial personal transition, both for the university as a whole and for the football program. Robert Wallace, for example, stepped down as principal in 1951 at the age of seventy (the mandatory age for retirement at Queen's in those days), to be replaced by William Mackintosh, a leading Canadian economist with a strong record of public service.[16] Mackintosh was to be a good friend to Queen's football, looking with considerable charity of spirit on the many minor crises that developed around the game (the most usual being drunkenness, graffiti painting, goalpost destroying, railway-car trashing, and other "prankery").

As regards the football program, "Senator" Powell, the legendary trainer of the late 1920s and 1930s, died after the war and was replaced by Stu Langdon, who was equally acerbic and thus followed a tradition of Queen's trainers that reached back to Billy Hughes. Langdon had worked for Dutch Dougall as part of the stadium grounds, arena maintenance, and overall equipment management crew.[17] His place there was taken by Tabby Gow, a well-known Kingston long-distance swimmer, who would in his time become the team's trainer.

With the addition of McCarney and Lenard to Tindall's coaching team after they graduated, and the presence of Edwards as the intermediate coach, the group that would guide Queen's football fortunes into the mid-1970s was in place.[18] All that was needed were players. The nucleus began to form in 1953, but they did not really make their presence felt until the 1955 season. Before turning to these well-known and much-loved teams of the mid-fifties, it is important to note one other transition, for it was during this time that Alfie Pierce finally passed from the Queen's scene. It will be recalled from chapter 2 that Pierce had been around the university since the time of Curtis half a century earlier. "A gentleman of colour," Pierce "was the son of a runaway slave who operated a livery serving coaches running between Kingston and Toronto."[19] Myth has it that Curtis recruited him at the age of fifteen to be the team handyman and masseur, posts he never abandoned until his death in 1951.

But Pierce became more than that. Living in the hockey arena in winter and the stadium in summer, and supported by the university for the various odd jobs he did, he was possessed of a peculiar gait (due to badly fallen arches – he had been an excellent athlete in his own right, playing in baseball and lacrosse leagues until well into his forties when injury finally caught up to him). He was instantly recognizable. Everyone knew Alfie Pierce, having come across him in one place or the other, exchanged pleasantries, and succumbed to the charm of his idiosyncratic speech and dress. By the end of the 1940s, then well into his seventies and "woven into the Queen's fabric,"[20] he had become a kind of talisman for the team, and indeed for the university as a whole.[21]

Pierce was the key to the spectacular ritual of the Gaels' entrance to the field during those years:

Alfie stood on the playing field to greet the players, headed by their captain, as they ran in single file from the dressing room under the stands. He was flamboyantly dressed in the University's colours – blue tunic with red cuffs, yellow waistcoat with red buttons, and red trousers – a tall, stooped, dusky man, with large feet, gnarled hands, and a certain nobleness of countenance and dignity of bearing. He threw a football to the captain, who then led his men into a pre-game warm-up. If this took place during the various times when the team boasted a bear mascot, the bear would be somewhere near the head of the procession.

Flanked by a couple of comely cheerleaders, Alfie then made his way in a plodding shuffle, as if his feet hurt him, and they did, to the bleachers on the student side of the field. The ritual that followed is engraved in the memories of thousands of alumni and Kingstonians.

"What's the matter with Alfie?" demanded the cheerleaders.

"He's all right!" The fans roared.

"Who's all right?"

"Alfie!"

"Who says so?"

"Everybody!"

"Who's everybody?" And the reply would come thundering back:

Mr Alfie Pierce and friends (QUA)

"Queen's! Queen's! Queen's!
Oil Thigh No Banrighinn Gu Brath!
Cha gheill! Cha gheill! Cha gheill!"

Alfie would stand there, while the Gaelic war cry reverberated around the stadium, brandishing his shako, student trophy of a football trip to Montreal, at arm's length, and as the noise died down he would turn around and hobble back to the grandstand side of the field. His part had been played, tradition had been observed, and the game could now get under way. The entire performance had taken only a few minutes, but it was an impressive ceremony, carefully choreographed, uniquely Queen's. It was an integral part of the football season and added much to the enjoyment of the spectacle.[22]

Pierce died early in 1951. Tributes poured in from across the country and abroad – from the principal and the trustees, from former footballers, and from many others in a "spontaneous expression of goodwill … a remarkable display of affection":

He was given a funeral that was impressive in its simplicity and dignity. For two hours his body lay in state on the ground floor of the Gymnasium. His long-time associates on the Athletic Board of Control stood guard as the lines of the many who came to pay their respects filed past. St. James Anglican Church, situated within a few hundred feet of the Jock Harty Arena, where he had lived and died, was well filled for the service. The pall-bearers were six student athletes: football captains Al Lenard, Ross McKelvey, Jim Charters and Sam Sheridan, and Alfie Pierce Trophy holders Tip Logan and Don Griffin.

He was buried in the Church of England Cemetery at Cataraqui, near his mother and father. The grave has been marked with a stone, the gift of the Class of Medicine '34:

Alfie Pierce

1874–1951

A faithful servant of Queen's University

Dead for many years, his legend still lives on. He is remembered by many as the personification of what has been called the Queen's spirit. Twenty and more years after his death a caricature still appears in student promotional publicity with the inscription "Alfie Sez." His ghost has been reported in the Students' Union by reputable witnesses. In his own humble fashion he has made a lasting impression on the University and the community. May his shadow never grow less.[23]

THOSE CHAMPIONSHIP YEARS: 1955–1956

In 1953 the tide, which seemed to have carried everything away from Queen's football, at last began to turn for the shore. That fall, the team went three and three, and substantially outscored the opposition in total for the first time since the war.[24] In 1954 it moved to a winning season (four and three) with the points for-and-against spread being even better. Indeed, the 1954 team almost won the championship, losing a close game to Western in a playoff in late November. The score was 20–18 won for Western on the last play of the game when Gino Fracas – with Don Getty, the future premier of Alberta, holding – missed an improvised 45-yard field goal, which Ronnie Stewart fell on in the end zone, only to have the wet ball squirt out from under him, whereupon Ed Killinger of Western fell on it for the winning touchdown.*

---

* *Queen's Review*, December 1954, 254. The *Review* reported that despite having lost, the team was "greeted on arrival at the train station in Kingston by a couple of thousand fans, led by the Queen's Bands. Coach Tindall was carried off on the shoulders of some of his admirers and Stewart was given a rousing

What explains this gradual turn of events for the better? In part it was due to a larger sociology. The Cold War had brought the Korean conflict in 1950, but the situation was beginning to stabilize by about 1953, and people could be reasonably sure that the steady economic progress made since the war was not in jeopardy from global conflict. Sons of the middle class could safely consider a university education, could afford it, and could venture somewhat farther afield to experience it. Of greater direct impact to the football programs was the availability of better coaching at lower levels as the graduates of the new university programs in physical education began to take their places, especially in the high school teaching and coaching ranks. Thus it was that, by about 1953, Queen's was beginning to see a better brand of football player overall.

None typified these influences better than the aforementioned Ronnie Stewart and his early teammates Gary Schreider and Lou Bruce. Stewart was a first-generation Canadian, the son of Scottish immigrants. His mother had raised the family through her own efforts, his father having abandoned them after the war, and there was always very little money. Stewart worked for the first half of his Grade 13 year, then finished high school, Riverdale Collegiate in Toronto, in the rest of it. In spite of this, he was still only seventeen when he left to go to Queen's in 1953. He had been encouraged to do so by his good friend and high school teammate, Lou Bruce, who had arrived the year before. Bruce knew what others could not see past (especially the University of Toronto, which did not pursue him despite his excellent high school reputation) namely, that Stewart was quick, tough, nasty even, and certainly durable in spite of his size. But he was small for an offensive back (5 ft. 7 ins., 155 lbs.) and did not impress them. It was a misjudgment that others, even at the professional level, would also make – to their chagrin. For "little" Ronnie Stewart was to end up in the Canadian Football Hall of Fame as one of the pre-eminent players of the middle of the century. But all this was still in the future that fall of 1953.

Part of the reason Stewart had been interested in Queen's was that he knew that the team was thin in halfbacks and he figured he could start playing as a freshman, which indeed he did. Another outstanding Toronto

---

ovation. It was a reception reminiscent of the days when the Batstone-Leadly-McKelvey teams were met on their return to Kingston." Football was important to Queen's, and it was "back" by 1954! As additional evidence of this fact, in a time when the university had a student body of about 1,600, Queen's drew 27,000 fans for its last game of the season against Toronto in Varsity Stadium – a record for college football that has only recently been eclipsed (with the Vanier Cup in the SkyDome).

high school player made his way to Queen's that fall by a very different route but with the same expectation of playing in the backfield. Gary Schreider was a St Mike's (Toronto) product who had been raised in Belleville and had briefly considered the priesthood before choosing Queen's. Like Stewart, he had blinding speed; he was a sprinter of national calibre in addition to having a reputation as a football player. He did not consider McGill or Toronto, and he found John Metras of Western arrogant (as did many others). By contrast, he liked Tindall as a person, and it did not hurt that Frank was a "good Catholic boy." There was also the fact that Johnny Munro, of 1930s fame, heavily recruited Schreider and helped with some of his expenses in his early years at Queen's; and that Queen's was willing to admit him quite late in September after he had abandoned his intention to become a priest.

Unfortunately, Schreider was plagued by injuries that first year; for instance, he broke his collarbone in an exhibition game against Clarkson Technical College of upper New York State early on. Consequently, it was not until the 1954 season, with a healthy Schreider, and a year's worth of experience, that he and Stewart began to make an impact. They were joined in the backfield by Bill Surphlis and Al Kocman, giving Queen's, by the time 1955 rolled around, "the most-feared backfield in college football at the time."[25] Others were added to the mix. Jimmy Hughes, and particularly Gary Lewis, Jr (son of Lewis, Sr, of earlier fame), along the line; Jay McMahan, a basketball player of considerable talent, as a pass receiver to complement Bruce; and Jocko Thompson, the quiet man from Western as punter and field goal kicker.

But in 1954 it was not quite good enough, and everyone pretty much understood why. What Queen's really lacked, what it needed to make everything whole, was a good quarterback. And so it was that in the fall of 1955, Gus Braccia came to town. Anyone who attended Queen's in the middle to late fifties knows "the Braccia story," the story of the man who came and went, helping Queen's to its first championship since 1937. Songs were even written about him:

BONNIE BRACCIA
(to the tune of "My Bonnie Lassie")

Somewhere the Tindall crew
Feeling a little blue
Dreaming oh dreaming
Of winning football games
Then with the drums a-drumming
Then with the pipes a-humming

> Our Bonnie Braccia's coming
> Coming to Queen's.
>
> Drums at the school were drumming
> Oh how the pipes were humming
> With Bonnie Braccia coming
> Coming to Queen's
> We hear the Yates he's bringing
> No more Toronto singing
> Bob Masterson is winging
> Towards Calgary.
>
> We'll meet him at the shore
> Playing the pipes for him
> Dressed in a kilt and a tam-o-shanter too
> That's why the drums are drumming
> That's why the pipes are humming
> Our Bonnie Braccia's coming
> Coming to Queen's.

What is less well known is how it came about that Braccia arrived that fall or where he went the Christmas following the season, never to return. But first let's look at the season itself, for quite a season it was. Recall if you will that Bill Haley and the Comets were in vogue; Paul Anka was bigtime; Elvis, "the King," was just starting to knock 'em dead; all the slow dances were to Nat King Cole; and the Gaels were on a roll, at last.

They opened at home against McGill on 1 October, winning handily with Stewart scoring three times, Schreider and Braccia once each. The second game, against Varsity in Toronto, was lost 10–6 even though they were leading going into the fourth quarter (touchdown by Bruce, convert by Thompson).[26] A home-and-home series with Western resulted in two wins. The first, in Kingston in a mud game "reminiscent of that game back in 1934 when there was sufficient water in the south end of Richardson Stadium for some wags to float a boat," was almost lost, until Surphlis delivered two touchdowns in the third quarter, the first after a 71-yard return of a kickoff by Schreider, the second 69 yards of his own making through the mud.[27]

It was a similar story in London the following week, except that in this case it was Stewart's chance to shine – he scored three times to avenge the fumble of the year before. Back in Kingston for reunion weekend, Queen's squeaked through 11–10 against Varsity with a last-second field goal by Thompson (and he would do it again to Varsity the following year in an even bigger game). Had the team lost, it would have ended up second and out of a championship. McGill was beaten the following week, setting up the need for a playoff against Varsity. It was no contest the third time around for the two teams, the Gaels winning 18–0 on touchdowns by Braccia and Surphlis (once again 77 yards from scrimmage), and a series of field goals by Thompson. Queen's had finally won, "ending the longest stretch without a championship in the history of the university … Queen's supporters went more than somewhat mad."*

The team was the toast of the town. "It seemed as if every organization wanted to buy the boys a dinner." At one such event, "various presentations were made to the players, including signet rings from the City of Kingston."[28] It was the old story repeating itself, this reaction of the city and the university. It had happened first in 1893 and was made all the more wonderful in this case by the eighteen dry seasons since 1937. Stewart, Schreider, McMahan, and others on the team, despite considerable later success both in football and in their professional lives, remember that season as a particular high point of their lives.

Stewart, who by this time was being more than favourably compared to Leadlay because of the number of points he had scored in his three years at Queen's, was a consensus all-Canadian (and Schreider was linked with Stewart, much as Batstone had been linked with Leadlay); Hughes, Lewis, and Bruce also made the all-Canadian team. The *Queen's Review* stated that "overlooked in the all-star selections was Gus Braccia, who came to Queen's via Temple University, but as far as the Gaels fans are concerned, Gus was the class of the league. He could pass, run, and kick, and his handling of the team on the field was a treat to watch."[29]

Hamilton, in his book on Queen's, also gives "a lot of credit to the quarterback, Gus Braccia, a transfer from Temple University in Philadelphia." He goes on to say, "Alas, Gus received his military call up and was

---

* *Queen's Review*, November 1955, 224. Indeed it would seem that supporters had gone "more than somewhat mad" at several points in the season. Gibson reports that after the reunion game (with Toronto) which was marked by well-publicized incidents of rowdiness, "Principal Mackintosh wrote in an entirely relaxed way to an agitated President Sidney Smith who felt perhaps the intercollegiate playoff match should be cancelled in reprisal … 'For me to concur in a statement in this sense would be sheer bluff on my part. Short of some shocking demonstration I could not carry through on it'" (*To Serve and Yet Be Free*, 409). As noted earlier, Mackintosh was sympathetic to football; he thought the concerns exaggerated and perhaps even thought Queen's had a chance of winning its first championship in a long time and didn't want that to slip away in such a silly manner.

"The Boys of '55" – champions. Braccia (55), Stewart (45), Schreider (48, left front), and Surphlis (64) (QUA)

gone after one season."[30] Actually, Gus had left by Christmas and there is considerable question whether he ever had that call up, despite the university's public version of the events. Equally disingenuous is Hamilton's description of Braccia's coming to Queen's "via, or as a transfer from, Temple University." Temple was certainly the last school Braccia attended, but he did happen to pass through the hands of the Ottawa Rough Riders in between!

In fact, after an unsuccessful pre-season experience with the Riders, Braccia had been at home in Philadelphia, despite a relatively large investment the club had made to bring him north. Queen's learned of this after an exhibition game in Sarnia early in September, when it was clear that the Gaels needed a quarterback. One of the Sarnia coaches, a friend of Braccia's, told Queen's about him; some phone calls were made, and by the following

Wednesday, in exchange for picking up what remained of Braccia's contract (thereby letting Ottawa off the hook), Braccia was in Kingston. He took over at quarterback from Claude Root and started that Saturday in the first league game.[31] As has been amply demonstrated, he helped the team gell into a winning unit. And then he was gone.[32]

The Gaels were back in 1956 having lost not only Braccia but Bruce and Schreider as well, both of whom went on to play professional football with Ottawa. While still having the nucleus of a solid team (Kocman, Surphlis, Lewis, Hughes, and above all Stewart), Tindall was once again at a loss over who to play at quarterback. His indecision showed as the Gaels opened against Varsity with Stewart at quarterback, alternating with a young Korean war veteran from Clayton, New York, named Johnny Moshelle,[33] who was in first-year commerce. While Stewart scored, it was clear he was no quarterback, and Queen's was lucky to come away with a tie thanks to a booming punt by Thompson for a single point very near the end of the game.

The following week with Moshelle now at quarterback full-time, the Gaels rolled over Western at home in the reunion game, 35–0, Stewart and Kocman getting two touchdowns each. Queen's then lost to McGill at home when Moshelle was hurt early in the first quarter and the offence could not get untracked. However, the following weekend in Montreal they regrouped around Moshelle's return, and despite an early injury, this time to Stewart, came back to score two touchdowns in the last ten minutes to win 20–15. The next weekend it was a similar story, with the Gaels fumbling twice inside their own 20-yard line in the dying moments of the game but still winning 20–13. This brought the team to the last game of the season, needing a win against Varsity to force a playoff. Queen's went out to a big lead early, only to see Varsity close the gap. However, Stewart scored late in the game, and the Gaels won 19–12, thus finding themselves in a playoff with Varsity for the third year in a row.

Played in Kingston, the game is long remembered for the way in which Queen's won. Thompson kicked a field goal from the 20-yard line with seconds remaining in the game. It barely cleared the uprights but was good enough for the win, 4–2. For those who were at the game or who played in it, the drama around "Jocko's kick" is one of the moments of their years at Queen's that they remember most vividly. It came at the end of an extremely hard-fought game that saw Queen's hold on its own 1-yard line early and move the ball 60 yards in the last three minutes, mostly on the strength of Stewart's running, to set up Thompson's kick. It was the kind of win against Varsity that was reminiscent of Reeve's teams of the thirties, and it set off similar expressions of hysteria: "And then, the pandemonium. The jumping and the shouting and the singing and the screaming, and the cheerleaders

Jocko's field goal: champions again in 1956 (H. McCarney personal papers)

so amazed they forgot they were cheerleaders. The players swarming around Jocko; and everyone hugging his neighbour, while the little voice inside says this is crazy, it isn't possible."[34]

Indeed, so sports mad was the campus that year (the basketball team actually won one of its few championships in the 1956–57 year as well) that the *Queen's Journal* felt compelled to write an editorial entitled "So Little for the Mind" on the subject of the relative sizes of the library and the athletic budgets (the former was 70 per cent of the latter, something the *Journal* found reprehensible despite its huge coverage of sport).[35]

While on the subject of budgets, it is interesting to consider the financial aspects of that 1956 season. Table 6 shows that the revenues from football that season were $39,415.84 ($242,202 in 1995 dollar equivalents), 40 per cent of the total athletic revenues (but 67 per cent of all revenues net of student fees); it was the only sport to show a working surplus (of $1,738.20, equivalent to $10,680 in 1995 dollars).[36] Virtually all the revenue came from gate receipts.

Table 6
Athletic Board of Control: Details of revenue and expenses for the year ending 30 April 1957

A   Distribution of total receipts and expenditures for 1956–57

RECEIPTS

Stadium revenue	$6,263.86
Rink revenue	11,043.55
Hockey revenue	668.88
Basketball revenue	381.00
Gymnasium revenue	1,626.75
Summer school	143.50
Students fees	37,909.50
Football revenue	39,415.84
Total revenue	$97,452.88

EXPENDITURES

Athletic equipment, uniforms, etc.	$9,952.07
Travel expenses	14,169.40
Training table, meals, refreshments	4,949.83
Movies	1,681.65
Maintenance, bldgs, flds, plants	5,425.54
Utilities	1,985.38
Advertising, printing, tickets	1,595.79
Medical, dental, etc.	487.95
Fees, guarantees	1,621.00
Trainers' supplies	630.93
Laundry	1,601.42
Tutoring	611.00
Floodlights	5,253.25
Postage, telephone, telegram	657.90
Awards	1,141.98
Referees, rules commission	2,189.77
Police and commissionaires	1,390.00
Coal	231.45
Tractor expenses	56.80
Chemicals and oil	618.74
Music (rink)	107.20
Insurance	81.00
Game & meet expenses	501.58
OQAA-CIAU expenses	536.80
Employees' insurance	112.37
Workmen's compensation	205.75
Grant to band, ambulance	325.00
Chlorinator expense	160.56
Auditing	250.00
Office supplies	228.95
Colour night expense	504.00
Pension fund	1,252.29
Depreciation, furniture and fixtures	300.00
Miscellaneous	727.27
	$61,544.62

Table 6
(continued)

SERVICES		
Coaches	9,142.00	
Trainers, assets	15,993.86	
Foreman, labourers		
General office:		
Secretary-treasurer	5,199.96	
Assistant	2,351.90	
		$32,687.72
		$94,232.34
Surplus for year		$3,220.54

B Football

REVENUES		
Gate receipts	$37,340.84	
Broadcast	525.00	
Programs	1,500.00	
Donations	50.00	
		$39,415.84
		($242,202.00)[2]

EXPENSES		
Coaches	$5,117.00	
Trainers and assistants	2,293.00	
Trainer supplies	630.93	
Medical, hospital, etc.	419.40	
Training table, meals	4,601.17	
Equipment	6,593.64	
Travelling	6,569.24	
Advertising, printing	1,023.93	
Laundry	1,032.02	
Tutorials	597.50	
Floodlights, P.A.[1]	2,650.00	
Postage, telephone, telegraph	257.05	
Movies	1,665.65	
Awards	412.78	
Officials	683.75	
Guarantees	1,550.00	
Police	857.95	
Rules Commission expense	458.50	
Miscellaneous	263.93	
		37,677.64
Excess of revenue over expenses		$1,738.20
		($10,680.00)

Source: Queen's University Archives, "Athletic Board of Control: Supplement to Annual Financial Report for 1956–57"

[1] Year new floodlights installed at stadium; half of the cost charged to football ($2,500) and all expenses

[2] Figures in brackets are 1995 dollars

It is interesting to compare these figures with the 1930s ones reported above in table 4. The results suggest that the revenues were slightly higher in the 1950s ($242,202 vs $218,095 – both in 1995 dollars) but that the surplus on football considerably less, even making allowance for the one-time-only nature of the lights in 1956 ($50,611 in the 1930s compared with $30,282 in the 1950s). All categories of expenses seem to be up relative to revenues in the fifties, but especially "equipment." By the 1950s, everyone was wearing a helmet and various other pieces of equipment, such as shoulder and thigh pads, the costs of which, relative to the thirties with their far simpler uniforms, were much more. Still, football was a net contributor to the athletic program (indeed, greater than student fees) and a central element in the cash flow of the athletics department.

THE AFTERMATH: 1957–1959

It was good that the sun shone when it did, for it went behind a cloud again and did not re-emerge until the 1960s. The 1957 season figured to be tough. It was thought that Stewart would be gone, along with Kocman, Hughes, and several other regulars including Lewis and McMahan, who would likely not play because of the advanced stages of their medical studies. Tindall would thus lose all the league all-stars he had.

As it turned out, Stewart was the only one of the group who stayed on. But that did neither him nor the team much good. The club lost all six of its games, managing to score just 30 points all season – the worst since 1938, when the team also lost all six games. As an indication of just how bad things were, it was reported at the time that Stewart started the season needing only a few points to eclipse Pep Leadlay's all-time scoring total.[37] But Stewart got exactly six points in that 1957 season (despite impressive yardage on kick returns, and other runs from scrimmage) and wound up still trailing Leadlay when he finally left Queen's for the Ottawa Rough Riders in 1958.

The 1958 and 1959 seasons were marginally better, the team winning two and losing four games in both. In the 1958 season Toronto took further vengeance on the Gaels for the earlier three years, drubbing them 44–0 and 32–3, going undefeated, and winning the championship handily. And in 1959 it was Western's turn, beating Queen's 20–8 and 55–13 to win the cup. In both seasons the team showed traces of form but was really racked by its failure to replace Stewart and the others with players of like calibre and by a steady turnover, through injury, of what good players there were. This was especially true at quarterback, a position which had become the key to the offence as the modern systems evolved (especially in all versions of the т-formation). In 1958, a young Cal Connor showed good promise, but he was ineligible in 1959 for academic reasons. So Tindall used his sixth new quarterback in as many years, an equally young Kent Plumley, who according to all reports performed well enough but lacked experience at the senior intercollegiate level. Injuries also plagued the 1959 team (knocking out Fred Endley, a promising young fullback, for example, in pre-season) so that despite some good performances by Mike Wicklum, Mike Pettit, Norm Dunstan, Dave Wilson, Terry Porter, and others, it was just not enough to carry the day against the more powerful Varsity and Western clubs, though McGill was beaten both times in each year.

However, the pieces were slowly being assembled for the "great leap forward," which would begin with the 1960 season and continue through the entire decade. Connor, the Plumley brothers, Porter, Dave Skene, and several others would all stay on to play important early roles in the successes that followed. But before turning to those years, it is worth pausing to look back at the postwar period, to reflect on the achievements of several of the players and their later histories, and to consider the development of the game at Queen's.

A REPRISE

There is little question that the premier player of the postwar period to the end of the 1950s was Ron Stewart. He scored more touchdowns than anyone before him, in fact so many more that the closest person paled by comparison: Stewart had over thirty to George Richardson's six! Had he had even part of Leadlay's kicking game, he would easily have surpassed him in total points scored (which, as we have just seen, he very nearly did anyway). Like Leadlay, Stewart played both ways, as virtually everyone was still doing throughout this period. Specialization into offensive and defensive teams ("platooning") developed early in the 1960s. In this respect, the *Queen's Review* reports that in that disastrous season of 1957, Stewart's last, he "was at the bottom of practically every pile-up on the field, he was in on most of the tackles, he was in many instances the last man between the attackers and the Queen's goalline. Without his services, the Queen's team would have been racked up a lot worse."[38] It is clear that Stewart ranks along with Curtis and Leadlay as one of the Queen's greats of all time.

There are two or three others who stand out, as well as several who certainly merit note. Gary Schreider was unquestionably of paramount importance in the years he played. Indeed, had he not had the misfortune to play somewhat in Stewart's shadow (even though they complemented each other well), his exploits might have been better known. Then, too, he was not at Queen's as long as Stewart. Equally deserving was Jocko Thompson, the punter and place kicker. As has been noted, he single-handedly

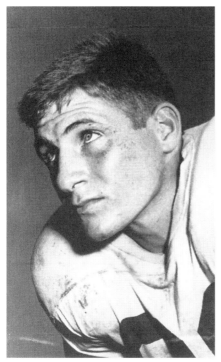

Ron Stewart (1953–57). Among the top scorers in Queen's history (152 points), he was named team MVP in 1954, 1956, and 1957, and was the first winner of the Omega Trophy as league MVP. He had an outstanding career with the Ottawa Rough Riders, was named Canada's outstanding male athlete in 1960, and is a member of the Canadian Football Hall of Fame (QFHF)

kept Queen's in many a game and was especially the nemesis of Varsity in the championship years. As well, everyone who played in those years mentions one other person, the centre Gary Lewis. A perennial all-star, Lewis anchored the line during the big years and was quite simply the team leader and captain throughout. There were others of course: certainly Lenard in the forties, and Bruce, Kocman, and Hughes in the fifties. All made important contributions.

"And where are they now?" is a question that is often asked. After leaving Queen's, Stewart followed Schreider and Bruce to Ottawa, where he lasted thirteen seasons, helped win three Grey Cups, and one day found himself in the Canadian Football Hall of Fame. Throughout his career he suffered virtually no serious injuries despite his size, and he left the game on his own terms before the 1971 season.[39] In recent times he has served the country as its federal ombudsman for corrections, a post that involves standing between the almost twenty thousand convicted persons in Canada's prisons

Gary Schreider (1953–55). From Belleville, he was part of one of the finest backfields at Queen's. He played on the 1955 team that won the Yates Cup for the first time in eighteen years. He showed his versatility in ball carrying, blocking, pass receiving, and punt returns, as well as place kicking (QFHF)

and on the street, the corrections system, and the government and public at large.

Schreider had an equally distinguished professional football career, making all-pro four times as a defensive back and linebacker. He was instrumental in establishing the CFL Players Association in 1965 and served as it first president. After his playing days were over (his last season was 1964), he practised law in Ottawa, representing many sports figures in their contract negotiations with professional teams. He also became quite active in larger legal circles and was appointed master of the Supreme Court of Ontario (General Division), a many-faceted job that includes resolving disputes between clients and solicitors over bills, arranging the court's schedules, hearing pretrial motions in civil cases, and so on. Like Stewart, he has retained an active interest in Queen's football, and he saw his son play for Queen's in the late 1980s and early 1990s.

The quiet kicker, Thompson, became a doctor and has practised medicine in Barrie, Ontario, for many years. The team leader, Lewis, who also became a doctor, practises in Seattle. Others, including Hughes and Bruce, became businessmen. As mentioned earlier, Lenard stayed at the university in the physical education department, helped coach the team through the years, and ended up as director of athletics before retiring in the early eighties.

Like the earlier players, they all speak well of the university, and especially of their football experiences. The period immediately after the war, with its returning veterans, had a different cross-section of students, but by the early 1950s most, like Stewart and Schreider, came from working-class families. They arrived at Queen's partly because of their athletic ability, to be sure, but also with good street smarts and with a strong desire to get ahead in life. In Tindall they found a father figure who was able to strike just the right balance between leader and friend. They were also befriended, though with a harder edge, by McCarney and the ever-present "doctors." Through the fifties the torch passed to a new generation of doctors: Dunlop, Kerr, Melvin, and Simurda taking over from the older group of the twenties and thirties such as Austin, Batstone, Carson, Houston, and Boucher. As we shall see, they did not lack enthusiasm for the team. If anything, the flame burned even brighter for them.

All these influences were needed. On occasion, things got out of hand. Kocman, for example, was suspended for punching Sgambati, the referee. And Braccia broke a guitar over a Western supporter's head in London (along the sidelines). But by and large they lived hard, worked hard, played hard. And most emerged from the experience with a greater sense of self-esteem, an appreciation of the need for there to be a "team" from time to time in human existence, and a sense that life had been very good for a certain period in their lives. In this sense, they were not unlike those who had gone before, except that they played in easier economic and political times than their predecessors of the thirties and forties. The larger environment supported a return to good times, college, football, and parties like those of the 1920s, except that a much broader part of society was participating.

As we have seen, the game was changing in several ways towards the end of the 1950s. By now, the forward pass and more "open" formations on offence were deeply embedded in the game; equipment was becoming more extensive and sophisticated; and the practice of platooning was beginning to show up, meaning that players could go much harder when they were actually on the field.

More important, perhaps, was the fact that television was beginning to bring the game directly into people's living rooms, not just at the pro level but at the collegiate level too. Queen's could be seen on CBC television in the Lakehead cities of Port Arthur and Fort William. College football and college life – with crowds of students in the stands obviously "enjoying" themselves (alcohol was an ever-present fact of life) – suddenly looked very glamorous to the many young people watching, and also to their parents, who likely needed little encouragement about the value of higher education. For many parents of the 1950s, a college education was a cornerstone of their belief about what was necessary for a better life for their children. Many students would go to Queen's as a result of this growing awareness of the university. Some, as we shall see, even played football!

5

The Golden Years

1960–1969

It is always risky to make claims about the "best" of virtually anything, for the term means different things to different people. In the present context, the "best" might refer to the quality of the experience, in which case everyone who ever played football at Queen's might describe that time as the best – and who could quarrel with them? But if one concentrates strictly on team results, if one refers only to the statistical record and assumes that decades are a reasonable time frame over which to categorize things, then it is the 1960s that have been the best decade for football at Queen's over the entire time since 1882 that the university has been playing the game in an organized way.

As table 7 shows, all the seasons were non-losing ones, and nine of the ten were winning seasons. The team won five championships in the ten years, and both its won/lost record (77 per cent won) and its points for/against record (1.94 points for vs. each point against) were better than in the 1920s, which is the only comparable decade (when only eight of the ten seasons were non-losing and when the won/lost and points for/against records were 69 per cent and 1.42, respectively). It is true that during the 1920s the team won one more championship than in the 1960s, but the nod of the objective outsider would likely go to the sixties based on the better won/lost and points for/against record.[1]

It is not clear why Queen's did so well in the sixties. To say that it had a better breed of football player than in the past or than other schools in the same period is to state the obvious. The question is why, and there is no ready answer. There is no doubt that coaching at the lower levels was raising the calibre of player who arrived at the university, but this was true at other colleges too. It may have been because of the better quality of coaching at Queen's, but the record and stability of the other coaches in the league – for example, Metras at Western – were equal to or better than Tindall's during the 1950s, and there is no evidence that the Queen's staff came up

The Golden Years

Table 7
Queen's football record, 1960–1969[1]

Year	Won	Lost	Tied	For	Against
1960N[2]	4	3	0	129	102
1961C[3]N	6	1	0	178	48
1962N	4	3	0	150	102
1963CN	6	0	0	154	82
1964CN	7	0	0	215	85
1965N	3	3	0	87	66
1966CN	6	1	0	207	75
1967N	4	2	0	135	87
1968CN	8	1	0	265	109
1969N	5	2	0	133	96
Total	53	16	0	1,653	852

Source: Queen's University, 75 *Years of Football + 10*
[1] League and playoff games only
[2] N indicates non-losing (i.e., winning or tied) season
[3] C indicates championship season

with any brilliant innovations in the game on a regular basis during the 1960s which others could not or did not copy.[2] Nor is there any evidence that Queen's had adopted different admission or "support" standards from the rest which might have drawn better players to it on a continuing basis.

There are, however, three factors (besides good coaching) that might help explain what transpired. The first is longevity. For reasons that again are not clear, Queen's seemed to keep more of its good players longer than others in the league did. Many stayed on to do postgraduate study at the university or to work for a degree in medicine or law after their four-year undergraduate degree. Since there was no ceiling on the number of years one could play (unlike the five-year limit today), Queen's could and often did find itself fielding a team with an average number of years of playing experience in excess of five. And given that each player was good and that some were outstanding, it was difficult to beat Queen's with a younger, more inexperienced team, even though that team might have some players who were better than the ones Queen's had to offer at their particular positions.

The second factor is depth, which is related to the first, for the longevity meant that good rookie players, who were arriving at the university with the ever-increasing flood of students, simply helped augment or deepen the team in ways that others could not match. But this still begs the question of why Queen's was able to hold its players longer than the other schools. For that there is no clear answer; it just did so, because of the nature of the players it happened to get.

Thus, the players themselves are an obvious third factor. For they were, for the most part, not only there for a longer time, but they were good and had chosen Queen's. They had done so partly because of vigorous work by alumni, especially ex-football players, high school coaches, and teachers. But other schools, of course, were equally active. So in part it was no doubt the luck of the draw – at first. And then, as the reputation built, it was because of the desire to play with a winning team.

For whatever reasons, the 1960s were to prove the truly golden years of Golden Gael football. As a result, there is much that one could say about them. We shall consider in turn the period 1960–62, when the main competition was McGill; 1963–64, the back-to-back undefeated seasons, one of only two such occurrences in Queen's football history (the other being 1923–24); then 1965–67, with the championship in 1966; and finally 1968–69, which includes the first Vanier Cup winning season for the university. Each has its own particular story to tell.

"JAMES McGILL, JAMES McGILL": 1960–1962

The decade that was to change not only the fortunes of Queen's football but society at large began innocently enough. John Diefenbaker and the Conservatives had been in power federally since 1957 (after a long run of Liberal governments since the war), and except for the controversy over American missiles and the cancellation of the Avro Arrow airplane construction project, the country seemed to be peacefully working its way along a prosperous timeline within well-defined political and economic norms.

Change was, however, on its way, bubbling up from the bottom and coming in from abroad, especially from south of the border. It is interesting to note that four novels were published in 1959 which readers today will recognize as important to Canadian literature: Hugh MacLennan's *The Watch That Ends the Night*, Mordecai Richler's *The Apprenticeship of Duddy Kravitz*, Brian Moore's *The Luck of Ginger Coffey*, and Sheila Watson's *The Double Hook*.[3] Several of these, especially Richler's, were to become important to the young in Canada in ways similar to T.S. Eliot's poem "Prufrock" or J.D. Salinger's work from the United States. And in the United States, visions of the new and possible were being played out in the 1960 presidential campaign that led to the election of John F. Kennedy in the fall of that year.

It would take a while for all this to reach Queen's in ways strong enough to make a real impact. Consequently, in the early years of the decade, things remained much as they had been, though signs of the "newer world" became more frequent and stronger as the decade moved along. One institutional change of note did occur at the beginning of the decade which provided some outward evidence at least of change. Principal Mackintosh retired in mid-1961 to be succeeded by James Alexander Corry, a political scientist of considerable repute. Corry, however, was a "quiet man," who although leading the university well during an important part of the decade (he had announced on taking the position that he would serve only one term of five years), took more of a bemused, detached interest in the revolution that was occurring around him rather than an active and directive role in shaping it, as did several other university heads, especially in the United States.

It was in this climate of dimly perceivable social revolution that Queen's began its first football season of the decade in the fall of 1960. Although the team had suffered three consecutive losing seasons, it had carried over a nucleus of good players from the 1959 club: Mike Wicklum, Don Robb, Kent Plumley, Robin Ritchie, and others. It also had Cal Connor once again at quarterback. It was clear, in fact, that both McGill and Queen's, which had been the doormats of the league over the previous seasons, had made substantial improvements.[4] While McGill started slowly, losing narrowly to Queen's and Western, it grew steadily stronger, beating Varsity and Western by large margins towards the end of the season. Queen's, on the other hand, won its first two games but then split with Western and lost to McGill in early November to force a playoff with McGill.

The game was played in Richardson Stadium, once again jammed to capacity, with more than two thousand McGill supporters among the crowd. Queen's was hopeful,* but McGill won 21–0 on the strength of Tom Skypeck's arm (all three touchdowns coming on passes), and a shutting down of the Queen's ground game. It had been twenty-two years (1938) since McGill last won a championship – an even more unenviable record than that of Queen's in the 1950s – and pandemonium broke out in Kingston, this time with McGill fans on the tear. As usual, it involved goalposts and graffiti; also as usual, things eventually settled down, were patched

---

* Mackintosh apparently "dispatched news of recent scores to a colleague in England, remarking in cheerful anticipation: 'If we can defeat McGill here this Saturday, our team shall have won a championship, which is a good thing once in a while'" (Gibson, *To Serve and Yet Be Free*, 412). He did not get his wish in that last football season of his principalship. This was unfortunate, for Mackintosh had been a good supporter of football, no doubt because he enjoyed the game but also because it likely helped keep the university in the public eye, which was important to him, for he was a "building principal" (Gibson, *To Serve and Yet Be Free*, 412) and needed the strong financial support of friends and alumni of the university.

over, but not forgotten. The need for revenge was carried over by players and fans alike.

Much was thus expected of the 1961 season. The team did not disappoint. As luck would have it, Queen's opened against McGill, winning 8–7 on the strength of a 110-yard return of the second-half kickoff by Pettit and Dunstan (a lateral was involved). The team then beat Western and Toronto handily in both of the games against each, only to lose to McGill in Montreal in the last game of the season, 15–7. This forced a second playoff in as many years, once again in Kingston. This time the Gaels won 11–0, avenging their shutout loss of the year before and winning their first championship since 1956.

The *Queen's Review* noticed for the first time what was discussed at the beginning of this chapter: "Such was the strength of Queen's that when injuries forced a man to the sidelines, there was a strong replacement … Every week Coach Tindall was faced with the task of making difficult choices, knowing full well that there was little if anything to choose between the man he finally decided to dress and those he didn't."[5] This depth of talent showed up in the scoring titles and all-star results, Bill Sirman of Queen's winning the former, and eleven Gaels (including Sirman, Erickson, Skene, Bethune, and Connor, who was also named the league's most valuable player) securing nominations to the latter.

It was more of the same in 1962. Both teams were back with veteran clubs sprinkled with good rookies. Of particular note was Jimmy Young, who was to distinguish himself over the three years he played at Queen's and who later had a long and successful professional career. However, the league was much stronger overall, and at the beginning of the final weekend of the regular season there was the very real possibility of a four-way tie for first place. Fortunately this did not happen; Queen's and McGill found themselves tied for first place and once again had to play off for the title.

Again the game took place in Kingston (Tindall having won yet another coin toss over the phone). But the Gaels lost, 15–13, when McGill, starting from its 7-yard line with less than three minutes to play, went the length of the field to score, and Queen's ran out of time to try for the field goal to win, with the ball resting on the McGill 30-yard line. "Close, But No Cigar," said the headlines. Once again it was McGill's turn: Skypeck, Lambert, Taylor, Stefl, Mackenzie were back on top; Connor, Plumley, Erickson, Sirman, the Quinns, and the Rasmussens on the losing end. It was particularly hard, especially for such long-serving veterans as Porter and Skene, for whom the game was their last (as it was for Plumley, Ritchie, the Quinn brothers, and Sirman, all of whom had done a great deal to rebuild the reputation of Queen's football).[6] For those who remained, it brought the same sense of anger and need for revenge as that which had motivated the 1961 club after the playoff in 1960. It also brought the same result.

UNDEFEATED, BACK TO BACK: 1963–1964[7]

Despite the losses to graduation, the Gaels were picked by many of the experts to win the title without a loss in 1963.[8] They still had a veteran team (that deep was the talent) going both ways, with standouts in Connor, Young, Norrie (the son of Bozo Norrie of 1920s fame),[9] Edwards, Ware, Erickson, Miklas, Thompson, the Rasmussens, Latham, Greenwood, Ferguson, and others. They started slowly and never really dominated (except against Western, 51–9, at the end of the season), winning by such close scores as 20–18 and 19–15 (see appendix A). But the end result was that they had in fact gone undefeated in league and playoff games for the first time since the 1924 season, winning the championship without the need for a playoff.

This was not the end of the story, however. To quote the *Queen's Review*: "If the Gaels had stopped with the Intercollegiate championship, they might have evoked some dreams of invincibility, but they accepted a challenge from the University of Alberta's Golden Bears for a post-season game to determine whether the West could play football with the East, something which had been decided decisively otherwise in previous encounters."[10] The *Review* went on to say that it was "a natural setup," since the Golden Bears and Golden Gaels were both undefeated and since there was room for one more game that year without violating Queen's regulation that only one post-season game could be played. It would be the first East–West college game in about five years (including the odd exhibition game), and it served as a precursor to the first Vanier Cup, which was played in 1965.*

The game was played in Edmonton on a clear but very cold mid-November day, and the result was 25–7 for Alberta. "Stunned Queen's fans were left grasping at straws to explain away the defeat. Coach Tindall offered no excuses, and neither did the team."[11] There were, however, a few mitigating

---

* Cosentino (personal correspondence) reports that the University of British Columbia and Western had played the odd exhibition game as early as 1956 and that they met in Varsity Stadium in 1959 for what was billed as the "first Dominion University championship." (Western won, the trophy for both this game and the exhibition ones being the Churchill Cup.) However, the practice did not take off until 1965, when the Vanier Cup began. The Gaels/Golden Bear game of 1963 would have undoubtedly been the start of today's nationwide playoff system if the 1964 challenge by McMaster had not transpired (see below). So in that sense it can be seen as the precursor to the Vanier Cup. It was certainly the first time *Queen's* had played anyone from the West since it beat Regina 54–0 to win the Grey Cup exactly forty years earlier.

On the trip west, November 1963, with Miklas in appropriate flying gear (QUA)

circumstances, which those who made the trip have usually been disposed to offer when the subject comes up. The principal problem was the airplane in which they flew West. In its strong desire to measure itself against the East, the University of Alberta and its alumni had arranged enough financing to transport about thirty-five Queen's players, coaches, and others at regularly scheduled TCA (now Air Canada) fares. Queen's chose instead to use the money to charter a plane so that as many as possible of the players, doctors, and others associated with the team could make the trip. They chartered a C-46, which Nordair was using to fly some of its polar routes. A vintage Second Word War plane, it shook, rattled, and bounced its way from Trenton to Edmonton, taking fourteen hours and two refuelling stops during the night to do so.

For many of the players, this was their first experience of flying, and few of them slept; a good many were ill. Add to this a time change and the fact that they had little opportunity to recover or acclimatize (for they arrived at midday on Friday for a game twenty-four hours later), and it seems likely that they would have stood little chance even against much weaker opposition than Alberta. Although the Golden Bears were much lighter than the Gaels, they were quicker and hard hitting, and they shut down the Gaels' running game running up 25 points by virtue of playing almost the entire game in Queen's end of the field.[12] The team was shattered by the result, angry about the circumstances, and fearful of flying home in the same machine. Some of the players refused to do so and took commercial flights at their own expense. The rest made the long trip back and spent the next month recovering from the ordeal.* All vowed that next year there would be a return game, in Kingston, and "God help those sons-a-bitches then!"[13]

Virtually the same cast opened the 1964 season for the Gaels with two narrow victories: over Western, 11–9, and over McGill, 13–12. Then the team hit its stride, winning the next four games with ease. It thus went undefeated for two consecutive years – only the second Queen's team to do so (the first having been the 1923–24 team forty years earlier). The Golden Bears kept pace, winning again out West, so the stage seemed set for the much-anticipated rematch of the two teams in Kingston.

However, it was not to be. Exercising a little-known and relatively recent option to challenge for the Yates Cup, McMaster (which was undefeated in its own conference of lesser-known football schools, the Intermediate Intercollegiate, and which perhaps hoped to emulate the success of Alberta and St Francis Xavier the year before) insisted on its right to play Queen's and would not give way. Nor would the administration relax its rule that only one post-season game could be played. As a result, Queen's was forced to play McMaster instead of Alberta. The players took out their fury on the hapless Marauders, winning 63–6, and walked away never to know whether the "stain would have been wiped away" (to quote the school song) had they had a second chance at Alberta.

In retrospect, it seems a shame that they were not given the chance, because in all other respects the 1963–64 teams were outstanding. Tindall referred to them as his "best teams ever since coming to Queen's in 1939," and the statistics bear him out.[14] Several players went on to have outstanding professional careers, especially Jim Young, who that year was the first Canadian college player to be drafted by a National Football League (NFL) team (the Minnesota Vikings). If he had stayed longer at Queen's, he would likely have challenged Stewart's and Leadlay's scoring titles. Heino Lilles, who would eventually do so, was also on the 1963–64 teams, as were Bayne

---

* The trip home was even more onerous than the one out. The plane circled the airport in Edmonton in a light snow, trying to retract the landing gear, then landing for repairs to it and the heater in the cockpit before taking off again. Over Sault Ste Marie it flew through a serious thunder and electrical storm, bouncing about like a cork in the sea – while Kerr, one of the team's physicians, helped matters considerably with continual verses of "When the Roll Is Called Up Yonder, I'll Be There"! Many of those on the team report that they had trouble flying for years afterwards. It is part of the reason why their inability to play Alberta a year later (see below) sticks so much in the craw of the 1963 players. A high price was paid with no chance for redemption.

Frank Tindall and Hal McCarney with the defence, 1964 (Wally Berry Photo Collection, QUA)

Norrie and Mike Law, both of whom later had good careers with the Edmonton Eskimos. As noted above, these were teams deep in talent in a way few previous Queen's teams had been.[15]

THE MIDDLE YEARS: 1965–1967

The 1964 season represented a kind of watershed for the team, just as the period did for the university as a whole and society at large. It would take a year or so in transition, but by 1966–67 the revolution that was the sixties had arrived at Queen's, and the newer influences began to replace the old.

It had begun with the Kennedy presidency in the United States and the new music out of Britain. A sense of idealism (tempered by one of betrayal, stemming especially from John F. Kennedy's assassination) and new and radically different styles of dress, music, talk, and behaviour (what historian

J.M. Bumsted has referred to as "an emancipation of manners") gradually began to be diffused through youth populations everywhere, primarily through the power of television: bell-bottomed jeans, longer hair on men and women alike, and the return of beards; the Beatles and the Rolling Stones; the casual use, by both sexes, of words not heard before in polite society; the appearance of drugs; and the greater sexual freedom of women as a result of the birth-control pill. All were present at Queen's by 1967.

So was a general distrust of older authority and values. This was partly a spillover from the Vietnam War protests in the United States – which by 1967 were becoming important as President Johnson, Defence Secretary McNamara, and others prosecuted an ever-larger war on the Asian subcontinent. The attitude also stemmed from the anti-materialistic, pro-people, and environmental concerns of the young. Also important to young Canadians was a growing sense of Canadian nationalism. The country acquired its very own new flag in 1965 (brought in by Lester Pearson's government), and it celebrated the hundredth anniversary of Confederation in 1967, during which year Expo '67 in Montreal came to symbolize a new sense of Canadian pride.

What swept all this forward at such a dizzying pace was the sheer weight of numbers. The baby boom had started at the end of the Second World War as the men returned home and as people became ever more certain of economic prosperity and political and military stability. By the late 1960s, the front of this wave, bringing with it the seeds of these new ideas and behaviour, was beginning to hit the universities. The impact on Queen's was dramatic: in Mackintosh's last year, 1961, enrolment had stood at 3,089 students – up about 900 from when he took over from Wallace ten years earlier. By 1967, Corry's last year as principal, it had nearly doubled to 5,838.[16] Construction and renovation were to be seen everywhere on campus: new residences (Victoria Hall, Leonard Field), new buildings (for mathematics, physics, engineering, among others), and extensive library renovations and other projects were the order of the day.

The football team reflected these larger influences. As mentioned above, most of the carry-overs from the fifties – such as Porter, Skene, Ritchie, Plumley, and Connor, who had helped the team to the 1961 championship – were gone. By the end of the 1964 season, so were the bulk of the late-fifties intermediate players (who had moved up to play important roles in the 1962–64 seasons) and some of the early 1960s stars. Included in this list was virtually the entire starting offensive line, including Erickson, Miklas, Shaw, Thompson, Rasmussen, Bruce Stewart, Beynon, and Jamieson, as well as Sirman, Edwards, and a number of others. And, of course, also gone from the team was Young, a decidedly new-generation player. While a few were left, particularly Connor, Ferguson, and Arment, the 1965 team, perhaps the

Left to right: Hal McCarney, Bill Miklas, Al Lenard, and Frank Tindall. Wally Mellor (not shown) was also a regular contributor to the coaching squad in this period (Wally Berry Photo Collection, QUA)

most transitional of the decade, had a different look. And by 1966, with the departure of Connor, the last holdover from the fifties, the team was demonstrably changed, all positions being filled by new-wave players who had arrived in the 1962–64 period.[17]

In view of all this changing and turbulent climate, it is a wonder that Queen's was able to continue its winning ways. Perhaps the saving grace was that the other schools were being buffeted by the same influences as Queen's. With the exception of the 1965 season, continue to win it did. In part this was due to the continuity of the coaching staff; in part, to the continuity of players. With respect to the former, Tindall, McCarney, and Lenard were by now old hands at the business, having been together for nearly fifteen years. They had a strong sense of the systems they wanted to run and of how to handle players.[18]

This latter point is of considerable importance, for both Tindall and McCarney were able to make the transition from their own time to that of Stewart and Schreider, then to that of Connor and Porter, and finally to that of Lilles and Bayne (in other words, from the forties to the sixties and seventies) so successfully that players from all these eras refer to them with the same kind of warmth years later. Theirs was no small management feat, as anyone who has tried to run an organization over such a long period will recognize. It was largely because of their personal integrity, which the players of all periods quickly sized up. It was very clear that Tindall cared about each one of his players in a kindly, fatherly sort of way, and McCarney equally so, if in a gruffer manner. Thus, Queen's was always known as a relatively happy place to play and one where there was a strong sense of team cohesion. The gradual turnover of players also helped in this regard. Rookies were often carried for a year or two before they actually dressed and played. They therefore knew the system and came to accept the norms of the club, and when the time came to play they were ready in most senses of the word.

The 1965 season is perhaps the best example of where this transition happened too quickly and was not handled entirely successfully. Because of the platooning, the team was essentially two separate sub-teams: the offence and the defence. In 1965 the defence was a veteran club with a considerable number of carry-over all-stars from the 1964 championship team. The offence, on the other hand, had been decimated by graduation, leaving very few veterans either along the line or in the backfield (Connor and Norrie being the only real exceptions). The season's results reflect this situation directly: the team had the second-lowest points-against record of the decade but could not score; it had by far the lowest points-for record of the decade. Indeed, it was the season between 1960 and 1994 in which Queen's scored the least points (see appendix A).

In a return to the performance of Reeve's teams of the 1930s, the club lost to Toronto 1–0 and beat McGill 8–0. To be sure, there was a blowout against Toronto, 31–0, and two larger-point losses to Western. But the team ended up three and three. And in a very confusing year, in which everyone was beating everyone else in a random sort of way, Toronto won the championship in a playoff against Western. It then went on to beat the Golden Bears in what has come to be recognized as the first Vanier Cup. The result was particularly unsatisfactory for Connor, who was in his last season, having played seven years for the Gaels at quarterback, been a league most valuable player (MVP), helped win three championships, and made an extremely important contribution to Queen's football during his time.

By 1966 the Gaels were back with another strong defence, led by Frank Arment, Larry Ferguson, Guy Potvin, and others. But now the offence was solid: led at quarterback by Don Bayne (in first-year law but with three years' experience as backup to Connor and with actual game experience as a wingback in the 1965 season); in the backfield led by Jamie Johnston and

Doug Cowan; and along the line by Brian Parnega, Bob Climie, John Gordon, and others. Potvin added a kicking dimension the Gaels had lacked in previous seasons, consistently converting touchdowns, adding field goals and single points.

It showed. The team scored almost three times as many points as the 1965 club had done, while holding the opposition (principally Bryce Taylor of Toronto, who set a modern scoring record, to that point, during the season) to nearly the same number of points as the previous year; and it won the championship in a playoff against Toronto in Kingston, blowing out Varsity (without the services of an injured Taylor) 50–7. It was the Gaels' fourth championship in seven seasons.* Queen's did not, however, go on to play for the Vanier Cup. Because participation at that time was by invitation only, Queen's found itself passed over by the Vanier committee in favour of McMaster, which lost to Alberta by one point. The Gaels thus lost yet another opportunity to avenge the 1963 defeat and win a national championship.

The 1967 season was a deeply frustrating one for all concerned. Picked to repeat as champions, the team opened with big wins against Western (42–12) and McGill (41–23), only to lose two very close games back to back to Toronto (19–14 and 16–13), thereby destroying its chances, though Queen's won both return games with Western and McGill. The second game against Toronto was particularly "quirky," involving a missed single from Toronto's 10-yard line, a muddy field, and so on. The whole season was in fact rainy, slowing down the very quick ground game with Johnson and Cowan which the Gaels might have had.[19] But their frustration at having lost what might well have been theirs in slightly different circumstances provided the same spur as it had for the 1961 and 1963 clubs, for in 1968 the team stormed back.†

---

* One wonders about the validity of the laws of probability when it is noted that these playoffs were always in Kingston. Each time, Tindall won the coin toss over the phone, and Queen's came to have home-field advantage – a not inconsequential leg up as visitors were quick to point out (see, for example, Metras, *The Metras Years*). It is worth mentioning that Tindall always called heads!

† It should also be noted that Stu Langdon, the longtime and much-respected trainer of the Gaels, passed away in 1967 and was replaced by Tabby Gow. In the tradition of Queen's trainers, Tabby also served a long time, finally leaving the team in 1980, to be replaced by the current trainer, Dave Ross. Thus, in more than seventy-five years of football, Queen's has had only five trainers: Hughes, Powell, Langdon, Gow, and Ross. That is surely a tradition of honourable and faithful service to one's calling.

QUEEN'S FIRST VANIER CUP: 1968

The chance finally came in 1968, but as fate would have it the Golden Bears fell just short of keeping up their end of the bargain to get there. As the season dawned, Toronto was favoured over Queen's to repeat for the championship. The league had been expanded to include McMaster and one of the newer universities, Waterloo.[20] Thus, the old six-game, home-and-home schedule had been amended for the first time since the war.

Queen's opened against Western, winning a close game 22–17 on the strength of three second-half touchdowns. The team then demolished Toronto, 35–0, "puncturing the myth of the Blue's invincibility,"[21] but lost the first of a home-and-home series with McGill at home, 28–21. Fortunately, the team won the second in Montreal in spite of a bizarre series of events at the end of the game. With the score tied 14–14 two minutes from the end, Keith Eaman scored on a run from scrimmage, only to have the play called back on a penalty. He then kicked a single point, which was again nullified by a penalty. With just twenty-three seconds left, he kicked a second time, this one finally doing the job: final score, 15–14. On such thin threads does glory hang, for, as it turned out, if the Gaels had tied, they would not have won their first Vanier Cup.

This was the first year in which the Vanier Cup was a truly national championship, won by a series of playoffs leading to a national final (rather than by invitation), and because of the very complicated won-lost records in the league, the team found itself in a series of league playoffs, first against McMaster and then against Toronto. Four years earlier McMaster had been humiliated by Queen's, and this time around it suffered the same fate: the score was 54–7. The team then turned to Toronto, and in shades of earlier encounters won a hard-fought game 14–6, allowing Varsity no touchdowns for the second game in a row.

The Gaels were then due to go west for a game, called the Western College Bowl, to decide who would play the winner of the Eastern College Bowl for the Vanier Cup. Until well into the week before the game (which was played on 17 November, the administration having by this time agreed to an extension of the season to accommodate the new national championship possibilities), the Gaels fully expected to be playing the Golden Bears, the top-ranked team in the country. Indeed, "some of the more enthusiastic afficionados" among the Queen's fans had already started hitchhiking to Edmonton in anticipation (in mid-November, mind!), when the University of Manitoba Bisons upset the Golden Bears to win the Western championship.[22] The Gaels thus changed travel plans and headed for Winnipeg, once again missing the chance to avenge the 1963 loss.

"A wave of football madness hit the campus … the band put on a blitz for funds … Some students went by thumb all the way."[23] And, one hastens to add, this time the team went by scheduled air. The Gaels beat the Bisons quite handily (29–6),[24] thus qualifying for the Vanier Cup in Toronto the following week against the winner of the Eastern College Bowl, one of the newcomers to college football in Ontario, Waterloo Lutheran (later Wilfrid Laurier) University, whose football reputation was beginning in this period and would continue down to the present.

The game was played at Varsity Stadium before 20,000 fans. The result was 42–14 for Queen's and its first Vanier Cup.* The game itself reflected the score, with Queen's allowing a touchdown early and late but in between dominating with a finely balanced strong offence that was reminiscent of the 1964 team. Led this time by another excellent quarterback, Don Bayne, with running backs Keith "Skip" Eamon and Heino Lilles, a good split end in Rick Van Buskirk, and a small but tough offensive line anchored (as always in Tindall's offensive system) by two good guards, Climie and Parnega, the team was also strong on defence, with Walker, Turnbull, Brooks, McKeen, and others leading the way. It thus had an overall balance second to none in Queen's history.

Bayne and Eamon had particularly good years, with Lilles steadily adding to his accumulating scoring totals. Bayne threw for fifteen touchdowns during playoff and league play (four in the College Bowl alone) and won the MVP of the Vanier Cup game, while Eamon added another eight along the ground (and tied for the best punting average in the league). Together they helped the team to the highest number of points ever scored by a Queen's team to that point (see appendix A; the all-time leader in this respect was to be the 1991 team).[25]

As might be expected, the city and the campus reacted enthusiastically to the hardware the team brought home. The team was praised in a manner more reminiscent of late-nineteenth-century rhetoric than of the radically chic 1960s counterculture:

Rugby football was introduced at Queen's in 1882, the college union in 1898, and football from the beginning has been the major sport on this campus despite the fact that Queen's played in what is said to have been the first hockey game in Canada in 1885.

----

* To suggest, as the *Review* and other sources did, that this was the "first national Intercollegiate championship" for the school ignores the many other times (1893, 1900, the 1920s, the 1930s, the 1950s) when Queen's could legitimately claim – and did, as we have seen – that it was the Dominion or national champion, professional, intercollegiate, what have you. What is correct is that "they won their first Vanier Cup symbolic of national Intercollegiate victory."

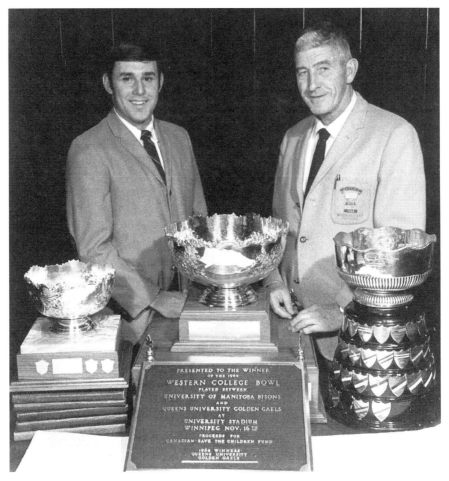

Don Bayne, Frank Tindall, and the 1968 championship trophies (Wally Berry Photo Collection, QUA)

Many and memorable have been the triumphs of the Tricolour on the gridiron dating back to the days of the legendary Guy Curtis. The old men in their chimney corners still boast of the teams.[26]

And that was just the beginning of the article! The team was also honoured by the city, which gave the players special achievement pens at a meeting of city council early in 1969.[27]

The team shared many of the traits (balance, star players, veterans working on second degrees, and so on) of earlier "big" teams, such as the Grey Cup clubs of the 1920s, the Reeve "fourteeners" of the 1930s, the Stewart-based champions of the 1950s, and the powerhouse clubs of the early 1960s; yet it was as different in its way as each of those former clubs had been from one another. In particular, this was the first fully "boomer" club (made up of certifiable baby-boomers). Whether because of this or because of the sixties counterculture from which they clearly sprang, they were a much more intellectual group than almost any Queen's team before them. Bayne, Climie, McCarney, and others who bridged several eras all note that the teams of the fifties and sixties still had "cowboys," "swashbucklers," "wild-assed boys," who often played their own game within the main game and were somewhat larger than life both on and off the field.[28] The 1968 College Bowl team had far fewer of these types and was described as more "mature," "sophisticated," "adaptable." In this respect, it was far more like the Queen's teams of later years, especially as admission standards tight-ened through the seventies and eighties. Indeed, it represents the fact that a kind of watershed in Queen's football – particularly with respect to the personality of the players the university was getting – was passed some-where in the middle sixties.

THE AFTERMATH

The 1969 season was bound to be a letdown, even though Queen's was picked to repeat for league honours at least. Several of the veterans were gone, including Bayne, so Tindall was faced with the same problem he had had in the fifties – having to find a new quarterback. Nine years of stability, first with Connor and then with Bayne, were now past history. Not surpris-ingly, the offence was inconsistent all season. Eamon had another fine season, making all-Canadian and running his points total to 84 for two seasons.[29] Climie, Van Buskirk, Sherritt, and Lambros made the league all-star team, the latter as a rookie, playing two ways and punting. In the end, however, the club could not repeat its success; it lost twice to McGill but won every other game and ended up five and two for the final season of the decade.

"So end[ed] the saga of the sixties. It was a Golden era for the Golden Gaels."[30] They won five league championships, were runners up in the other five, and won the College Bowl in 1968. In regular season and playoffs, the record was 53 wins and 16 losses. As in past decades, the game had been an all-consuming part of campus life. *Maclean's* characterized Queen's as "football-crazy" in a slightly hysterical 1965 piece that described the team as follows:

Undefeated in the last two seasons, the best college team in Canada has been the Queen's Golden Gaels. It may be again this year, the result of a phenomenal football machine working for the university. The Principal never misses a game, and every alumnus is expected to be a scout, directing strong high-school boys into the autumn football camp of experienced coach (17 years) Frank Tindall, who was recruited from the U.S. Even the university Padre, the Rev. A.M. Laverty, pushes football when he visits high school and alumni meetings.[31]

While clearly exaggerated, this does give a flavour of the importance of football to the university during the sixties. Richardson Stadium was still sold out for every game, and there were pep rallies before and football "tea dances" after all home games. Even as the decade drew to a close, with the new mores pressing in on athletics as on everything else, football fever continued to burn strongly at Queen's.

The *Maclean's* article went on to suggest that the Athletic Board of Control was a "profit-making operation for the university," implying that this was so because of the football program. In this respect the article was incorrect. Table 8 shows, for example, that in the championship season of 1966, although the Athletic Board of Control did run a surplus, the football team was in deficit to the tune of $5,739 ($30,250 in 1995 dollars). Revenues from football were still a healthy $29,610 ($156,075 in 1995 dollars), but by the mid-sixties, because of the explosion in the number of students attending the university, student fees for all athletics were by far the most important source of revenue for athletics. Naturally, some of these applied to free admission to home football games. There seems to have been no accounting attempt to allocate such revenues out of fees to football (or to any other program – for example, hockey, which would have had a similar claim). Obviously, had the university done so, the football program would have been decidedly in the black.

If one compares this to the 1956 championship season, it is clear that revenues were down, in 1995 dollar terms, by $86,127 (about 35 per cent), despite the same number of games and an increase in general inflation of about 19 per cent (revenues should have been about 20 per cent higher in 1966 to account for inflation). Expenses in 1966 were $186,326 (in 1995 dollars), down about $45,196 (about 20 per cent) from their 1955–56 levels in comparable dollars. In short, while less was being spent on football,* even less was being collected at the gate. Since there is considerable personal

---

* Milne (personal interview) reports that strenuous efforts were made to hold costs down, especially by Dutch Dougall, the head of stadium and arena operations: "We never had the right stuff to do the job. One day I was working on the stadium stands, cursing and swearing away about the lack of tools and everything else. This old girl come wandering along, hears me bitchin' away, and chats for awhile. I think nothing of it, we had all kinds wandering through the old stadium in those days. Next day, there's a big truckload of lumber there, the tool supply guys are there, all hell is breakin' loose! Dutch is mad as stink at me: 'What the hell did you say to old Mrs Richardson anyway? The Administration is all over my tail about going over their heads!'" Evidently, other benefactors were less directly up on conditions – or less sympathetic.

Table 8
Athletic Board of Control: Details of revenue and expenses for the year ending 31 May 1967

A Distribution of total receipts and expenditures

	Actual, 1967	Actual, 1966
REVENUES		
Student fees	$101,993	$91,794
Surplus: gymnasium	2,157	1,677
Surplus: summer school	3,227	3,694
Surplus: swimming class	311	709
Total revenues	107,688	97,874
EXPENSES		
Football	5,739	9,758
Basketball	4,015	4,133
Hockey	5,899	7,604
Jock Harty Arena	1,019	(133)
Wrestling	989	1,696
Track	1,772	1,496
Cross-country race	610	938
Badminton	380	427
Intramural sports	4,145	3,472
Colour night awards	2,164	984
General administration	25,306	19,400
General stores	1,978	473
Dues and travel (OQUA-CIAU)	945	1,262
Levana	12,983	10,951
Stadium	7,281	11,856
Training room	1,062	1,465
Rugger	2,200	1,599
Graduate society	–	149
Intermediate basketball	650	878
Medical supplies	–	673
Contingencies	2,425	1,033
Miscellaneous sports	6,493	3,571
Total expenses	88,055	83,685
Net revenue (expense for 1967)	19,633	14,189
Deduct provision for future operations of Women's Athletic Board of Control	147	424
Net surplus (deficit) for the year	$19,486	$13,765

evidence that the stadiums were usually full during the 1960s, one suspects that the price of tickets had not been increased to keep up with inflation. Whatever the explanation, although the program still contributed by far the largest revenue of any of the athletic programs, the financial power behind Queen's athletics in general was beginning to shift from being very much

Table 8
(continued)

B Football		
	Actual, 1967	*Actual, 1966*
REVENUES		
Gate receipts:		
exhibition and regular season	$25,171	$27,119
playoff	3,372	–
Excursions and program sales	1,067	1,129
Total revenues	29,610	
	($156,075)[1]	28,248
EXPENSES		
Medical and hospital	–	198
Training table meals	7,431	7,640
Equipment	4,885	5,451
Team travel expense	6,165	4,143
Other travel expense	474	460
General travel expense	–	263
Advertising, printing, postage,		
telephones, etc.	1,837	1,720
Tutorials	–	46
Salaries	8,235	9,362
Movies	1,461	1,373
Officials and police	3,687	3,431
Rules committee expense	574	681
Exhibition	600	3,100
Miscellaneous	–	138
Total expenses	35,349	38,006
Deficit	$5,739	$9,758
	($30,250)	

Source: Queen's University Archives, "Athletic Board of Control: Statement of Revenue and Expense,"
year ending 31 May 1967
[1] Figures in brackets in 1995 dollars

a function of football – and hence of those who controlled football revenues
– to whoever controlled the disbursements of student fees to all aspects of
athletics (including salaries for the general administration of sports). And
while its deficits were still about the same size as those for hockey and
basketball, they were now deficits and thus were identifiable as a drain on
the overall budget, despite the fact that football still supplied 25–30 per cent
of the Athletic Board of Control's cash flow.

Meanwhile, changes were afoot elsewhere. Canada had a new prime
minister, the dashing young Pierre Trudeau, and the United States had a

John Metras and the "kindly old coach," 1963 (Wally Berry
Photo Collection, QUA)

new president, Richard Nixon, a horse of rather a different nature. The former
was bringing a breath of fresh air to Canadian politics, while the latter was
taking the United States ever deeper into Vietnam. Nearer to home, the
university had a new principal, John Deutsch, an economist who succeeded
Corry in 1968. In football, Tindall's longtime friend and opponent John "Bull"
Metras, the coach at Western, retired after the 1969 season, ending more than
thirty years' service to his university.[32] Tindall himself was aging. As well,
there was talk of again enlarging the league and of splitting it into two
leagues oriented to the geographical realities. Finally, at the turn of the
decade, the university decided to relocate the stadium to a new West Campus
it was constructing, preferring to use the land under the old stadium in the
middle of the campus for new buildings and parking. These latter two
developments, together with a change in admissions policy and a shift in
the philosophy about the role of athletic programs at universities, were to
bring major changes to Queen's football in the seventies and beyond.

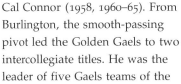

Cal Connor (1958, 1960–65). From
Burlington, the smooth-passing
pivot led the Golden Gaels to two
intercollegiate titles. He was the
leader of five Gaels teams of the
Silver Sixties and was captain in 1965. He has gone on to a successful medical
career in Kingston (QFHF)

WHERE ARE THEY NOW?

Recording what has become of the major players of the sixties is a more
difficult task than doing the same for the earlier periods. First, because
of platooning and the strength of the program during this period, there
were many more "outstanding-at-their-position" players who passed
through Queen's than there probably were in any earlier period – and,
arguably, than there have been since. Secondly, many are still in the prime
years of their professional lives and may well go on to further noteworthy
achievements, which of course cannot be noted here. Nonetheless, as with
the earlier decades, it is important to identify a few of those who made
noteworthy contributions and to record their activities since leaving
Queen's.

   Keeping these limitations in mind, it is possible to argue that four players
stand out from the rest and that twenty or so others are certainly worthy of
note. The four are Cal Connor, Jim Young, Don Bayne, and Heino Lilles.
The "honourable mentions" go to Porter, Skene, Ritchie, Sirman, Edwards,

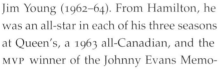

Jim Young (1962–64). From Hamilton, he was an all-star in each of his three seasons at Queen's, a 1963 all-Canadian, and the MVP winner of the Johnny Evans Memorial Trophy in 1964. He had a natural talent for scoring, and he scored touchdowns the first time he was given the ball in each of his first three games at Queen's (QFHF)

Erickson, Miklas, Peter Thompson, Bob Latham, Norrie, Potvin, Ferguson, Arment, Johnston, Parnega, Climie, Eamon, and Van Buskirk.

Connor came to Queen's from Burlington, Ontario, in 1958 after a year at Royal Roads Military College. He played well that year but had academic problems and missed the 1959 season. Back again in 1960, he quarterbacked the Gaels to three championships (and two near misses) in the first six years of the decade. Tough and resilient, with a strong arm and a Sonny Jurgenson attitude towards life, Connor was the first quarterback of note that Queen's had in the modern passing era.[33] Time and again, his ability to score long with the pass or to scramble to avoid losses, plus an obviously competitive and combative nature, made all the difference to those winning teams of the first half of the decade. Connor graduated in medicine after playing seven years for Queen's (ranking him with Batstone, to that point, behind Curtis, as those who had played the longest number of years for Queen's). He has had a successful career as a general practitioner in Kingston, where he is in partnership with another Queen's player of the 1960s, "Little" Frank Poce, a defensive half.

Jim Young was the acknowledged wunderkind among the players of the first half of the sixties. From Hamilton, he could have played professional ball for the Tiger-Cats straight out of high school but wanted a university education. Offered a scholarship to Syracuse, he chose instead to attend Queen's – on the advice of the Tiger-Cats' team physician, Jim Charters, a Gael from the 1950s. From the very first game against Toronto in 1962, it was clear that Young was capable of single-handedly breaking open a game, much in the way that Stewart had done (and as, later, Eamon, Jock Climie, Elberg, and several others would do). Young could do it from virtually every position. He was also a punter and regularly quick-kicked out of various different formations, recalling Pep Leadlay. Big, fast, and durable, with a kind of nervous enthusiasm and pleasantness, Young was a unanimous all-star pick each year he was in the league. If he had remained longer, he would certainly have set several Queen's scoring records.

He left with a BA after the victorious 1964 season, was drafted by the Toronto Argonauts, who badly mishandled the negotiations (as they regularly seemed to do in those days), and ended up with the Minnesota Vikings, who had taken him in the U.S. college draft. After several seasons there, mostly as a special teams player, he was traded back to the Canadian Football League (CFL) and eventually found his way to the B.C. Lions, where he enjoyed a long and successful career. He has written of his experiences in football, including his time at Queen's,[34] and after his playing days were over he served for a while in a management capacity with the Lions. He later went into the hospitality business in Vancouver and retains an active interest in Queen's football.

Connor and Young were mirrored by another quarterback and running back duo, who can be said to have shone as the brightest of many bright lights in the second half of the decade: Bayne and Lilles.[35] Don Bayne was from Ottawa but spent most of his high school years in the United States. Like Connor and Young, he came from a working-class family. Knowing little about Canadian universites, he resisted several recruiting offers elsewhere, choosing to come to Queen's on the strength of his high school history teacher's recommendation and in the belief that Queen's was a "quality place, with a quality program."[36] As noted, his time at Queen's consisted of two distinct phases: the first, 1963–65, when he was an undergraduate and for the most part served as a backup to Connor or played another position; and the second, 1966–68, when he was in law school, quarterbacked the team to two championships and the College Bowl in three years, set passing records, and was an all-star and MVP throughout.

On graduation, Bayne returned to Ottawa, hoping to play professional ball, article, and then practise law as Schreider and others had done. But he experienced the unwillingness to develop Canadian quarterbacking talent that has plagued the CFL, so he quit the game to concentrate on the law. A decidedly new-generation player who shared a sixties concern for social involvement, Bayne set up a "storefront" legal practice concentrating on litigation. He has since developed into one of Canada's better-known trial lawyers, participating in several high-profile war-crime trials as well as other criminal and diplomatically sensitive trials. He has retained an active interest in Queen's football and was involved with Lilles and McCarney in establishing the Queen's Football Club (for ex-players concerned with the continuing welfare of Queen's football) and the Queen's Football Hall of Fame. He views his football activities at Queen's as having been a "terribly important experience in life, not just in respect of the winning and the sports, but mostly in terms of the people I met and the friendships I established."[37]

Heino Lilles, from Beamsville in the Niagara Penisula, came to Queen's in 1963 with his friend John Latham, younger brother of Bob who had been with the Gaels for two seasons. From fruit-farming family stock, Lilles had enjoyed a good high school career but found it hard to crack a backfield with the likes of Edwards, Young, Norrie, Ware, and others firmly ensconsed. However, the club was thin in defensive backs, having lost Plumley, Quinn, and others from the 1962 team, and Lilles thus played his first season at Queen's as a defensive back.

In 1964, with Edwards gone, Tindall and McCarney decided to move Young to wingback and use Lilles as their fullback – one of their most astute player-position decisions of those years. Lilles ran with that slashing, high-knee action which football players especially love to watch (Roger Craig, late of the 49ers in the NFL, and Emmitt Smith of Dallas were the same kind of runners), and he quickly emerged as a scoring force, getting six touchdowns in the 1964 season (to Young's nine, Connor's four, and Norrie's three).[38] In 1965, with the general lack of offence, he scored only four times, and in the championship year of 1966 he was out for most of the season with the first of a series of serious knee injuries. But back he came in 1967, scoring four more times, and in 1968, the College Bowl year, he added another eight touchdowns to his total (to Eamon's eleven). Out again with injuries in 1969, Lilles returned in 1970 for one last time before injury finally forced him to retire (much like Batstone many years earlier). "No knees and all," he scored six times in the 1970 season. This was the same as Eamon's total for that year, and it placed Lilles just shy of Stewart as the player to have scored the most touchdowns for Queen's to that point.

Heino Lilles (1963–70). From Beamsville, he was an integral part of the Gaels team during the Silver Sixties. He was awarded the MVP Johnny Evans Memorial Trophy in his final year and remains one of the all-time highest scorers in Queen's history with 168 career points. He also received the Jenkins Trophy in 1971 as Queen's most outstanding male athlete (QFHF)

(Elberg would later surpass them both.) As well, Lilles ranked with Connor, though behind Guy Curtis, as having played the longest at Queen's: seven years. His was a steady major contribution made over a number of years in the face of considerable physical risk and pain.

Like Bayne, Lilles was a "scholar," taking a bachelor's and master's degree in chemistry, followed by a law degree – all at Queen's – and then a master's degree in law at the London School of Economics. He taught for some time in the law school at Queen's, becoming ever more involved with the university's developing legal department, before being appointed to the bench as a justice in the Yukon. He has been active in supporting Queen's football and not only helped form Queen's Football Club and its Football Hall of Fame, but served as the club's first president.

And what of the others? Porter, Skene, Ferguson, and Climie are doctors. Ritchie, Sirman, Erickson, Thompson, Potvin, and Parnega are lawyers. Edwards is a high school teacher, and Miklas, McKeen, and others are university professors; Latham, Norrie, Johnston, Eamon, and others are successful businessmen; and some, including Bob Howes, have remained associated with sport.* Like the players who went before them, they and many of their 1960s teammates, despite being very different kinds of personalities, have in almost all respects gone on to successful and rewarding lives.

---

* In perhaps the most idiosyncratic experience of the 1960s, Bob "Bo" Howes (who in early 1996 was appointed head coach of the Gaels) played steadily (at centre) in only one of his three seasons with the team (1965), preferring basketball instead. After kicking around Europe for a year or so, he returned to the University of Waterloo for a physical education degree, was drafted by Calgary, traded to British Columbia, and eventually ended up in Edmonton with the Eskimos. He played professional ball for fourteen years, winning five Grey Cup rings (the most of any Gael ever) from eight Grey Cup finals, before returning to Queen's in 1980 to help Hargreaves coach the Gaels. His experience is dramatic proof of the existence of "late bloomers" in athletics and of the fact that one's college career should not necessarily be taken as a prediction of one's eventual place in the history of sports – or, for that matter, in any other endeavour.

6

A Time of Transition
The 1970s

The 1970s were perhaps the most turbulent years in the history of the game at Queen's, to say nothing of the chaotic nature of events in the world at large. The pressure of events had a variety of effects on football: Queen's traditional schedule of playing Western, Toronto, and McGill was replaced, after several years of transition, with to-day's Ontario Quebec Interuniversity Football Conference (OQIFC); the eligibility requirements were amended to place a cap on the number of years in which a player could compete (five, the last two to be played at the same institution); the old stadium at Queen's was abandoned for a new one far removed from the heart of the campus; and Frank Tindall retired as head coach and was replaced by Doug Hargreaves.

If these developments were not enough to contend with, football faced other problems too. Early in the 1970s the university decided to restrict enrolment to 10,000 students, with the inevitable result that academic admission requirements (principally high school grades) began an inexorable climb. By the 1990s, the potential flow of players to the university had become limited is the very best academics among the scholar-athletes. Another problem was the fundamental change in physical education and athletics philosophy, following the influential Milliken Report, which favoured broadening the athletics program to include the active support of many intercollegiate programs, rather than maintaining a "deep and focused" concentration on a few sports such as football, hockey, and basketball. In almost all these cases, the result was injurious to the football program, though some were eventually to have more effect than others. It is almost as though fate had set out to destroy football as a sport at Queen's and began sowing the seeds in the 1970s.

Meanwhile, turbulent events were occurring in the world at large, especially of an economic nature. They brought to an end the relatively tranquil years of continued economic prosperity that had been enjoyed since the war

Table 9
Queen's football record, 1970–1979[1]

Year	Won	Lost	Tied	For	Against
1970c[2]n[3]	6	2	0	203	116
1971n	6	3	0	310	162
1972n	3	3	0	121	129
1973n	5	3	0	181	184
1974	2	5	0	111	168
1975	2	6	0	121	177
1976n	5	2	0	128	105
1977cn	7	2	0	259	132
1978cn	10	0	0	282	84
1979n	7	2	0	202	101
Total	53	28	0	1,918	1,358

Source: Based on individual game reports (appendix A)
[1] League and playoff games only
[2] c indicates championship season
[3] N indicates non-losing (i.e., winning or tied) season

and threw the world into an era of terrorism and regional wars, shortages, cartels, dramatic inflation, and ultimately, by 1980–81, the worst economic downturn since the Great Depression of the 1930s. This would lead governments to begin running deficits on their accounts (after years of careful management of their revenues and expenses) and to begin cutting back on their spending for higher education, two factors that have continued to worsen in the intervening years. Coupled with these economic events was a sudden political uncertainty in Canada and abroad, which developed around the Americans' withdrawal in disgrace from Vietnam and saw the United States abandon the gold standard backing to its currency. Other developments included the resignation of President Nixon in order to avoid impeachment proceedings (1974) and, in Canada, the October Crisis (1970) and the election of the Parti Québécois in Quebec (1976).

Perhaps because we survived and have moved on, it is all too easy to forget how chaotic the 1970s were in many respects. In fact it is surprising that the football program at Queen's was as successful as it was during the seventies. As can be seen from table 9, although the seventies were not as outstanding as the twenties or sixties, Queen's did have eight out of ten non-losing seasons, and it won three championships and another College Bowl. The decade therefore compares favourably with the 1930s and was certainly better than the 1950s.

There are several clear divisions in the timeline of the 1970s. In the first place, there was the year 1970 itself, which could easily have been appended to a discussion of the 1960s because it was a championship year and the last of an era in several important respects. The year 1971 also stands by itself, for it was a beacon of change with a completely new league, new eligibility requirements, and the new stadium. Following it were the four seasons of decline to the end of Tindall's career, especially 1974 and 1975, which were the two clear losing seasons, the first since 1958–59. Then there was a dramatic turn for the better as Hargreaves took over as coach, this stage culminating in the 1978 undefeated Vanier Cup season. Finally, the decade closed on a very good but ultimately disappointing 1979 season.

START OF A DECADE, END OF AN ERA: 1970

The first season of the new decade dawned with the league configuration that had been adopted in the 1968 season – Queen's playing the traditional three (home-and-home against Toronto and McGill, and a single game against Western), plus McMaster and Waterloo. Eaman was back, as was Lilles, though off an injury yet again and thus in some question. Otherwise, the offence was an unknown quantity, Innes at centre being the only returning starter along the line). The defence, however, was full of veterans.

As luck would have it, Tindall found himself a quarterback, Skip Rochette, a native of Quebec, who had three years' experience at the University of Bridgeport, Connecticut, and was a late cut from the Montreal Alouettes. Rochette was enrolled in the newly created, one-year education program at Queen's and brought a veteran's hand to the position if only for that year. McCarney also made some inspired adjustments along the offensive line, moving the veteran McIntyre from end to tackle, picking up Wayne "Ace" Powell from the University of Ottawa (he, too, enrolled in education), and moving yet other players, including Stoneham, from their former positions to guard. With Eaman, Lilles, Tom Chown (a receiver), newcomers Stu Lang (later of Edmonton Eskimos fame) and Tom Shultz at the ends, and Doug Cozac kicking, the Gaels patched together an offence. It managed to stand up to the year, despite injuries to Eaman (and Lilles on "no knees"), getting steadily better as the season wore on. "And while it seldom proved capable of a prolonged performance, its moments were well chosen and proved sufficient. The defensive squad played heroically and effectively and scored a lot of points and saved a lot of games on fumble recoveries and pass receptions while waiting patiently for the offense to get started."[1] In a preview of the 1990s teams, it relied heavily on its linebackers, who included Mike Lambros, Gord Squires, Jim Murphy, and others as well as a corps of experienced defensive backs led by the five-year veteran McKeen.

The team opened with a win against Western, lost to Varsity in the second game (giving up a quarter of all the points-against for the season in that one game alone), and then went undefeated the rest of the way – including a return win over Varsity in Kingston before 14,000 fans – to win the championship, the Yates Cup. Then it was on to post-season play, with once again a return to Winnipeg for a rematch against the University of Manitoba Bisons in the Western College Bowl. This was an evenly fought game all the way, with some questionable calls by the officials, and it resulted in a tie (on a single point by Manitoba) at the end of regulation time. Queen's went ahead with a field goal in the first half of the overtime, but Manitoba scored a touchdown with two minutes left in the second to go up 24–20. In shades of the 1950s and 1960s playoffs against Varsity and McGill, Queen's stormed back from the ensuing kickoff to find itself on the Bisons' 19-yard line with one play left. Rochette went to Brian Warrender, another new back playing for an injured Eaman, deep in the end zone, "but the ball slipped by his outstretched fingers and the game was over."[2] It could well have meant another national championship for the Gaels if that pass had connected, because the Bisons went on to beat the University of Ottawa the following week for the Vanier Cup.

The season thus ended on a disappointing note. But Eamon had a good year – his last – despite bad hamstring injuries, as did Lilles, who also was in his last year and who won the league MVP honours that year. Lilles scored the last touchdown in the old Stadium – against Waterloo on 7 November in the final league game of the season. The *Review* reported: "Among the spectators at this final game was Dr. W.A. Campbell, Captain of the 1923 team that won the first of three Dominion Championships and the player who scored the first touchdown in the stadium when it was opened in 1921."[3]

THE FIRST YEAR OF TRANSITION: 1971

The 1971 season found the team competing in the new Ontario Universities Athletic Association (OUAA) with only the traditional Varsity Blues left from the old schedule. The University of Western Ontario was in the western division of the four-division OUAA, which now included a total of twelve universities. And McGill was part of a new Quebec grouping. Under the new arrangement, Queen's played home-and-home with Toronto and Carleton, and one game each with Ottawa, Laurentian, York, and Waterloo. It was a bizarre arrangement and required the Gaels to play three games in eight days at one point. It did not stand the test of time, but it took five to ten years of experimentation before the scheduling committee eventually settled on which universities would continue to play and what was the best arrangement of conferences and games.[4]

Queen's opened on the road against Laurentian, destroying the new university from the north 65–6. Rochette was gone, replaced at quarterback by his back-up from the previous year, Tom Taylor. Eamon and Lilles also were gone, but that made little difference, for the Gaels had a new "dynamic duo," Brian Warrender and Gordie McLellan, who proceeded to tear the league apart, scoring twelve touchdowns each in the course of the year. Added to these two were Dave "the Beast" Hadden (later of Toronto Argonaut fame) at fullback; Stu Lang; Alex Melvin and John Hollingsworth at ends; and Doug Cozac (who was steadily adding to his scoring totals almost exclusively from field goals and converts) with Mike Lambros handling a strong kicking game. Taken together they gave the Gaels a highly potent offence, which that season scored the most points ever for a Queen's team, though there would be four seasons in the 1980s and 1990s when the team managed even more (see appendix A). This was perhaps easier to do than in earlier times, given the nature of the opposition; a review of the season shows that the Gaels won by large scores in several games besides that against Laurentian: 36–0 over Waterloo, 48–25 and 22–0 over Carleton, and 62–7 over York. Nevertheless, the quality of the offence in 1971 was certainly extremely high.

Unfortunately, the defence was not quite of the same calibre. Indeed, it set a record of its own that year, giving up the highest number of points (162) that had ever been scored against Queen's. In fairness, it should be noted that the two league losses (to Ottawa and Varsity) were close affairs (27–16 and 31–29). The really disastrous outing was a 42–3 loss to Western in a playoff (for the right to go on to the College Bowl round of playoffs), in which the offence, for once, was shut down completely and the defence simply could not stand up to the steady pressure.[5]

Whether or not any of this could be put down to the fact that the team was playing on new ground is impossible to know. But new ground it was. On 18 September 1971, on the occasion of the first home game against Ottawa (which was lost 27–16 in what some still consider a telling omen), the old stadium was officially closed – in a ceremony that saw the lowering of the flag, several pieces of sod removed for transfer, and the playing of a piper's lament – and the new one on the western fringes of the campus was officially opened. Despite some of the acknowledged disadvantages of the old stadium, especially its tendency to poor drainage, virtually everyone connected with Queen's football, including many alumni, staff, and townspeople, rue the day the decision was made to close it. One still hears numerous complaints about the closing: "People never ever again came in the same numbers" … "The new stadium was cold and distant and no longer seemed part of the town or the school" … "The old stadium was the heart of the campus. They tore the heart right out of it."

In view of such strong feelings, it is worth digressing to comment on the change of stadium.[6] To begin with, it is important to note that Queen's was the only one of the "old four" (Queen's, Western, Varsity, and McGill) to move its stadium during the building boom of the late 1960s and early 1970s. In fact, Varsity, Molson, and Little stadiums remain to this day in their original locations at the centre of their respective campuses, as do most Ivy League and Big Ten stadiums. Thus, it would seem that Queen's went its own way in this respect. The interesting question is why.

The story begins with the establishment by Corry early in his principal-ship of the Long-Range Facilities Planning Committee to coordinate the obviously explosive growth that was taking place and was expected to continue well into the 1970s. By 1967 this committee, under the chair of the dean of arts and science, George A. Harrower, had concluded that, among other things, a new arts and social science complex (ASSC)[7] was needed, that the university could most likely get funding for it from government, and that it should be built somewhere on the existing stadium and playing field area.

The committee brought the issue to the Board of Trustees in November 1967, and after a report by Harrower, which included the observation that "spectator sports were losing their popularity and a playing field with a very simple and limited bleacher arrangement might meet our future needs," the board passed a motion to go ahead with the ASSC and build a new stadium elsewhere.[8] There was no discussion of the stadium's socio-logical or psychological importance to the university in its existing location, or of its importance to the town; nor was there any comment on traditions; or, in fact, any discussion around the issue at all, except to note that a new stadium had to be available before the old one was closed. Nor did the *Queen's Journal*, the *Alumni Review*, or the Kingston *Whig-Standard* choose to comment on the decision (either at the time or for some considerable period thereafter).

What could have led to such a "quiet going in the nite"? Or, in its more extreme form, to Harrower's opinion about spectator sports, especially in view of the large attendance at home games and the extensive coverage of the football team by the media? To understand this, it is necessary to recall that this discussion had begun in the 1960s, a time of social revolution, when personal philosophy was swinging towards self-indulgence, individuality, and "people power." One of the many areas it touched on was sport, its purpose and role. At Queen's, questions of this sort had led Corry to request a report on university athletics, the Curtis Report, and it had resulted in the establishment of a "committee of implementation of the report on athletics" called the Principal's Advisory Committee on Athletics, which first met in 1967 and contained among its members Harrower and the new head of physical education, Donald MacIntosh. It is interesting to note that although both Tindall and McCarney requested to be included, neither was appointed to the committee, despite their long experience at the university and the central importance of football to the total program.

After much confusion, a new chairman was appointed – Jack Milliken, a local doctor – and on 9 November 1967 the committee issued an interim report in which it stressed the need for more recreation space for students and advocated that new playing fields for rugger and field hockey be established on West Campus, but made no mention of relocating the existing stadium; in fact, recommended that its lighting be improved.[9] It was one week after this that Harrower went to the Board of Trustees, said that "spectator sports were losing their popularity," and had a motion passed to build the new ASSC on the site of the old stadium.

One can only conclude that Harrower had his own agenda and found the interim report useful in this respect. It may well have been that he and, possibly, others personally disliked the large intercollegiate spectator sport that was football and genuinely believed that his comments to the board were correct. But they would also have been aware that it was far easier to get government funding for academic buildings than for athletic facilities. By the mid-1960s, the provincial government had stopped funding athletic facilities directly, making these entirely the responsibility of each university. The fact that football had become a net drain, that the stadium would need continual maintenance, and that a far cheaper facility elsewhere might do, would have made it all too tempting to shuffle off the existing stadium to a far corner of the campus (where new fields needed to be built in any event) and to replace it with a nice new academic building, and parking, for which funding seemed easily obtainable and for which there was an evident need. In retrospect, it was a tragic mistake.

From then on, the project to close the stadium and to build the ASSC and a new stadium gathered momentum. Through 1968 architects were hired and estimates obtained, and the university made ready to move the moment funding for the ASSC finally came through. (The new stadium's opening was very much a hostage to the funds being made available for the ASSC.) The project received further impetus from the final report of the Milliken Committee in April 1969, which strongly recommended a much broader emphasis on athletics at Queen's at the expense of existing intercollegiate sports, particularly football.

Needless to say, the Milliken Report caused considerable controversy. Three student representatives on the committee resigned, to be replaced by three others. Alarm bells began to ring elsewhere as well. In October 1969, John Deutsch, who was by now principal, wrote in a covering memo to Milliken: "Enclosing Copy of letter of October 23 from Peter H. Quinn concerning sports at Queen's. I have been getting this kind of reaction from a number of quarters and I thought you should see a sample of it."[10] In February 1970, Deutsch received a long letter from Peter Thompson, a Gael from the early 1960s, representing "concerned alumni in Ottawa" and requesting the right to speak to the Senate when the Milliken Report was considered for implementation.[11] Deutsch informed Thompson that his concerns would be passed on to Milliken, who would no doubt give them serious consideration. Little was changed, however, when the report's major conclusions and philosophy were adopted by the Senate in the fall of 1970.[12]

It was clear by early 1970 that the university would get funding for the ASSC.[13] Construction thus went ahead on the new stadium that year and the next, while the university made every effort to hold the outlays to a minimum. It even resorted to using its own Department of Physical Plant to do the construction, after getting an estimate from private contractors that it considered too high.[14] It is clear from a careful reading of the record, as well as from the media reports, that neither the peculiar importance of the location of the old stadium nor the uniqueness of Queen's actions vis-à-vis the other three "old schools" was an issue at all. Accordingly, the old stadium was closed with the last game of the 1970 season, and the new one was opened with the first home game of the 1971 season.

Attendance began to drop almost immediately as the disadvantages of the new stadium became clear. It was situated a considerable walk from the residences and houses of the main campus; the sound of the crowd no longer boomed through the campus and into the downtown to draw spectators; the new stadium was open to the elements with none of the intimacy of the enclosed and partly roofed old stadium. But Queen's had its new ASSC underway; the rugger, field hockey, and soccer teams had new playing fields, and the track teams had a new all-weather track. Besides, the football team could take solace from the fact that it had a new field and stadium. Meanwhile, the world moved on to other things, such as Vietnam, oil cartels, and inflation.

In time, though, the change of stadium came to be recognized as a mistake, one that other colleges did not make and one that Queen's need not have made if more thought had been given to the matter or if events and personalities had not conspired to bring several agendas together. One cannot help but speculate that if just one of the major actors – whether Deutsch, Harrower, or MacIntosh – had had a stronger appreciation of the role of football in the university's life and traditions, the decision would have gone against the change. But it did not, and the university has suffered in consequence. Future consideration should be given to returning the stadium to its rightful place, on Tindall Field in the heart of the campus.

THE FINAL TINDALL YEARS: 1972–1975

In the four years that were left of the Tindall era, the Gaels did poorly on the whole. The last two of the years, 1974 and 1975, were clear losing seasons (two and five, and three and six, respectively), while 1972 was a non-losing season (three and three), one of only four such seasons between 1945 and 1994, the others being 1945, 1953, and 1965. Only in 1973 did the team win more games than it lost (five and three), and even then it was outscored by the opposition, as indeed it was in the other three years as well. A careful review of the individual game records (see appendix A) shows that Queen's lost big to Toronto in all but one of its eight games over this stretch and that it generally had equal trouble with the University of Ottawa. For the most part, it did reasonably well against Carleton but lost more than it won against the eclectic mix of other schools which the new scheduling threw its way (Loyola, Guelph, McMaster, York, Laurier, occasionally McGill, and in 1975 for the first time, Concordia and Bishop's). The season length was also highly irregular; for example, in 1972 the team played only six games, but in 1975 it played nine. These factors no doubt made preparation difficult in every respect (lack of knowledge about the opposition, injury occurrence, and so on).

It is not clear why these years were so barren. Both Hadden and Melvin were at a loss to explain the dry spell,[15] much as Lenard and McCarney had been unable to explain that of the late forties and early fifties. In almost identical language they noted that "somehow it never quite worked out," adding: "In '73, for example, we had a good offence, but it wasn't good enough." There is no doubt that injuries to key players were part of the story; for instance, McLellan was lost for the entire 1972 season after scoring twelve times in 1971. Similarly, Hadden was gone for most of the 1974 season. But Queen's had some fine ball players throughout this period – Hadden, for one, who was later a CFL player – and many others: Darrell Penner (son of "Bo Bo" Penner of the late forties teams), Stu Lang, Alex Melvin (son of team doctor Jim Melvin and the first Queen's water boy ever to "graduate" to playing for the Gaels), John Wintermeyer (who set a new league record for field goals in a season, getting eighteen), Dave Whiteside, John Waddell, and others. And, of course, there was Doug Cozac, who graduated in 1972 and who, over his five seasons, 1968–72, was able to accumulate 204 points, almost entirely from kicking, a feat that placed him fifth on the all-time scoring list (see appendix B).

Very likely, the explanation for these barren years lies simply in the fact that a certain vacuum existed at the top of Queen's football family.[16] McCarney decided to leave the coaching staff at the end of the 1972 season after twenty-one years of service as Tindall's right arm and fixer, and the necessary heavy.[17] He could not easily be replaced, despite the continuing contribution of Miklas and help from various sources such as Climie, McKeen, and others. Undoubtedly Tindall missed him, and he was himself tiring. In that 1972 season he won his hundredth game. By 1974, his twenty-eighth season, he had 108 to make him the most winning coach in Canadian intercollegiate history. There was considerable speculation whether he would return for the 1975 season, especially as he was past the normal university retirement age. Ultimately, the university prevailed on him to complete one more season while it struck a search committee (in February 1975) to find a successor. This proved to be Frank Tindall's worst season since 1957, almost twenty years earlier. The team went two and six, losing the last game 57–26 to Ottawa.

And then Frank was gone. By this time he was sixty-seven years old, the "kindly old coach," often also known as "the Mentor." He had put in twenty-nine seasons counting his prewar year, had won eight championships (28 per cent of his seasons), brought home nineteen non-losing seasons (66 per cent), and won one hundred and ten games (56 per cent of the total), losing eighty-five with two tied. It was quite some achievement, and it brought him accolades from every quarter. At a testimonial dinner for him early in 1976, which four hundred people attended, Stewart said, "We're all better people for having known Frank Tindall … I have never met a man who didn't like Frank Tindall." Hadden had similar words of praise: "You could finish second best and experience something your opponents wouldn't – playing for Frank Tindall … Frank Tindall is a special man and I gained something very special playing under him."

In reply, Tindall was gracious as always in giving credit to everyone who had helped him down the years: "Good players make good coaches. I'm also grateful for the friendship and moral support I received over the years from the principals [Tindall had seen five, from Wallace to Watts], doctors, trainers, and my assistant coaches, especially Hal McCarney who was with me for twenty-one years." When asked about the disastrous final game against Ottawa, his habitual wit did not desert him: "It would have been nice to go out in a blaze of glory. But, then again, it didn't do Joan of Arc any good!"*

---

* These quotations are from a review article on Tindall in the Kingston *Whig-Standard* (16 August 1985) on the occasion of his induction into the Canadian Football Hall of Fame. Tindall was always welcomed as a speaker at alumni, service club, and other functions. Famous for his wit and his ability to tell a humorous story, he had a kind of George Burns or Will Rogers delivery in which the punch line was always slightly delayed. Many of the stories were no doubt impromptu, but when searching through his files for this book, I found a whole collection of cartoons and stories, many from the *New Yorker* (always a source of high-quality humour), which Tindall had collected over time and from which he drew some of his many stories.

Frank Tindall, the "kindly old coach," "the Mentor"
(Wally Berry Photo Collection, QUA)

It was typical of the man that he did not disappear completely but remained strongly connected with Queen's football in succeeding years. Finding the area to his liking, he retired to a summer home on Downie Island, where he took up landscape painting and other activities. He was elected to the Canadian Football Hall of Fame in 1985, both as a player and coach, and in 1989 was awarded an honorary doctorate by the university. He occupied a special place in the "Queen's family" until his death in 1993.

A NEW BROOM: 1976–1977

As had sometimes been the case in the past, the transition from one coaching era to the next was not without its bumpy aspects. In this instance, the committee had made its choice quite early, settling on Garney Henley, a well-known CFL star with Hamilton who was coaching basketball elsewhere in the college ranks. Henley, however, wanted an extra year "to arrange his affairs," and it was for this reason that Tindall had been encouraged to stay on for the 1975 season. Fully expecting Henley's appearance for the 1976 season, the committee and the university were shocked when Henley informed them, in the late spring of 1976, only several months before the season was to begin, that he would not be coming to Queen's after all. He had accepted a position at Mount Allison University as athletic director and head football coach.

The committee scrambled to find a replacement of quality who could be available on short notice, and it settled on Doug Hargreaves, who was head football coach and athletics director at Dalhousie University. This was to prove an inspired choice and one that by 1978 had made Queen's forget it had ever considered Henley for the position. Hargreaves was a veteran football coach and a Queen's person to the core. Originally from "the Soo," he had played for the Gaels on several occasions, first as a young undergraduate in 1951, again in 1953, and then briefly in 1959 as a mature student before injury forced him out. He had coached in the high school ranks in the Kingston and Sault Ste Marie areas, and also off and on for five years at the Royal Military College (RMC) as well as with Tindall at Queen's when his military activities permitted. In 1965 he had been appointed head football and basketball coach at RMC, and in 1972 had moved on to Dalhousie.

So Hargreaves had a long record of handling young men of a university age, and an intimate knowledge of the Queen's football program. He had a great deal of respect for both, thought highly of Tindall, and set out to make sure that the team would do as well as it possibly could. He was under no illusion that he had been the first choice and was determined to prove himself.[18]

On arriving at Queen's, Hargreaves found himself a nucleus of coaching help in the persons of the veteran line coach Bill Miklas and John Thomson, a professor in physical education who had strong opinions on defensive football theories and a good way with the players. Several other former players also pitched in during Hargreaves's first seasons to help with the transition.* He made his mark early, bringing a highly organized approach to practices and game preparation, introducing three-times-a-day practices during camp (whose length he extended) and a change in both defensive

---

* The "old guard" passed to the new in other respects as well. For example, Tommy Hopkins, who became the team's equipment manager in 1977, also began his time at Queen's when Hargreaves started; and as noted above, the trainer Tabby Gow would retire by 1980 to make way for Dave Ross. In yet another domain, it is also worth noting that the principals of the university had changed in this topsy-turvy time. In late 1974, Ronald Watts, a political scientist on faculty at the university, was appointed to succeed Deutsch. He remained at the helm until 1984.

Doug Hargreaves, the new broom (Art Martin)

and offensive strategy; for example, the blocking rules on offence were completely formalized. All were important changes from Tindall's final years, and they showed that there was a new broom now in charge, with a strong hand.

Hargreaves had a nucleus of good players – Bob O'Doherty, Randy Edgeworth, and others – and things very quickly turned around.[19] The team went from three and six in 1975 to five and two in 1976, outscoring the opposition for the first time since 1971. It was greatly aided by an exceptional crop of rookies, who were to help carry the team back up to the heights over the next several years. Dick Bakker, Jim Muller, Ross Francis, Pat Plishka, Jim D'Andrea, Jim Rutka, Ed Andrew, Paul Langevin, Dave Marinucci, Tony Manastersky, Blaine Shore, Bob Mullen, John Vernon, among others, all arrived more or less at the same time (1976 and 1977) and suddenly gave the team a depth and strength it had not seen since the late 1960s.

The curve swung steadily upwards, Queen's winning seven and losing two in 1977. Rutka, a native of Toronto who had come Queen's after two years at Princeton, was now at quarterback. There was a strong backfield, consisting of Marinucci, Manastersky, O'Doherty, Best, and others, not to mention Shore, who also handled the field goal and convert duties and was quietly amassing points towards the all-time Gael points-scoring leadership he would achieve by the time he left. There was a solid offensive line, anchored again by good guards such as Edgeworth and John Wilson, and a steadily maturing defence, especially along the line, with Bakker, Muller, and Francis, at linebacker with Andrew, Langevin, and Vernon, and in the deep backs with D'Andrea, Tyczka, and Mullen.

By this time Queen's was playing a mixture of Ontario and Quebec teams, which included Bishop's, Ottawa, Carleton, McGill, and a newcomer in 1977, the Université du Québec à Trois Rivières (UQTR). The latter remained for three seasons and was beaten convincingly by everyone, including Queen's (45–1, 46–7, and 42–7), before it withdrew in 1980. Queen's 1977 club came very close to making the College Bowl for the first time since 1968. Opening with solid victories against Bishop's and Ottawa, it then lost a heart-breaking 5–4 game against McGill in Montreal, which was avenged two weeks later in Kingston with a 21–9 victory, Queen's having beaten Carleton 40–1 in the meantime. After a walkover of UQTR the following week, the team was into the playoffs, where it won a hard-fought game against Ottawa, 27–14, and then a relatively easy one against Bishop's, 45–27. For the first time since 1974, the Gaels found themselves in a playoff outside their own conference, deep into November, as they headed to Halifax to play Acadia for the right to go to the College Bowl.

Played in the abysmal grey and wet that is often typical of Canadian November days, the Gaels went out to a comfortable half-time lead, only to see the Axemen recover in the second half to win convincingly, 35–22. The loss was a bitter one for the players to absorb,[20] but as was so often the case in the past, it became a rallying point for the team, which was to achieve a very different result when it reached post-season play the following year.

THE VANIER CUP: 1978

Coming off two solid seasons with virtually the entire 1977 team intact and with some good new rookies – in particular, running back Tom Macartney – the Gaels were ranked in the top ten nationally before the season began. (This issue of ranking was to be a bone of contention, as well as a strong motivating factor, by the end of the season.) The team had a feeling that something dramatic was going to happen.[21] The defensive line, which the press dubbed "the Gold Rush," was particularly strong, anchored by all-Canadian Bakker (who was the Metras Trophy winner for the best lineman in Canada) and including Muller and Francis (both of whom would go on to careers in professional football) as well as Rob Ball. The defence was rock solid overall as well, with seasoned veterans such as Andrew, Langevin, Vernon, D'Andrea, Tyczka, Mullen, Al Jette, and Bruce Balson, at work behind the front four. The defence was to hold the opposition to just 84 points over ten games, the second-best average points-against per game in the postwar period (the best being Queen's 1961 team, which allowed just

48 points in seven games, see appendix A). The team came to rely on its defence as the bedrock of its game, much as Reeve's teams of the 1930s or the undefeated clubs of the early 1960s had done.

The season opened with five victories in a row, with large scores over the first two opponents: UQTR and another newcomer from Quebec, Concordia, which was playing for the first time. These were followed by three solid victories over Queen's regular rivals, McGill, Ottawa, and Carleton, the scores being 27–17, 28–16, and 26–3, respectively. At this point things looked good. The team was delivering on its pre-season promise, the only worry being that Rutka, the starting quarterback, was out with injury and Mullen was having to fill in. The offence sputtered somewhat but was still putting points on the board.

Then things seemed to turn for the worse. Journeying to Lennoxville for a game against the steadily maturing Bishop's football program, the Gaels had to come from behind for a 15–14 win. Chances were especially squandered on offence, but the defence held firm. Tim Wardrop, the kicker, scored a single point on a 48-yard punt to tie the game with minutes left, and he then won it on the last play of the game with another towering punt which the Bishop's return man elected to run out of the end zone rather than punt back and was tackled a yard short of getting out. The Gaels thus came away with a win and had home-field advantage for the playoffs.

The first game of the playoffs was against Carleton, a game that by all rights should have been a given, for the Gaels were unbeaten, were ranked fifth nationally, and had already beaten Carleton. But it was a close call. The final score was 17–13 for Queen's, which again came from behind to win – this time, in the second overtime period. To be fair to the offence, it was severely handicapped: Rutka could not play; and Lynch, who backed him up when Mullen was not available, went out for the season during the game when he injured a knee ligament that he had first torn in the 1976 season. As well, Macartney, Best, and Shore were all unable to start, and O'Doherty and Mullen were playing with important injuries. Once again the defence came up big, for example, holding the Ravens on third and one from the one on the last play of the first overtime period. It was the second "heart-stopping victory" in a row – the Gaels were "puzzling as ever but still unbeaten."[22]

Then it was on to McGill the following week. Rutka was back in the saddle at quarterback, and the offence finally came untracked. With the defence playing its usual fine game (four more passes were intercepted, adding to the record number already accumulated so far that season), the final score, 23–1, left little doubt that the Gaels were soundly back on form. In addition to the usual veteran contributions, rookies Macartney and Fred Prinzen on defence made solid contributions.

The time had thus come to return to Halifax where, the year before, the Gaels had blown a solid first-half lead to lose their Atlantic Bowl contest against Acadia. In 1978 the team "washed away [that] bitter memory and replaced it with the taste of victory" by "blitzing" St Francis Xavier 35–10 before a record Atlantic Bowl crowd of 8,500 people.[23] Rutka had another fine day, throwing for two touchdowns and winning MVP honours in the game for his performance; the defence allowed but one touchdown in its continuing strong performance.

This brought the Gaels to their first national College Bowl appearance in ten years. This time, it was against the University of British Columbia Thunderbirds, who had beaten Wilfrid Laurier in the Western Bowl for their right to play. Despite their unbeaten record of nine wins and no losses, the Gaels were not ranked as the favourites. They were also underrepresented in both the national awards and the all-Canadian picks, which were announced during the week of festivities leading up to the game.[24] There is little doubt that the anger these slights generated provided the team with a strong desire to prove to the selectors just how wrong they had been.

The game was played before 19,000 fans at Varsity Stadium on a brisk clear Saturday afternoon. An estimated 8,000 Queen's students had descended on Toronto in a convoy of thirty buses, vans, cars, and motor-cycles. In shades of the annual Toronto weekend of earlier years, there had been a big pep rally and dance at St Lawrence Market on the Friday evening before the game attended by 4,000 people, and by kickoff time the Eastern-ers' side of the stadium was a sea of red, yellow, and blue jackets. With banners everywhere (most of which could not be shown to the nationwide television audience that was watching the game!), with the obligatory smoke bombs at half-time, and with a successful assault on the goalposts at the end of the game, it was a show of Queen's spirit and tradition at its finest.[25]

As implied, the team did not disappoint. Once again led by the defence, who never allowed UBC inside the Queen's 35-yard line and gave up only three points (a record, which Queen's would reset in 1992 with its shutout victory), the team won 16–3, capping its undefeated season with the Vanier Cup. It was Queen's first undefeated season since 1964 and the first time a Queen's team had won ten games in a season. In honour of the defence's contribution, Ed Andrew, the Gaels' middle linebacker, was named the game's MVP. With the victory, "Queen's was finally recognized as No. 1 in the country."[26] "Hargreaves could finally relax."[27] With the victory he had erased whatever lingering doubts remained about the circumstances of his original appointment. He had matched Tindall's 1968 Vanier Cup victory and was at last free to move on.

True to Queen's tradition in other respects, the crowds of students spilled out onto Bloor Street after the game, snake-dancing their way in celebration. The following Monday a pep rally was held back in Kingston, after which the champions were paraded around the campus. Both the university and

The Vanier Cup held aloft by Randy Edgeworth (59) and Jim D'Andrea (26), co-captains 1978 (Art Martin)

the city eventually held dinners and presentations to honour the team. Ross Francis reported that fellow students, the faculty, and staff, were pleased with the victory, "knew who we were," and seemed to feel it was important to the school. There was a feeling around the university that was reminiscent of Queen's football in earlier times and completely belied Harrower's arguments to the Board of Trustees that spectator sports, and particularly football, were dying out at the university.

VERY NEARLY AGAIN: 1979

With Rutka gone in 1979,[28] there was some concern over who would play at quarterback. But Hargreaves found a suitable replacement in freshman Bob Wright (son of a longtime Queen's staff member and avid football fan, Bill Wright) who was to quarterback the team for the next five years. Also expected to be missing, either through graduation or because they had used up their five years of eligibility, were Edgeworth, O'Doherty, Shore, Plishka, Manastersky, Shugart, Tyczka, D'Andrea, and several others.[29] It was thus a very great hill that Hargreaves, the coaching staff, and the team expected to face as the 1979 season rolled around.

Fortunately a sizable number of this group decided for various reasons to return for one last season, and the Gaels very nearly pulled it off again in 1979. After the usual opening walkover against UQTR (which left the league at the end of this season), the Gaels lost a very close game to Ottawa, 21–20, when Hargreaves chose to go for the win late in the game with a two-point conversion attempt that came up short, rather than settle for the tie with the convert. This was the only time all season, until the last playoff game against Western, that the opposition scored more than ten points in a game. The defensive unit, virtually intact from the 1978 club, thus helped lead the way to four more league victories (16–10, 23–7, 23–8, 17–6) and two playoff victories (Carleton was beaten 25–5, McGill 22–5 for the Eastern Conference championship). With seven wins and one loss, the team was headed for a confrontation with an old rival, Western, for the right to go back to the Vanier Cup.

Enthusiasm for the game ran high. The *Whig Standard* reported that over a thousand students were headed to London for the game. The *Globe and Mail* noted that it was "the long-awaited revival of both the Yates Cup game and one of the country's greatest college football rivalries." And Queen's athletic's director Al Lenard, a former Gael, was heard to say: "We've got alumni constantly giving us hell about how we destroyed the best football deal going [a reference to the one-time 'Little Big Four' of Queen's, Toronto, Western, and McGill] and, if we could, we'd like to reinstate everything that was in the past."[30]

Little Stadium was crowded to overflowing for the game.[31] Unfortunately for the Gaels, the defence, which had performed so well for virtually two complete seasons, suddenly could not find its way on a muddy field against a very good Western ground game led by Potter and Marshall. They both had over 100-yard games, broke the game open, especially in the second half, with long runs from scrimmage, and simply could not be contained even by the veteran Gael defence. Although Wright and the offence had a good day passing and although the game was close at the half (15–7), the final result was never in doubt, and the team down to a 32–14 loss. "There was a haunting atmosphere in the Gaels' dressing room after Saturday's loss … Most players were sullen, saying little while others wept. Some just sat and stared, oblivious to all else in the room. Many journeyed through the room from fellow player to player thanking them for three, four, five years of good football together."[32]

No doubt, the veteran players were recalling the euphoria of the previous year's Vanier Cup celebrations, finding themselves more appreciative of the true meaning of the *Wide World of Sports* slogan "The joy of victory, and the agony of defeat." This was doubly so since there was no chance of revenge for the many who were moving on. To be sure, there were individual recognitions gained. Muller, for example, won the Metras Trophy as the best lineman in Canada, the second time in three years Queen's had done so. But the game was to leave a bad taste in the mouths of those who played in it, especially those for whom it was their last as a Gael.

A SEVENTIES RETROSPECTIVE

The loss to Western was not the best of all possible ways to end the decade. Then again, neither was a second large increase in the price of oil, engineered by the OPEC cartel, or inflation running at 15 per cent, both of which also occurred in 1979. But both the bittersweet reversal of Gael fortunes and the semi-hysterical nature of the world at large were somehow a fitting end to a decade that had been marked by just this type of occurrence.

There were other influences too. Steroids and the use of other performance-enhancing drugs began to show up in sports. There was no reason to expect that Queen's football would remain immune from this development any more than it would be isolated from any other. Personal interviews with several players from the seventies indicate that there was knowledge of what could be gained from the use of steroids and a suspicion that two or three of those who played during the decade might have actually used them. However, it was the emphatic opinion of all concerned that the practice was never widespread among the teams. In the first place, most of the players had gone to Queen's as much for academics as athletics; they did not expect to go on to play pro football (where you needed all the muscle mass you could get), so they had no need of steroids. Also, because of the rising admission standards, most players were probably better informed about the possible dangers of excessive usage and were therefore unwilling to endanger their future careers for the sake of increased performance on a college football field.

Then, too, Hargreaves was especially emphatic about the importance of avoiding these drugs, and he introduced a drug education and counselling service for the players three years in advance of the one mandated by the Canadian Intercollegiate Athletic Union (CIAU). He also put a stop to the small monetary incentives that may have been offered to some of the players, and he stepped up his campaign against recruiting incentives, which he felt would eventually cheapen the college game in Canada. Not that he felt recruiting per se was bad. On the contrary, it was becoming increasingly obvious that if Queen's was to have any hope of competing against schools that took competitive football seriously but had lower admission standards, recruiting would have to become a key part of his activities. By the end of the decade, he was on the road much of the winter and spring, visiting potential prospects across Canada, talking to high schools and alumni, and generally beating the bushes for the ever-elusive scholar-athlete football player who might want to come to Queen's and might actually be able to get in, but who could not in any way be influenced by any financial aid other than an academic scholarship for which he would have to qualify. It was not an easy task, and it grew worse with time.

Equally bothersome was the business of financing the program. As noted above, attendance at games, except at truly major events such as the 1978 College Bowl, fell as soon as the new stadium was opened. This cut into the direct cash receipts from the program. Moreover, the gate receipts from such events as the College Bowl could no longer be split between the two teams playing. The CIAU's new policy of revenue sharing from these large events meant that Queen's football never received any more than its expenses (and not even all of those) from playoff and post-season Vanier Cup appearances. Instead, the money went into a general pot to subsidize all football and other sports programs across Canada. As well, the university began to compete in a much broader range of intercollegiate sports, and this diluted the amount of student fee revenue that in earlier years would have been devoted to the main spectator sports such as football, hockey, and basketball. Finally, the raging inflation throughout the decade drove up the cost of all components of the program (equipment, travel, and so on) dramatically.

These circumstances, together with a change in financial reporting at Queen's in the early 1970s (which abandoned detailed financial reporting by individual sports in favour of a more general university-based financial reporting system), and a certain absence of records in the physical education department, make it impossible to know exactly how profitable or, more importantly, how expensive the football program was during the 1970s.[33] It is likely that it was costing the university more than it brought in, but one cannot know with certainty what the real economic situation was – what it would have been if the program had received its traditional part of post-season revenues rather than directly subsidizing others; if an attempt had been made to allocate student fees to the program in direct relationship to the student admissions at games; and if all expenses had been recorded and paid by the program itself.[34] Perhaps it still would have been a losing proposition. As it was, all that the sports administrators at Queen's could see were the budgeted expenses for their own programs, which in the case of football were larger by an order of magnitude than any of the other programs, as indeed they always had been. This did not make football a much-beloved part of the family, even though it was still bringing into the university far more in the way of cash receipts than any other program. This was yet another difficult reality that Hargreaves faced, which his predecessors had not had to worry about.

Even with this steadily worsening situation, the team still managed to provide a quality experience to those who played, and indeed to be highly competitive and victorious, especially in the second half of the decade. Echoing the sentiments of earlier players, the men who played in the 1970s speak of the special experience that was football at Queen's. "It was the best football experience I ever had including the pros," said Ross Francis. "It changed my life," stated Randy Edgeworth. There was a sense of quality, of tradition, family, and personal concern, which virtually all the players cherished.

As in the case of earlier eras, it is interesting to know what became of the players of the 1970s. Which of them were the best? And where have they all gone? Because of the large number of hugely talented players in the second half of the decade, it is extremely difficult to single out any one of them without doing several of the others considerable injustice. Certainly, in the early part of the decade it is possible to settle on perhaps Hadden, Penner, Lang, and Cozac. But then the task becomes impossible: Bakker, Muller, Francis, Andrew, Tyzcka, D'Andrea, Mullen, Edgeworth, Marinucci, Rutka (in a shortened career), O'Doherty, and Shore. All were outstanding performers. Many won repeated all-star nominations, were game and league MVPs, set scoring records, and so on. Which out of all these to choose? I have settled on the following, who will just have to represent the rest: Hadden; Muller, Bakker, and Francis combined; O'Doherty; and Edgeworth.

Dave Hadden came to Queen's from Upper Canada College (UCC), principally because his school friend Lang had chosen Queen's the year before. Once Hadden had seen Queen's, he "loved it and only really ever thought of Queen's." He had played football at UCC but found the game a lot faster and more sophisticated at the university level. He was one of the first of a string of hard-charging Queen's fullbacks that would include such players as Marinucci, Bob Bronk, and Larry Mohr, all known for their particular toughness and durability and a flat unwillingness to go down. It is said about Hadden, who loved contact, that Miklas once stated, during his pregame coaching instructions: "Warrender, McLellan, get out of bounds when you get the chance. Hadden, you, you stay *in* bounds!"

During his four years at Queen's, 1971–74, Hadden was a league all-star on several occasions, as well as captain and MVP. Moving on to the pros, he caught on with Toronto and spent two years with the Argonauts,

Dave "the Beast" Hadden, 1971–74
(QFHF)

followed by one each with Saskatchewan and Hamilton. Always wanting to be a teacher, when offered a teaching post at UCC he left the game as a player, though he continued to do some coaching. Moving on from UCC, he became head master at Lakefield. In retrospect, he feels that the true value of the game to him was that it contributed to his sense of self-esteem and personal strength. It also helped him appreciate that one cannot hide, that often in life one is part of a team, that the game "soon lets you know when you're being a jerk," and that "you can actually grow and be better from this knowledge."[35]

Bakker, Muller, and Francis (with Ball filling out the front four in their later years) are inseparable in the minds of almost everyone associated with Queen's football in the late 1970s. Indeed, it is ironic that three of the best defensive linemen ever to play for the team all happened to play at the same time. Bakker was from a Dutch farming family from Manotick, outside Ottawa, and he came to Queen's in 1975. He really blossomed with the 1977 season, when he won the Metras Trophy as the best lineman in Canadian college football and went on to be the first Queen's player to compete directly against American college players in the Can-Am Bowl game.[36]

Muller and Francis arrived the following year – Hargreaves's first year – and late that season and for several afterwards they made up the core of

Ross Francis, Dick Bakker, and Jim Muller, 1975–80 (Art Martin)

the "Gold Rush," a defensive front line unrivalled in the country. Muller was also from Ottawa and also won the Metras Trophy (in 1979). He wrestled for the university, enjoyed rock climbing during his summers, and graduated in chemical engineering. Francis, the biggest of the three and probably the most intellectual, was from outside Oshawa and came to Queen's partly because of Miklas but principally because he saw it as an "intelligent" place, one where the program and the school had a sense of "quality and class to them." Like Bakker and Muller, he won his share of awards, including lineman of the year, MVP (twice), and a Jenkins Trophy. After an undergraduate degree, he stayed on to complete his MBA.

All three went on to professional ball for varying amounts of time. Francis's career lasted the longest; he played four seasons with Hamilton and two with Ottawa. While doing so, he completed law school, quitting the game when the time came to article in Toronto. After practising law for some years with Osler, Hoskin, a large Toronto firm, he became a corporate counsel to several large companies. Muller also played professionally with Hamilton and was named their rookie of the year in his first of several years there. Eventually, his work carried him west to make his living "in the oil patch" as an engineer, where he was tragically killed in an automobile accident early in 1996. Of the three, Bakker spent the least time in the professional ranks. He moved through a series of interesting jobs, which included marketing Canadian satellite technology to Asia, consulting, a series of other business exploits, and, finally, one that is involved with the internet. But he and Francis remain strong supporters of the Gaels. Francis summed up a common attitude when he said, "I loved the game at Queen's,

Bob O'Doherty, 1974–78 (QFHF)

the sense of tradition, the teamwork. I also enjoyed Queen's more generally. I got a sense of self out of it, what I was capable of, and a lot of lasting friendship. I'll certainly send my kids there, if they'll go!"

O'Doherty and Edgeworth were also key members of those late-1970s teams. O'Doherty, who came from a strongly athletic family in St Catharines, enrolled at Queen's partly because of Jim "Hairbone" Harrison, a Queen's grad and a legendary high school coach in St Catharines.[37] O'Doherty was part of that wonderful group of rookies in the fall of 1974, which included Edgeworth and others. He played five seasons for the Gaels, surpassed Lilles and Stewart as the leading touchdown scorer (until Elberg) in Queen's history, won numerous honours, including all-star and MVP awards (one of them in the Can-Am Bowl), graduated with an MBA, and went on to play professionally with Winnipeg, where he lasted several short years before a knee injury took him out of the game. One of the distinctive "characters" of the teams in those years, O'Doherty was a wonderfully gifted athlete, excelling at tennis as well as football. He had a smooth, easy-going, almost laconic manner that hid a fiercely competitive spirit. For several years after his playing days, he was involved in a franchise operation, after which he moved to Football Canada as its technical director.

Edgeworth, from Ottawa (but originally British Columbia), was a "small guard" and one of the acknowledged leaders of the teams in the late seventies. Arriving in 1974, he worked steadily to build up his strength and technique while "getting beat up a lot by some very big guys." By the time 1978 rolled round, he was offensive captain, "street-smart," able to hold his own, and one of a group of three or four who worked steadily within the team to provide coordination and a sense of team, family, and common purpose. Unlike the others mentioned here, Edgeworth did not go on to a professional career, nor did he even consider it. Proud of never having missed a game or practice in five years, playing in pain with a pinched nerve in his neck much of 1978 season, and having absorbed enough punishment from much bigger defensive linemen, he concluded that "the day it was over, it was over." Having done a four-year degree in physical education and one year in education, he began teaching in the Kingston public school system and coaching football in the local area. In 1979 he coached at the Royal Military College, where he helped them to a championship, and he was with Queen's from 1981 to 1986, as an offensive line coach much of the time. He has said that the latter activity was an attempt to give back something for the "wonderful time" he had as a member of the team: "We ate together, played together. We were a family. At the tenth reunion, there was only one guy missing! It was something else."[38] Edgeworth was later appointed principal of Joyceville Public School north of Kingston. He still runs a lot, having competed in several marathons during the 1980s, and retains a very active interest in Queen's football.

And what of some of the others? Plishka is a high school teacher, Rutka a neurosurgeon in Toronto at the Hospital for Sick Children. Tyzcka has his PHD and is an entrepreneur, as is Andrew, who runs the family business. D'Andrea, who holds the all-time pass interception record at Queen's, is a partner in a major Canadian law firm; Manastersky also is a lawyer. Langevin and Ball are practising engineers; Sops is in banking, and Shore in the airline business. Shugart is with the Canadian Olympic Association, as was Best for a while; Hanlon is principal of a high school. And these are only some of them. They were a fine group of Gaels. Several are in the Queen's Football Hall of Fame already, and many more will surely follow. Some in the group have taken over the running of the Queen's Football Club from the late 1960s generation of players and are thus making their contribution to the continuation of the tradition.

7
Over the Century Mark
1980–1994

The writing of history so close to the present is always dangerous, principally because the passage of time has not yet bestowed its gift of perspective on events. But in this case it seemed a logical thing to do, for the close of the 1994 season marked the end of the Hargreaves era in Queen's football. Over this entire period of the 1980s and half of the 1990s, "his" teams would add their own chapter to Queen's football history, winning six more league championships and two more national semifinal (Churchill) bowl titles, as well as another Vanier Cup in 1992 (see table 10).

Through the program would pass some outstanding players: Mike Schad, the first Canadian college player to be chosen in the first round of the NFL draft; Brad Elberg, who was to become the leading touchdown scorer in Queen's history; Jamie Galloway, the team's leading all-time scorer; Charlie Galunic, the first Gael to win a Rhodes Scholarship in the modern era; and also Jock Climie, Bob Bronk, Larry Mohr, and several others, all of whom made large contributions and went on to pro careers. There was also a host of good solid quarterbacks to lead the offence, notably Bob Wright, Peter Harrison, and Tim Pendergast, and some outstanding linebackers and other defensive ballplayers to backstop the offence and make their own contribution – most recently, Mike Boone, Eric Dell, and, in the backs, Joel Dagnone, Mark Morrison, and others. Their history and the story of those who played with them is as important to the overall tapestry as the remembered glories of the 1920s or, even farther back, the exploits of Guy Curtis and his mates.

The reference to Curtis and the early days is apt, for the history of the 1980s and 1990s marks the passage of more than a century since football was first played at Queen's (1882) and since Queen's won its first Dominion championship (1893, exactly one hundred seasons before it won another in the Vanier Cup of 1992). Moreover, if one discounts the nine war years when football was not played (1915–18 and 1940–44), there is another centenary of note, for the completion of the 1990 season marked the end of a century

Table 10
Queen's football record, 1980–1994[1]

Year	Won	Lost	Tied	For	Against
1980N[2]	5	4	0	178	141
1981C[3]N	6	4	0	278	210
1982	4	5	0	235	213
1983CN	7	2	2	316	192
1984CN	7	3	0	368	205
1985N	6	2	0	207	143
1986	3	5	0	222	195
1987	3	5	0	165	178
1988N	6	3	0	183	132
1989CN	9	1	0	294	148
1990N	5	3	1	192	116
1991CN	7	3	0	359	240
1992CN	10	1	0	334	145
1993	2	5	0	122	168
1994	1	6	0	136	188
Total	81	52	3	3,589	2,614

Source: Based on individual game reports (appendix A)
[1] League and playoff games only
[2] N indicates non-losing (i.e., winning or tied) season
[3] C indicates championship season

of seasons. These are important landmarks in the passage of time in any human endeavour, and they represent a continuity scarcely found elsewhere, if at all, in Canadian sport.*

Like the earlier periods, the 1980s and early 1990s were played out against a larger complex of events which gave their own shape to the times.[1] It will be recalled, for example, that the 1980s began with interest rates approaching 20 per cent and with a referendum (in May 1980) on sovereignty in René Lévesque's Quebec. Pierre Trudeau had just been re-elected prime minister after the debacle of Joe Clark's failure to count properly on the budget vote in 1979, and cancer-stricken Terry Fox was making his courageous attempt to run across Canada. In 1981, thanks to the governor of the Federal Reserve system in the United States, the Canadian economy went into a nosedive and by the following year had witnessed the second worst collapse in gross domestic product since the Great Depression of the 1930s. The year also saw the famous federal-provincial conference that led to the 1982 repatriation of

---

* Regrettably, these landmarks have all passed without recognition of their importance, largely because of a lack of appreciation of their historical significance. Now that they have been noted, it is to be hoped that the university will find cause (and be able) to make use of the upcoming 125th year anniversary in 2007, for example, to celebrate.

the constitution (without Quebec) and entrenchment of the Canadian Charter of Rights and Freedoms.

FOOTBALL AT THE BEGINNING OF THE 1980S:
1980–1982

Within this larger environment, the Gaels found themselves coming off the 1979 season with a conference championship but a loss to Western in the run-up to the Vanier Cup. They were a little uncertain about what the first year of the decade would bring, primarily because they had lost a sizable number of important players from the late-1970s clubs – Bakker, Muller, D'Andrea, Marinucci, Manastersky, and others. However, there was a good degree of carry-over, with Francis, Wilson, Andrew, and Mullen still on the team, and with Macartney in the backfield (where, during the early 1980s, the Gaels would once again come up big).

After an exhibition loss to Western (which meant that Queen's had had two successive losses to Western), the Gaels opened at home against Ottawa before 8,000 fans and lost 21–11. But just as doubts were beginning to surface about the offence, Queen's unloaded for 34 points against Concordia, with rookie Larry Mohr and Macartney, Bob Bronk, and others contributing to what looked like the makings of a good ground game for the Gaels. However, the team promptly went back into the offensive tank the following week against McGill, losing 22–12 after leading convincingly at the half. The game had to be called with time still on the clock because visiting Queen's students stormed onto the field and would not return to the stands. The *Queen's Journal* described it as "perhaps one of the dirtiest matches ever played in the OQIFC." Obviously, the young sportswriter had never seen one of the 1880s games!

In serious danger of having its first losing season in five years, the team turned around with a decent win over Carleton, only to lose yet again to Ottawa, this time in a close 10–9 game. At this point the team, primarily on offence, finally jelled around the ground game that it had shown some promise of throughout the season. With Wilson, Francis, Tony McDowell, and others up front and with the "four horsemen" of Bronk, Greg Baun, Mohr, and Macartney carrying the load, the Gaels rolled off three wins in a row, carrying themselves to a final playoff game against Ottawa to move forward into post-season bowl competition. Playing on an icy, rainy field for the second time in two games against Ottawa, they lost by one point, 13–12, failing to score from inside the 25-yard line three times in the last seven minutes. It had been a winning season even though it had produced the worst won-lost record (5–4) since the 1975 season.

In 1981 the team stormed back. After two opening losses to Concordia and McGill, it won four games in a row on the strength of the ground game, led by Mohr, Bronk, and Macartney and with Wright's solid passing. After a "nothing game" loss to Ottawa, the Gaels found themselves once again in the playoffs, and this time the offence continued "hot" deep into the post-season. The team beat Concordia 39–14, and it then won 26–19 in Montreal against an undefeated McGill club in a miraculous comeback (behind rookie quarterback Pete Harrison and the triple option) from two touchdowns late in the game. To Hargreaves's amazement (for he had felt all through the season that it was a young club), they were off to the Atlantic Bowl in Halifax to play Acadia for the right to go to the Vanier Cup game.

Fan support ran high. Bus-loads of students made the long trip, and Principal Watts was there with three thousand signatures on a good-luck letter. But fortune did not look kindly on the Gaels twice running. They were off to an absolutely appalling start – by the end of the first half, fumbles and punt blocks had the score at 26–8 against – and they duly lost 40–14.[2] In the post-season awards, Bronk and Mohr were made league all-stars, and Macartney received a much-deserved all-Canadian designation.

Thinking perhaps that the team had been young, and mindful of the time when the Gaels had lost badly at the Atlantic Bowl in Halifax in 1977 only to bounce back to win the Vanier Cup in 1978, Hargreaves was hopeful for the 1982 season. However, the "bounce-back miracle" was not to be repeated this time (though it would be in 1992–93). Ottawa was once again a problem. The Gaels lost twice, 22–20 and 35–32, but won the playoff 31–30.[3] In fact, 1982 was a season of close scores and big offence (with the exception of one game). Wright, in his fourth season, led the country in touchdown passes, finding receivers such as Scott Bissessar. Mohr, who had a record-breaking season on the ground (he narrowly missed winning the overall Canadian university rushing title) and Macartney, in his final year, were also big factors in an offence that scored a lot, even though the team so often lost late in the game. The single exception was the first playoff game against Ottawa in which, in a repeat of the McGill game a year earlier, Harrison came off the bench for an injured Wright and ran the option to secure a one-point victory. Still injured a week later, Wright was again out early in the game, but Harrison and the Gaels could not repeat the result of the previous week. Better prepared to deal with the option, and capitalizing on several Queen's turnovers (especially a badly mishandled punt in the end zone midway through the fourth quarter), Concordia won 25–15 to put an end to Queen's 1982 season.

SOME BIG YEARS: 1983–1985

By 1983 the economy had made a strong recovery. The country had finally had enough of Trudeau (this was the period of his "fuddle duddle" and his one-finger gestures), and in 1984 Brian Mulroney and the Tories won a landslide victory. They seemed to fit the times, which were coming to be characterized by a 1920s-like crassness that was typified by "yuppies," certain BMW-driving, and aggressive, youthful, "barbarians at the gate" of both sexes, who belonged to health clubs, played squash, and bought and sold huge companies before lunch. Increasingly influential feminist and aboriginal concerns came to the fore as the decade wore on; so did the scourge that was AIDS. They brought with them, respectively, a particularly harsh debate on abortion, a standoff at Oka in the early 1990s, and fear and death throughout the hard-hit homosexual and artistic communities.

Throughout much of this period the university had to deal with a steady erosion in its funding as the government continued a process of tightening up that had begun in the 1970s. Queen's suffered especially because of a decision that had been made by Principal Deutsch in the 1970s to restrict the total enrolment to 10,000 students. This measure did achieve Deutsch's intended effect of not "overrunning the city of Kingston's capacity" and of raising entrance standards (and hence another kind of reputation for the university), but because government grants continued to be partly tied to enrolments, Queen's found itself more strapped for funds than might have been the case if it had grown steadily throughout the period.[4]

There was also a change of principal during this period: from Ronald Watts to David Smith, an economist at the university, in 1984. Smith held the position for the next ten years, passing it over in his turn to William Leggett in the summer of 1994. Much of the flavour of the period 1980–94 thus comes from the Smith principalship, which was marked by yet another, and largely successful, university fund-raising campaign, a steady push to improve graduate studies and research, and an ever-increasing need to extract every possible economy out of a very tight budget. As noted, admission standards, especially for undergraduate programs, rose steadily, bringing the university a very different kind of student body than in earlier times and making it ever more difficult to find young men who could both meet the admission criteria and play football (or any other sport, for that matter) at a competitive level against schools with lower admission standards.[5]

There were several issues that preoccupied the university during this period: the problem of investment in South Africa, which triggered demonstrations and sit-ins at the principal's office as well as other manifestations of confrontation; marches to "take back the night" (in support of women's issues, especially security on campus and a need to increase the number of women faculty members); assertions of gay and lesbian pride (a strong theme in the *Queen's Journal* for a considerable number of years); concern over racism and the "non-representativeness" of Queen's when compared to a newer Canadian multicultural reality; and, among other issues, problems in the Law School and elsewhere over promotion decisions and over faculty representation more generally.

Of particular importance to the football program, besides the admissions criteria, was a steadily increasing attempt to control student behaviour on campus, especially drinking and celebrations such as street parties, and relations between the sexes. Partly motivated by considerations of town-gown relations and alumni-giving impacts, partly by a fear of legal litiga-tion, efforts such as the "No means no" campaign (to counter concerns about date rape) were made to change all aspects of male-female relationships on campus. Also, a kind of Puritanism spread across the campus, affecting such diverse activities as freshmen initiations, street parties at Homecoming, and student behaviour at football games. With respect to football, drinking was very seriously proscribed and penalties assigned, fans were forbidden to come on to the field after the game, and so on. By 1994, there was virtually no student attendance at home football games except during Frosh Week and at Homecoming and other reunions.

Through all this, Hargreaves, his coaches, the players, and those who supported Queen's football, whether through the Football Club or simply by their loyal attendance at the games, soldiered on. It was never easy, and it grew harder as time passed. But it was surprisingly successful, as became evident in the period 1983–85. The 1982 football season had been decep-tively disappointing in view of the number of points scored. Moreover, it had been Hargreaves's first losing season since taking over in 1976. Macart-ney (nick-named "the Franchise" while at Queen's) was now gone, and several of the others were uncertain of returning. In the face of this, Har-greaves was not at all optimistic about the 1983 season, but he knew that he still had Wright, Mohr, and Bissessar and was therefore hopeful. The defence, behind a rookie middle linebacker from Belleville named Mike Schad, and some good deep backs, including Rick Prinzen, Jeff Kyle, Ian Deakin, and John Corrigan, would continue to improve over the good signs it had shown late in the 1982 season. What Hargreaves could not have foreseen was that he had a team that would go 7–2 all the way to the Vanier Cup, only to lose there to Calgary.

Queen's began the season with back-to-back victories against Carleton.[6] The Gaels were led by Wright's passing to Bissessar and fourth-year tight-end Jim Pendergast (who showed big in 1983 after being a late cut of the profes-sional Hamilton Tiger-Cats and returning to Queen's), and they benefited from Mohr's continuing contributions along the ground; obvious from this was the play of a vastly improved offensive line, led by Tony McDowell, Steve Porter, Mark Oakley, Steve Hudson, and Tom Stefopulos. The Gaels opened with a "made-at-Queen's" defence, which had been designed by the returning defensive coordinator John Thomson to counter the offence game plans that later came to be called "run and gun," though at the time they were simply known as "pitch and toss" or "touch" football, because of all the passing. Essentially, it was an eleven-man defence with a very deep safety. Hargreaves called it the "lonesome polecat." It gave the Gaels' opponents something very different with which to contend.

The improved play of the offensive line was particularly evident in the next win, which was against Concordia the following week. Without the services of Mohr (hurt the previous week against Carleton, as was the other back, Scott Stirling), the Gaels nevertheless won 26–23 – against what Hargreaves called "the biggest team he had ever seen in Canadian college football"[7] – by carrying a first-half passing attack lead of 24–0 (on two touchdown passes to Bob O'Doherty's younger brother Ross) through to the end, and by benefiting from a failed Concordia attempt to win rather than settling for a tie with a field goal, on the last play of the game.

After another big-point victory over Bishop's in Lennoxville, again on the strength of the pass, the Gaels seemed to go flat in the back-to-back ties with Ottawa. Wright was again hurting, and Harrison could not seem to move the club. The defence kept the Gaels in both games, with the offence getting just enough for the ties (it helped that Ottawa missed two field-goal attempts at the end of the second game to preserve the tie in that one). At this point, the team was thus 4–0–2 and lucky to be so (just as it had been unlucky, the previous year, to have lost so many close games).

With first place sewn up, the next outing against McGill was really a "nothing" game, but it was one the club wanted to win in order to preserve the undefeated season. Despite being played before a capacity Homecoming crowd of over 10,000 people, it was not to be; the Gaels lost 34–33 on a converted touchdown by McGill with no time left on the clock. In retrospect, it was a good thing, because after disposing of Carleton for the third time in the season in the first playoff game, the Gaels roared back in revenge against McGill in the second, this time winning 36–5. They were thus league champions and moved on to post-season play, first against their old rival and nemesis the University of Toronto. It had been eight years since the Gaels had last played the Varsity Blues, and "only a residue of that fierce rivalry remained," as sportswriter Trent Frayne so vividly described:

Memories and a greased goal post are the only residue of a 77-year football rivalry that involved Queen's University and the University of Toronto all the way back to 1898.

That was a time when pigskin really came from pigs (now, on exceptional punts, it moos) and players were festooned in canvas vests and ankle boots, and their padded pantaloons inspired one of the game's great clichés: Gridiron heroes seldom retired; they hung up their moleskins.

Chill winds and snow flurries are expected in tidy little Richardson Stadium this afternoon when the Varsity Blues meet the Golden Gaels for the 148th time – but the first in eight years. That's because they are in different divisions. After the final intercollegiate game of 1975, Queen's was shifted to the Ontario-Quebec league's Eastern Division, snapping a rivalry with the U of T unbroken by anything but two world wars in this century.

Here they are again, though, because in last Saturday's division finals Queen's hammered McGill 36–5 (or, as the *Queen's Journal* crowed in a front-page box: Queen's 36 McGill who cares?) and Varsity shaded McMaster 20–16. The survivor of today's game plays next Saturday in the national final, the Vanier Cup, in Toronto's Varsity Stadium, against the western champion, the winner of last night's involvement between UBC Thunderbirds and University of Calgary Dinosaurs.

Once, the rivalry was intense. Dr. Jack Sinclair, a retired physician known in his playing days at Varsity as Long John Sinclair, remembers that when the team headed here from Toronto in the late twenties it took a bus to Belleville, stopped there overnight and came on to Kingston on the Saturday morning.

"Why was this?" your agent inquired. "The trip was too long?"

"Are you crazy?" the good doctor replied testily. "Because the bloody Queen's students wouldn't let us sleep if we went to Kingston. They'd blow horns and raise hell under our windows all night long."

The current Queen's coach, fiery Doug Hargreaves, who played against the Blues 30 years ago, says he misses the old wars. "But, listen," he amended, "I'm a throwback. You can't build instant tradition. The old rivalry is meaningless to the current kids. Hey, I'm so far out of date that I still think the run belongs in football."

Hargreaves remembers when college ball outdrew the pros in this country. "We had just under 26,000 for our game with Toronto in Varsity Stadium in 1954," he recalled. "But about that time the pros began to introduce skilled marketing and promotion ventures. The college people sat on their hands, expecting fans to come whenever they opened the gates. First thing you knew, they were staying away, and they still are. The new alignment didn't help, in the mid-1970s, and now Varsity is just another team in the other division."

As if to emphasize the point, Geoff Heinricks, Queen's linebacker on the 1980, '81 and '82 teams, says the only conscious reminder he has of a Queen's-Varsity rivalry is the tale of the greased pole.

"One time, years ago, Queen's beat 'em in their park and some of our engineering students stole a goal post and brought it back here to Kingston," he said. "Every year since, the engineers bring it out of its hiding place, cover it with oil and grease, nail a Queen's Scottish tam on top of it and set it up on end. Each new class of engineering frosh has to climb it as part of initiation week, trying to retrieve the tam. After that, the goal post is hidden away again."

Where?

"In its secret place."

The 1980s: pipers and cheerleaders (Art Martin)

Of course.

In Toronto, Rick Kollins, assistant to Blue head coach Ron Murphy in 1977, once put together a brief history of the game at the U of T, uncovering in his research that the Blues were called the Beavers in 1936, prompting a heading in the student newspaper after a defensive struggle with Western: BEAVERS DAM GOOD AGAINST MUSTANGS.

Not a moment too soon; the ink was still drying on the headline as the Beavers became the Blues again.

Over the years, there was occasional dismay in some schools that the U of T should appropriate the word Varsity naming its stadium and sports teams. Other schools, obviously, have varsities, too. But the explanation, as uncovered in Kollins' research, is innocent enough:

"From its earliest days, U of T was known as Varsity in recognition of its status as the first and, for many years, the only accredited university in the province. It was natural, then, for the football team to adopt this nomenclature."

Nowadays, it is doubtful that the ancient nomenclature matters. It's like where the Varsity Blues laid down their heads and closed their eyes last night.[8]

It snowed! And the Gaels, with less reliance on the pass and outside running – using a balanced, old-time offence attack led by a veteran quarterback, some fine kicking by Bill Barrable, and above all a strong defensive effort, especially by Steve Bodnar and others from northern Ontario, who were used to playing in snow and slippery conditions – won 22–7 before 8,500 fans at home in Kingston. So on they went to the Vanier Cup at Varsity Stadium the following weekend, against the University of Calgary Dinosaurs. This was Hargreaves's second appearance in the national final in the eight years since he had taken over from Tindall.

Football fever once again gripped the campus, and there was the usual rush for tickets. Souvenirs were made and sold. Many of the fans developed plans to travel to Toronto for the game, while others decided to watch it on television. The CBC, holder of the rights to the radio broadcast, refused to allow CFRC, the Queen's student-run radio station, to carry the game, a decision that caused quite a controversy in the week leading up to the game. During that week, at the awards banquets, Hargreaves won the CIAU Football Coach of the Year Award, but otherwise the Gaels were ignored in the all-Canadian selections.

All of this should have helped; and for a very short while it did. So, very likely, did the fact that the 18,000 fans in the stadium included "a reported 80 percent of Queen's 11,000 student body."* Down 17–3 at the start of the

---

* *Toronto Star*, 20 November 1983. There had been a huge parade down Bloor Street before the game and Vanier Cup organizers afterwards said that thanks to

fourth quarter, the Gaels roared back behind a stiffened defence and a ball-controlling shift to the option to go up 21–20 with three minutes left to play. However, when faced with possible ignomy, Calgary, which had moved the ball at will much of the day, came back to life with eleven points in those last three minutes to kill Queen's chance of a "Cinderella finish" to the season. Although it was supposedly a "no name" club, which had lost its biggest back (Mohr) early in the season and its middle linebacker (Schad) several games from the end, the club had been "gritty" all year, and by the end it had made a mark as the team that had quite likely done the most, with the least, in the history of Gaels football. O'Doherty, McDowell, Wright, and all the others had every reason to be proud of what they had accomplished.[9]

In 1984 the Gaels were back knocking on the door again. Despite losing some important veterans to graduation, the team was in many ways stronger than the 1983 club. This was partly because of the presence of some outstanding rookies, notably Charlie Galunic, who in combination with Schad (who had been moved to offensive tackle to protect his knee) and Oakley, Stefopulos, Porter, Vince Panetta, and Frank Kakouros, gave Queen's the size on the offensive line, from end to end, in a way that it had not seen since the early 1960s. Returning veterans who had sat out a season or two (Baun, for example) were also to play a big role.

The Gaels opened the season by losing a close but high-scoring game to Bishop's, 39–36,[10] after blowing a 12-point lead. However, the next week they stormed back against McGill, setting a modern-day total yardage record of 752 yards, 633 of it on the ground, and winning 59–30. Harrison ran the option, and Baun by himself accounted for a record-setting 247 yards, despite not playing the fourth quarter.[†] The following week was the

---

Queen's, the Vanier Cup had finally come of age as the national college football spectacle that everyone had always hoped it would be. Clearly, the *Globe and Mail* was in awe of the "purple-faced hordes" which, it reported, stormed the field afterwards and tore down the goalposts, but were very respectful of the police. Taking into account the Toronto game the week before and the fact that the Queen's band went to the Macy's Thanksgiving Day parade in New York the week after the Vanier Cup, it was likely one of the finest few weeks in modern times to have been around Queen's.

[†] After the game, the Queen's students erupted in yet another in a long line of "disgraceful" post-game demonstrations against McGill: goalposts were destroyed, washrooms trashed, and so on. A new and somewhat more questionable aspect of these affairs was obscenity, simulated gang rapes of the McGill mascot and like activities, which showed the arrival of a new "age" of students with different mores and different ways of shocking and affronting

one real disaster of the season (until the final game). Perhaps flat and overconfident, the team lost a one-point game, 10–9, when the offence came up empty against a Carleton team that stacked the line against the option and found that Queen's couldn't pass that well.

The loss seemed to snap the team to attention. It proceeded to destroy Ottawa in two successive games, by large scores, and then to beat Concordia and Carleton (in a return game) in close and hard-fought games. Connie Mandala, a rookie punter and field-goal kicker who would go on to become the Gael's third leading-point scorer of all time (behind two other place kickers, Galloway and Shore), won both of the latter with clutch field goals late in the game.

So it was into the playoffs, the Gaels once again annihilating McGill, 65–29, but only narrowly defeating Bishop's, 37–35, to win the conference title. After blowing a 30–1 lead, Harrison, the conference all-star quarterback, brought the Gaels back 72 yards with just 82 seconds left on the clock for a touchdown pass to Bissessar – and the win. This took the Gaels to the Atlantic Bowl and a game against the Mount Allison Mounties for the chance to return to the Vanier Cup for the second year running.[11]

The Gaels were clear favourites going in and were on form until the fourth quarter, leading by nine points despite a stubborn Mount Allison defence, which pretty much took away the option. They then self-destructed, with six turnovers in the last quarter and two fumbles (by Baun) that yielded two touchdowns 70 seconds apart with just 3 minutes left. It was not the best way to end a season, especially for Baun and the record-setting offence. The defence had, however, played well, and this was some solace to those who were playing their last game as Gaels (including Ian Deakin, Jeff Kyle, Rick Prinzen, and Norm Pfenning, who would be named an all-Canadian for his efforts).[12]

---

their elders. In what was also something of a first, the university – through its new principal, David Smith, and the Alma Mater Society – issued a public apology to McGill. Thus, it is quite likely that the increasingly strict procedures which the university was to put in place, along with the public apology which followed this and future episodes – and which together led to a precipitous drop in attendance at games – date from this 1984 McGill episode. It should also be noted that the McGill game was only the first of a series of activities in 1984 that contributed to the situation. Several large Homecoming street parties "got out of hand," and the university found itself under siege from its immediate neighbours and from the city. Again, it was the obscenity and destructiveness that seemed to be the most upsetting things.

Mohr headed off-tackle against Carleton (Art Martin)

In 1985 the club was not nearly as dominant as it had been in the two previous seasons. Mohr was back from injury, and with Baun, Harrison, and a strong offensive line, it looked to be the best team the Gaels had had in some time. For example, the *Globe and Mail* said of Queen's: "They're The Montreal Canadiens, the New York Yankees, the Boston Celtics of Canadian College football. And they're the team other teams love to beat."[13] The team lived up to these expectations, opening with five straight victories and beating McGill 41–7 in the Homecoming game that year. Ranked second in the country at that point, the Gaels then proceeded to lose 20–17 to a winless Ottawa University club, thanks in part to some questionable refereeing and to Hargreaves's decision, in the last minute of play, to go for the win on third down rather than settling for a sure field goal and the tie.

Bouncing back with a win against Carleton that took its toll (Harrison went down with a kidney injury, Baun with a knee), the Gaels opened the playoffs at home against Concordia. Although heavily favoured, they let the win slip away, giving up a touchdown to tie the game in regulation time, and losing it 15–14 when a missed field goal by Mandala with 37 seconds left was run back out to prevent both the win and a tie to force the game deeper into overtime. It was a shockingly sudden end to a season which at six and two was certainly respectable but which should have led to more.

Mohr did, however, have a wonderful year in this his fifth and last season, winning the Hec Creighton Award as the outstanding player in the country, and setting an all-time Queen's rushing record. Schad, also in his last year, was an all-Canadian, won the Metras Trophy as the best lineman in Canada, and was chosen in the first round of the NFL draft by the Los Angeles Rams (after being scouted throughout the season by visitors to Kingston from the Packers, Falcons, and various other NFL clubs). Schad was the first Canadian college player ever to be so honoured. Others, such as Sheridan Baptiste, Bernie McDonald, and Randy Zarichny, who would make important contributions in succeeding years, were rookies on the 1985 team. All in all, the team should have achieved more than it did. But perhaps the nature of the loss to Concordia was an omen of things to come, for two season would pass before the Gaels were once again back in the conference finals, and not until 1989 did they go even further.

A FLAT SPOT, THEN MORE LIGHT: 1986–1990

Indeed, 1986 and 1987 would both be losing seasons for the team, a rarity during Hargreaves's period as head coach (which saw only five losing seasons out of nineteen). In 1986, without Mohr, Baun, Schad, Harrison, and the others who had contributed to the success of the wing-T/option ground game of the previous several years, the offence switched to a more modern, "search," passing attack, which came to life only briefly in mid-season. This was also a young team. Almost predictably, the Gaels opened with three straight losses before winning three in a row to make the conference playoffs for the tenth year in succession. The last of these games saw a 69–16 pasting of Concordia, a satisfactory revenge for the playoff loss the season before. But it was to little avail, for the team went down to defeat, 31–28, to Bishop's in the first round. Of note in the season were the steady additions to the scoring totals of Mandala (who also profited from the new offensive system to add some touchdown points to those gained from his kicking game) and the presentation of the first Russ Jackson Award for the player in the CIAU who best combined athletic ability, scholarship, and leadership. It went to Galunic, who that season again made the league all-star team (along with Kakouros, Tom Langford, and Steve Stewart).

By 1987, the team had matured somewhat – a great deal, if average age is a measure, since Baun, at twenty-eight and jokingly referred to as "old man," had made yet another return, this time for his last year of eligibility. As noted above, he had begun in 1979 but for various reasons had not played in certain years.

It will be remembered that the fall of 1987 saw the stock market crash, though it recovered when the monetary authorities took prompt action. That same year, at Meech Lake, Mulroney made his first attempt to bring Quebec into the fold with the rest of the provinces, but failed. And still the economy rolled on, largely fuelled by ever-greater accumulations of debt to finance the spending of governments, corporations, and individuals alike. Successive Canadian victories in the Canada Cup and the record-breaking sprinting of Ben Johnson made Canadians proud. There was a surge of self-confidence, a feeling that Canada could compete internationally, which as much as anything else led to the signing of the free trade agreement with the United States.

With Paul Senyshyn now in his second year at quarterback, and with a steadily developing core of receivers led by Jock Climie (son of Bob Climie of 1960s fame) and Sheridan Baptiste, among others, the Gaels ran off three wins in a row after a relatively close opening-game loss to Concordia. Unfortunately, they then lost three games in a row. Even so, they had managed to make the playoffs. But in a hard-fought game against McGill they went down to defeat 27–24, despite having led at the half 24–7 (on the strength of Baun's effort in his certifiably last game as a Gael, coupled with some fine running by Ted Bergeron).

So the team again finished early. Nevertheless, the closeness of the score and the gradual maturing of many of the key players pointed to better results in the immediate future. Of particular note at the end of the 1987 season was a first for the team in the postwar era – the awarding of a Rhodes Scholarship to Galunic, the Gael's captain and a four-time league all-star at guard.[14] The only other Gael to have been a Rhodes Scholar was Skelton in the 1920s.

The 1987 season was to be Hargreaves's last losing season for six years. In 1988 his pre-season "good feeling" about the club was justified, for the team was to win six games with three losses, getting to the conference finals behind a strong defence (coordinated for the first time by ex-Gael Bob Mullen, who would go on to make his mark on defensive football in the conference and beyond over the next five years); there was also some good work on offence, especially by Climie, with some help from Dan Wright, a big second-year end.

Led by two rookie blitzing linebackers, Mike Boone and Dan Pawliw, the Gaels defeated Ottawa in the opening game of the season but lost a close game to Bishop's when they went for the win with 24 seconds left rather than settling for a field goal and a tie; in this same game, Climie set an all-time record for receptions in one game: 13 for 244 yards. The Gaels then knocked off McGill, the defending Vanier Cup champions, this time scoring on a pass to Climie at the end to win it, and they repeated the dramatics a week later with a similar last-minute victory in the return game against Ottawa (going 103 yards, and again to Climie, for the touchdown). After a defensive letdown against Concordia, the team won back-to-back large-margin victories against Carleton behind Climie. In the second of these two games, Climie set a Queen's and CIAU regular-season record for total yards receiving, just narrowly missing the record for most number of catches.

Then it was on to the playoffs, where the Gaels won their first game in overtime on a field goal from their new-found place kicker, Jamie Galloway (who, by the time he left the team in 1992, had become Queen's leading scorer of all time). The Gaels then moved on to their first conference final since 1984, playing against Bishop's in Lennoxville, in a game telecast nationwide on TSN. The late-season weather that can be either an enemy or a friend in Canadian football, depending on the nature of one's team, turned against the Gaels. With the wind howling at fifty kilometers an hour, the Gaels' passing attack stalled completely, coming up empty-handed in a 16–7 loss in which only one touchdown was scored all day by either club.

This playoff loss to Bishop's was, however, just the kind of spur that in the past had so often caused the Gaels to be outstandingly successful the following season – and 1989 would be no exception. Indeed, one could argue that the effects of the 1988 loss would be felt all the way to 1992, because of the continuity provided by a carry-over in many of the players, who were rookies in 1988 and veterans of five years' play by 1992.

The Gaels came to camp with a solid defence – it had been the best in the league in 1988. Led by Boone, Pawliw, Zarichny, Matt Clifford, Dirk Brubacker, Gavin Higgs, and others, it was to be strengthened by Eric Dell and other rookies. Climie, who had won the conference MVP and been an all-Canadian, was back on offence, along with Paul Beresford, Bernie McDonald, Ron Herman, and Tim Pendergast (who, now in his third year, would be the starting quarterback). The rookies who came to camp included some talented players, especially Ed Kidd and Don Rorwick. Hargreaves correctly predicted at the beginning of the 1989 season, "This is going to be a great football team. It's just a question of when."[15] Over the next four years, essentially the same group of players went to the conference final each year in three out of the four years, moved on to the national semifinals (now called the Churchill Bowl), and finally won it all in 1992.

They started off in 1989 by winning nine games in a row (ten if one includes an exhibition game against Varsity). The first two were close enough, 13–9 over Ottawa (indeed, Ottawa proved tough in the return match as well, 28–24) and 28–17 over Bishop's. But there were blowouts too: 51–7 and 38–11 in the Carleton games, and 25–5 and 29–0 over Concordia and McGill, respectively. Both playoff games within the conference were sizable victories, 33–17 over McGill and a 39–18 verdict (at last!) against Ottawa in the conference final (now known as the Dunsmore Cup, having been donated and named for Bob Dunsmore, Queen's oldest living football player at that time).

Needless to say the defence, under coordinator Mullen, played extremely well while the offence, led by Climie, Beresford, Pendergast, and the others, mounted a balanced passing and running game which was difficult for the opposition to defend against. Climie was making his normal yardage through the air (along with Reid McGruer); Beresford, Kidd, Steve Yovetich, and Doug Corbett supplied the ground game behind McDonald, Herman, and the offensive line.

Then it was on to Saskatoon, with a game against the University of Saskatchewan Huskies for the right to visit Toronto's newly completed SkyDome, where the Vanier Cup final was to be held for the first time. In shades of earlier years, many made the long trip west, including the band, who spent forty-three hours in a bus and then, while in Saskatoon, slept in the university's Physical Education Centre. Unfortunately, the Gael magic of that 1989 season did not carry them through. Facing a big, strong defensive club and without the services of Pendergast, who was injured (Kidd, the rookie, was at quarterback), and with Climie being double- and tripled-covered on virtually every play, the Gaels could not produce the ground game they needed. While the defence allowed only two touchdowns, the offence turned the ball over six times, and the Gaels eventually lost 40–10 to the Huskies. It was a game that many of the players would carry with them for years.[16]

The following year, 1990, was not a good year for the country and was only somewhat better for Gael football. A number of events conspired to make things difficult everywhere. Not only was the free trade agreement (FTA) having a marked effect, but new tax measures were on the way, most notably the dreaded GST. Unfortunately, the added tax burden, the structural readjustments triggered by the FTA (which brought layoffs, among other things), and a determined effort by the governor of the Bank of Canada, John Crow, to foreclose any monetization of the debt that would cause inflation like that of the 1970s, turned the economy into a prolonged downturn and recession, which was exacerbated by a falling U.S. economy a year later. It would be several years before the economy recovered, by which time the Tories would be gone, virtually obliterated from the political scene by a combination of events: the impact of the recession; yet another failed attempt to bring Quebec onside (at Charlottetown); an almost universal personal dislike of Mulroney by the voters (which his replacement, Canada's first woman prime minister, Kim Campbell, could not save the party from); and a growing realization that something had to be done about the debt, particularly that of the federal government. All these factors would lead to victory for Jean Chrétien's Liberals in 1993 and to an era of recovery, but one of reduced expectations.

As for the football team, the 1990 season represented a hiatus between the surprisingly successful 1989 season and the successes of 1991 and 1992. Climie was gone and with him a big part of the offence; so too was McDonald. However, there were some promising replacements. One was Brad Elberg, who had been a highly touted rookie the year before but had suffered a severely broken arm early in camp and had not played a game in 1989 – but who was now healthy and ready to go. There was also Mark Robinson from Haliburton, a big rookie tackle who made McDonald's absence a bit less noticeable. The defence was steadily maturing, and although in 1990 it would hold the opposition to the least points against (116) in over ten years, the lack of scoring was ultimately too serious to be completely offset by this extraordinary defensive effort. For example, the team lost 6–1 to Ottawa, 20–11 to Concordia, and, at the end, in the conference final when it counted the most, it lost 20–9 to Bishop's (after a regular-season tie with Bishop's, 20–20). Still, this had been a winning season (5–3–1); the team had reached the conference finals yet again, and the efforts of the defence were recognized in part by Boone being named an all-Canadian after the 1990 season. Also of note was the fact that Elberg scored six touchdowns in his rookie year.

THE LATEST VANIER: 1991–1992

The 1990 season set the scene for the two most recent big years in Queen's football, 1991 and 1992. Evidence of this was quick in coming when the Gaels opened the 1991 season with a convincing exhibition victory over a shocked Western club in London, 36–24, the first such victory over Western since 1970. The win seemed to ignite the team, which then ran off three big-score wins over McGill, Carleton, and Concordia, which seemed to suggest that it was 1989 all over again. As in 1989 the defence was solid, for Dell, Boone, Pawliw, Morrison, and the others had matured into a sound unit. And the offence was better balanced than in 1989, with both a running and passing game that relied on Beresford, Rorwick, and Elberg (when he was healthy), as well as on Kidd (now at flanker), Wright at tight end, and Pendergast, who was steadily maturing as the signal caller.

Ranked number two in the country at this point, the Gaels came up flat against a previously winless Ottawa, turned the ball over twice late in the game, and lost by a close 19–15. Stunned, they proceeded to two convincing victories before losing to Bishop's, again in a close game (29–26), in the last regular-season game, thereby losing home-field advantage in the conference final if it came to a Queen's-Bishop's playoff. At this point, the Gaels' poor luck in close games swung the other way. In their first playoff game against Concordia in Kingston, they won 25–23 when a last-minute Concordia rally fell short. And a week later they came away with a 34–31 victory in the conference final against Bishop's in Lennoxville on the strength of a strong second-half rally.

This put them back into the post-season Churchill Bowl game against Wilfrid Laurier in the SkyDome (a first for the team) for the right to go to the Vanier Cup. It was a game that the players and many Queen's supporters recall with considerable chagrin. Fired by a desire to atone for the 1989 loss to Saskatchewan, the Gaels went out to a 22–3 first-half lead that looked unassailable – only to collapse in the second half, turning the ball over numerous times through bad snaps, fumbled punt returns, and interceptions. As well, the defence suddenly turned porous. The final score was 42–22 for Laurier, and it left a Gael team with considerable egg on its face.

This did not sit well with any of those on the team in the months between the end of the 1991 and the beginning of the 1992 season. Given that there was a reasonably consistent cohort who had played from 1989 on and had seen two big-score Churchill Bowl losses (the first of which might have been excused because of Pendergast's injury and the inexperience of all of them as rookies, but the second of which had no such convenient avenue of psychological escape), it was perhaps reasonable to expect that there were off-season meetings at which commitments were given by everyone that in 1992, the fifth and last season for many of the veterans, things would be different.[17]

One activity that seemed to draw the team together even more in a common purpose was a trip to England made in the spring of 1992 to play an exhibition game against the Brighton B-52 Bombers, a team in the newly developing European North American Football A league.[18] Much in the way of the more traditional rugby tour, the team travelled together, stayed at a university near historic Runnymede, and played the first ever football game of any Canadian college football team outside North America. Before 2,000 of Queen's British and Continental alumni and fans, the Gaels rolled over the hapless English team (which was bolstered by two American ex-professional backs, who could do little to help the Brits). Queen's won 48–8, playing everyone, including many of the Hamburg Squad (the practice squad), who had travelled with the team and who, for the first and only time in their lives, had the opportunity to dress for Queen's. Excursions by some of the players to Oxford and elsewhere, as well as the general sense of camaraderie and the historic nature of the occasion, helped to solidify the team in a way little else could have done.[19]

Once again, the Gaels opened the season with an exhibition game against Western. This time they were beaten, as they were two weeks later by

Bishop's. These two losses were the only ones they had all season. The stumbling start galvanized the veteran club, which then decided to get serious.[20] They ran off five decisive victories in a row, led by Elberg, who went on a tear, scoring fourteen regular-season touchdowns (to go with his eleven to date) behind a veteran line led by Tom Black, Mark Robinson, Dan Wright, Kevin Parker, Stu Dafoe, Ken Kirkwood, Jason Moeller, and Dan McCullough. The offence also had considerable help from Kidd and Yovetich, and there was a corps of dependable receivers for Pendergast. Galloway took care of the place kicking, and the defence played strongly throughout, again featuring the blitz spearheaded by linebackers Boone, Pawliw, Peter Pain, defensive ends such as Jamie Lewin, a fine corps of veteran defensive backs, and Dell, the all-Canadian defensive lineman.

The Gaels were thus off to the playoffs, where the season very nearly ended prematurely in the first game, against McGill. It looked lost with 40 seconds left, when Galloway's punt was blocked and the ball was run in for a touchdown. But a flag on the play brought the ball back to Queen's 46-yard line, with McGill in possession and with 16 seconds and no McGill time-outs left. Lewin sacked the McGill quarterback on the first play, and the Gaels intercepted the last play "Hail Mary" to save the victory. On such narrow threads hang many larger things …

Bishop's was beaten handily, 31–6, in the conference final. Then it was back to the Churchill Bowl, which was a closer-run affair. Experienced now with the Churchill Bowl (for this was their third appearance in four years) and also with the SkyDome, the Gaels beat a stubborn Guelph Gryphons club 23–16. Once again the team went out to a big lead at half-time, 17–2, only to have to scramble at the end. This time, Aron Campbell, another defensive back (the week before it had been Braden Dent) made a last-minute interception to secure the victory and put to rest the "Ghost of Churchill Bowls past" (as one writer put it), especially that against Wilfrid Laurier the previous year.

This brought the Gaels to the Vanier Cup the following week, where they found themselves decided underdogs in the pre-game run-up to the unde-feated Saint Mary's Huskies. However, come Saturday, before one of the largest crowds ever in the history of the Vanier Cup (about 29,000 people) and on nationwide television, the Gaels put on "as good a show as it gets," blasting the Huskies 31–0. Playing team defence, stunting and blitzing to take away the run, and getting timely interceptions and sacks to stifle the passing attack, the Gaels set a Vanier Cup points-against record which can only be equalled, never beaten. Led by Pendergast (whom the *Globe and Mail* described as "a model of efficiency and economy"), the offence ran roughshod over a Saint Mary's defence that had allowed an average of only nine points per game all season. Behind strong offensive line play, Elberg tied a Vanier Cup record with three touchdowns (which brought his season's total to twenty-two, an almost unbelievable number by any Queen's standard) and he was named the game's most valuable player. Galloway converted all the touchdowns (giving him a perfect 44/44 on the season) and added a field goal. Brian Alford scored the Gael's fourth touchdown.

"For people who [had] Queen's in their blood, this was heaven."[21] Indeed, for many who had followed Queen's football for generations, it was a wonderful moment, "beyond one's wildest dreams." Despite the relatively poor attendance at home, the Vanier Cup game seemed to have caught the fancy of the student body. The SkyDome was jammed with Queen's students and alumni waving the new tricolour flag, dancing, singing, and watching themselves on the large Jumbotron screen. As the game progressed and the score mounted, and the possibility of a collapse receded, their enthusiasm could not be contained. In time-honoured fashion, the fans flowed out of the stands at the end of the game, onto the floor of the Dome, celebrating and sharing in the unbelievable nature of the win.

It is not too much of an exaggeration to say that the country itself was impressed with what it saw of Queen's that day. In a column entitled, "A Canadian Experience," George Gross of the Toronto *Sun* commented, "I feel sorry for all those who missed yesterday's Vanier Cup between the Queen's University Golden Gaels and Saint Mary's Huskies of Halifax. There was a lot more to the game than it being a wipeout, the first shutout in the history of the event … The Vanier Cup is Canadiana at its best. It proves to us that we do not have to worry about our young people no matter what panicky folks are trying tell you."[22]

In the same paper, Jay Greenberg, another columnist, made the following remarks about Queen's in a piece he titled "Best and Brightest":

The brains went on to beat the jocks 31–0. So sleep well tonight, Canada, your future is in good hands. The next generation of engineers and doctors outran, and blocked, and, of course, outsmarted their employees of tomorrow to win the CIAU championship before 28,645 scholars and other strangers at the Sky Dome …

At the final gun, the Queen's kids gathered on the field for group discussion of existential philosophy, then spilled joyously out on to John and Peter Streets, obviously looking for the nearest library …

The truth that Canada's best college football team is also undoubtedly its brightest says a great deal for Queen's. But the fact that this is possible says volumes about a Canadian education system that keeps academics and athletics in proper perspective.[23]

In time-honoured fashion, the university and the city were proud of the team and showed it. A large post-game celebration was hosted by the

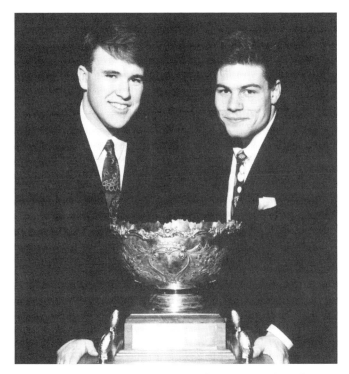

The 1992 Vanier Cup: co-captains Mike Boone and Brad Elberg (Art Martin)

That 1992 championship season! (Art Martin)

university at the team's hotel in Toronto, and Mayor Cooper of Kingston held a reception for the team the following week (at which she shared some of the seafood she had won in a bet with the mayor of Halifax over the result of the game). For the many on the team who were graduating, it was a storybook ending to their years as a Gaels, one that would live with them for a very long time after the championship season of 1992 had passed into the record books.

THE END OF YET ANOTHER ERA: 1993–1994

Since almost half the 1992 team graduated, it is perhaps not surprising that the next two seasons were anticlimatic. What is noteworthy was the degree of the falloff. Both years saw losing seasons, the first since 1987. The 1994 season was particularly bad, the club falling to one and six, the worst record since the no-win season of 1952 almost forty years earlier.

It is difficult to explain so dramatic a turnaround. Key players on both offence and defence, including Pendergast, Elberg, Boone, and Pawliw were gone, but as in other dry periods, there were still some fine ballplayers at certain positions (one thinks of Jonathan Taylor, for example). But there is no question that the old guard had not been replaced, despite Hargreaves's best efforts. It is possible that the increasingly difficult recruiting situation, with academic standards being what they were, was beginning to tell.[24] Then again, it may simply have been one of those times in the history of the game at Queen's when the team just did not win. On such occasions, if the school persists through the bad times, the circle turns, and the good times return. It is to be hoped that this will happen again.

As noted above, the irony of having two losing seasons at the end of the Hargreaves era did not pass unnoticed by Hargreaves or others. Tindall, it will be recalled, had a similar experience in the early 1970s just before he stepped down.* There was also the fact that it was so unlike Hargreaves to have a losing season, let alone two in a row. In his nineteen years at Queen's, he had had only five; he had taken the Gaels to the playoffs in sixteen of his nineteen years and had won nine conference championships, three national semifinal Bowl titles, and two Vanier Cups. In his career as a whole, he had coached the most games and been the third most winning of any

---

* It is to be noted with sadness that Tindall passed away in 1993. There was a
  large outpouring of grief from many quarters, and his memorial service at
  St Mary's Cathedral in Kingston was filled to overflowing with alumni, university officials, former players, and many others who recalled his long years of
  service to the game.

CIAU coach ever, being awarded (appropriately) the Tindall Trophy for the best coach in the CIAU in 1983. "At the national level, he was instrumental in starting the national coaching certification program and he was a pioneer in exporting the game overseas."[25]

But by the end of the 1994 season, Hargreaves was gone. At the conclusion of his speech at a retirement roast given him early in 1995, he quoted Tindall, his mentor and friend, who in ruminating on Joan of Arc's manner of leaving had decided that perhaps "a blaze of glory" was not always the thing.* There is little doubt that Hargreaves had given enormously to the game, not only at Queen's but nationally. A sense of "the honour," character, and reputation of the program was always foremost in his mind.

CONCLUSION

This brings the narrative up to the present era, completing more than a century of play with a discussion of the predominately successful Hargreaves years of the 1980s and early 1990s. As noted occasionally in passing, the attendance at games fluctuated quite dramatically but saw a fairly steady drop in average attendance, especially after the university tightened stadium security and regulations in the late 1980s and again with the 1993 season. In view of what was pointed out in the previous chapter about changes in the nature of financing the game and its accounting, one faces a similar difficulty in attempting to say exactly what the financial situation surrounding the game at Queen's actually was over this period. It cannot be assessed with anything like the certainty of the Athletic Board of Control years.

The *Whig-Standard*, reporting after the 1989 Churchill Bowl game against Saskatchewan in Saskatoon, quoted Queen's chair of athletics Rolf Lund as saying, "You never make any money on these things." However, the newspaper concluded that "apparently you don't go to the poorhouse either."[26] The article pointed out that although the Canadian Intercollegiate Athletic Union (CIAU) subsidized travel to all national playoffs up to a certain limit (in essence never 100 per cent of expenses), it took all the revenue from those games as well, including television and gate receipts, redistributing it

---

* Hargreaves was known for his own particular wit, which came in the form of cryptic sayings: "The players can't understand why we're losing. They have to remember we're just not that good"; "If you can't stay awake, stand up"; "I'm so forgetful now I can hide my own Easter eggs"; and my favourite, a most perfect characterization of the ideal strategic plan, "Be flexible, and have a sense of humour" (Kingston *Whig-Standard*, 10 April 1995).

Table 11
Some details of revenues and expenses for the 1992 regular season: Football

REVENUES	
Tickets	$28,804
Booster club	3,824
Tricolour booster	2,160
Total revenues	$34,788
EXPENSES	
Travel	13,303
Equipment	20,403
Officials	5,073
Film	8,908
Training meals	23,724
Total expenses	71,623
Surplus (deficit)	($36,623)

Source: School of Physical and Health Education/University Council on Athletics, Queen's University, graciously furnished by Prof. J. Albinson and Mr B. Sparrow

to all schools in the union according to an agreed-upon formula. Since football is by far the largest revenue earner for the CIAU, it, along with the individual universities (who support athletics over and above this source of revenue and whatever other revenue they can develop, such as local gate receipts, booster clubs, and so on) effectively help to carry the many other sports which the CIAU sanctions.

An approximate picture of the financial situation around Queen's football can be obtained by looking at the figures for the 1992 Vanier Cup season. Figures are available only for the regular season. As can be seen from table 11, revenues during the regular season were about $35,000 ($37,100 in 1995 dollars), while expenses of various sorts were $72,000 ($76,300), leaving a deficit of about $37,000 ($39,200). Because Queen's played four more games up to and including the Vanier Cup (and based on the way the CIAU subsidy scheme works) the size of the deficit will almost certainly have been larger.

Considerably more space is devoted to this question of finances in the next chapter, but even a cursory glance at the earlier data (see, for instance, tables 4, 6, and 8) suggests a number of things. First, revenues appear to have dropped quite dramatically, though it is difficult to tell exactly, since the 1992 figures do not include any post-season gates or the CIAU subsidy, whereas the earlier figures include all sources of revenue. Clearly, Queen's benefited a great deal more from the earlier arrangement of splitting gate revenues directly with the opposing team at all games, rather than by the present system, with its more diffused indirect subsidy from the CIAU.

Secondly, expenses too are dramatically lower, primarily because almost all coaching and other overhead costs are paid out of the Department of Physical Education's general departmental budget. One more or less constant expense category might be thought to be "equipment," although even here one must be careful about what is meant by the term in different periods. Again, in comparable dollars, expenditures would appear to be down on average compared with the figures of the 1950s and 1960s.[27] For the time being, it is perhaps best to leave it at this. That is, although one cannot make a definite comparison because of the different accounting systems, it does seem that the program has in recent years been running a deficit, albeit on dramatically lower revenues and expenses than in earlier decades.

Turning now to the question of which of the players may be said to have left their mark on the period and what has become of them, one is again struck by the embarrassment of riches. The record clearly points to those associated with the early 1980s clubs and, most recently, to the 1989–92 teams. Here one is venturing even farther out on a limb than the considerable distance taken in the last chapter when suggesting which of the 1970s players made the greatest impact. But despite the hazards, some effort must be made to assess which of the many in the latest era were most memorable; it would be grossly unfair not to treat these Gaels in the same way as those in every other era. Again, five or six merit that consideration, while at least eight to ten others deserve a strong honourable mention. The first group includes Mohr, Schad, Galunic, Jock Climie, Elberg, and Galloway; the second would add Bob Wright, Bronk, Baun, Mandala, McDonald, Pendergast, Boone, Dell, and probably several others.

Mohr was from a farming family near Baden, Ontario (outside Kitchener). He came to Queen's to do honours economics and stayed on for his MBA. A hard-charging fullback in the early to mid-1980s, he won numerous all-star nominations, the Tom Pate Award from the CFL for "the university player best combining academic and athletic excellence with community leadership and the potential to play professional football" (1983), and the Hec Creighton Trophy as the most outstanding player in the CIAU (1985). Had he not been plagued by injury in the middle of his time at Queen's, he would undoubtedly sit higher on the all-time touchdown list. After graduation, he played several seasons with the Ottawa Rough Riders before leaving the game for the public service. At present he is in the banking business in Ottawa.

Schad is the player in Queen's history who may well have reached the highest level of the game after his time at Queen's, albeit with less success than he had hoped, principally because of injury. It was clear from his earliest days at high school in Belleville that he would be a premier athlete,

Mike Schad, 1982–85: Philadelphia Eagles (Art
Martin)

and Hargreaves worked hard to get him. Schad chose Queen's because of
its interest in him, because he knew he would start in his rookie year, and
because of the influence of the assistant principal at his high school, who
was a Queen's graduate and stressed the academic emphasis, character, and
tradition of the football program.[28]

He played well at Queen's, starting on defence but eventually switching
to offence to protect his knee (which had been injured in the early going)
and because it was clear that this was where he would play in the pros. In
his last year with the Gaels he won the Metras Trophy as Canada's outstanding college lineman, brought all manner of NFL pro scouts to Queen's
for the first time ever, and was drafted in the first round by the Los Angeles
Rams, the first Canadian university player ever to be so chosen. He went
on to several troubled seasons with the Rams before being traded to Philadelphia, where he played several seasons under Buddy Ryan. He was then
traded to the Cleveland Browns, and in recent times has returned to Canada

Charlie Galunic, Rhodes Scholar (Art Martin)

to play for the Ottawa Rough Riders. Like many other professional athletes, he also has business interests; he owns and manages a chain of stores in the country and western apparel business.

Drago "Charlie" Galunic was of solid, working-class, immigrant stock and, like Schad, came to Queen's a highly regarded high school athlete. He was also an outstanding student and very involved with outside activities. He carried on in this way all through the years he was at Queen's, taking an extremely difficult chemical engineering degree with high honours, making all-star every year he played (and second team CIAU all-Canadian in 1987), and winning the CIAU's Russ Jackson Award in 1986 (the first year it was offered) "for excellence in academics, athletics and community service" – Galunic was extremely active in volunteer work on campus and in the Kingston community while he was a student). And, of course, there was his Rhodes Scholarship in 1987. After completing his studies at Oxford, he moved on to Stanford University for his PHD, and went on to be a professor at one of the leading business schools in Europe.

Jock Climie, 1986–89 (Art Martin)

Jock Climie was probably the greatest receiver ever to play for the Gaels.[29] As noted above, it sometimes seemed that he was all the offence Queen's had. In 1988 he set a new CIAU record for single season reception yardage, was conference MVP, and an all-Canadian. He won the Russ Jackson Award in 1989, when he again made all-Canadian. Climie was from Ottawa and came to Queen's because of his parents' influence, his father being Bob Climie, a 1960s Gael. An intelligent and sensitive black man, Climie was particularly attuned to the race issue that was developing on campus during his time at Queen's. Like his teammate Sheridan Baptiste and the very few other black athletes at Queen's over the years, he found himself in what was essentially a completely white environment. Having been raised in just such an environment, he did not find his Queen's experience all that different, at least in a racial sense. But like other visible-minority students, he felt that Queen's had to make itself more representative of a changing Canadian population, and he tried in his own way to further that end.[30] Naturally enough, Climie was drafted by the CFL, and he went on to play with the Ottawa Rough Riders and the Toronto Argonauts. He also completed his law degree, working at it part-time in the off-season, and then articled with the Ottawa law firm of ex-Gael Don Bayne, preparatory to taking up a career in the law.

Elberg was from Regina and came to Queen's as an indirect result of a recruiting trip Hargreaves made to look at another player. Stocky, of medium build, and possessing blazing speed and seemingly boundless enthusiasm, Elberg began by breaking his arm severely in his rookie camp and never seeing the field his first year at Queen's (1989), a particular regret of Elberg's in view of the playoff that year in Saskatchewan. He was back for his rookie season in 1990, and he performed well if not spectacularly both that year and in the 1991 season (when he missed five games with a leg injury). In the 1992 Vanier Cup year, healthy all season, he exploded for twenty-two touchdowns, including three in the final game, in which he was the game MVP, and he won all-Canadian honours. He was taken second overall in the CFL draft by Saskatchewan. The following year, 1993, after a short visit to the NFL and being a late cut from the Saskatchewan Rough-riders, he returned to Queen's but was again injured and played very little. Overall, however, his total of thirty-five touchdowns in four seasons makes him the all-time Gael touchdown leader. He has moved on to play with the Hamilton Tiger-Cats while intending to pursue a career in business.

Finally there is Galloway, Queen's all-time leading scorer with a total of 369 points accrued over the five seasons 1988–92. The story of Galloway's coming to the Gaels was, as Claude Scilley, the fine sportswriter of the *Whig-Standard* put it, "like finding a long-lost lottery ticket in a shirt you almost threw out."[31]

Galloway had never played football before (indeed, the first time he wore gear was as a Gael). He had been a rugby player at high school in Barrie, where he was known to Dr "Jocko" Thompson (of 1950s kicking fame) who worked with him a bit. Jocko told Hargreaves that Galloway was coming to Queen's, and the coach extended an invitation to camp. Galloway showed up, was impressive, but was given permission to play for the Ontario side in a provincial-level rugby tournament midway through camp and never returned to football practice again. Hargreaves assumed that Galloway was no longer interested – was probably playing rugby for the university. But several games into the season, with no kicking game to speak of, he remembered Galloway and went to a rugby team practice, only to find that no one there remembered the player.

Galloway was eventually located by using the university's general student directory. He said he wanted to concentrate on his studies, but Hargreaves, grabbing at straws, allowed him to set his own schedule for practising as long as he delivered in games. Galloway showed up, hit his first seven in a row – and "the rest," as the cliché goes, "is history." He was to account for 369 points in his five seasons with the Gaels, remaining

Jamie Galloway, 1988–92, all-time leading scorer (Art Martin)

always and only a kicker, with his own practice schedule. He graduated in engineering and education and then returned to Barrie to teach high school.

And what of some of the others? Wright is in the public service, Baun in the franchise business (with Tim Hortons donuts); Harrison works in the insurance industry, Mandala with computers. McDonald has both his PH D and is a medical doctor (Rutka from the 1970s is another Gael with this particular combination of credentials); Boone is working on his chartered accounting accreditation with a large accounting firm. Dell, after taking a degree in mining engineering and spending two years in northern British Columbia, returned to the university for his MBA.

These Gaels from the eighties and nineties and their colleagues would appear to be no different than any of their predecessors in their post-playing experiences, but in point of fact they have had to struggle through one of the most difficult labour market situations for young people since the 1930s. Yet virtually all of them seem to have found positions and are pressing on with their lives in a socially rewarding manner. In this respect, they are an honour- able addition to the family and will no doubt be recognized as such when, in the fullness of time, they become eligible for Hall of Fame membership.

They are also similar to their predecessors in at least one other way – in the general respect they seem to hold for their football experience at Queen's. The words used to describe experiences separated by decades are virtually identical. For instance: "I learned a sense of self-respect, of caring, of working with a group of guys" … "I learned how to bounce back, that losing was just as much a part of trying as winning" … "It beat anything I ever ran across at the pro level."

As stressed earlier, it is easy to discount much of the modern rhetoric of sport, with its talk of "giving 110 per cent every time he's out there" and the parallels that ex-presidents of the United States like to draw between football and life, war, or just about anything. What is more difficult to dismiss is a whole history of impressions from intelligent men – doctors, lawyers, university professors, some old, some young – all of whom have come to the same conclusion about the value of their football years at Queen's.

Conclusion

The preceding chapters document the historical record and texture of the game at Queen's, describing how, with the exception of the war years 1915–18 and 1940–44, football has been played continually at the university since 1882 – more than one hundred seasons. During that time the school has grown from its small beginnings to stand in the top ranks of Canadian universities. There have been wars, depression, rapid industrialization, immigration, humans on the moon, and the threat of thermonuclear extinction. But through it all, except for those two short periods, Queen's has played football.

There have been good times and bad: wonderful years when the games seized the attention not just of the student body but also of the city and indeed the country; bad times when things went seriously wrong or, worse still, when the game was almost ignored. Always one remembers the good times: that first Dominion championship of 1893 with Curtis and his boys, with the wire dispatches posted on the windows of the *Whig-Standard* for all passers-by to see, the victory parade to City Hall, and the sermons preached on lessons learned from the victory; or the early twenties, with three consecutive Grey Cup wins, as well as several near misses, when Queen's was known to everyone across the country. And who can forget the courageous and principled victory of the Fearless Fourteen in 1934–35, which was immortalized in newspapers across the land by, among others, their own coach Ted Reeve, columnist for the *Telegram*; or that wonderful year of 1955 when Braccia, Stewart, Schreider, Bruce, Kocman, Jocko, Lewis, and the rest of that band of merry men brought Queen's back into the limelight after nearly twenty years of depression, war, and athletic obscurity?

Then came the truly golden years of the 1960s, with undefeated seasons, championships aplenty, and Queen's first Vanier Cup in 1968. And there were the more recent victories in 1978 and 1992, as well as many close "knockings at the national championship door." But, of course, there were the bad times too: the debacles of the postwar years of 1919–20 and 1945–50; other seasons when the team never won a game (1911, 1938, and 1951, for example); that infamous year of 1971 when they moved the stadium; and the losing seasons at the end of both the Tindall and Hargreaves eras.

On balance, though, fortune has been kind to Queen's* in at least two ways: the bad times were always followed by good; and overall there were more good than bad. This can be clearly seen from the statistics for the 102 years (93 seasons in all) from 1893 to 1994 for which good data are available: of the 612 regular-season and playoff games during that time, Queen's won 335 (55 per cent), lost 262 (43 per cent), and tied 15 (2 per cent). In 59 (63 per cent) of those 93 seasons, it won more games than it lost (47 such seasons) or had a break-even record (12 seasons), and in 30 (33 per cent) of them it won a championship of one sort or another. During that time, it outscored the opposition team 10,366 to 8,590. Thus, Queen's won considerably more than it lost; it had a winning season every other year or so; and it outscored its opponents by about 17 to 14 in the average game. Finally, its thirty championship seasons compare favourably with the record of the other two schools that played throughout the same 102-year period: Varsity, with twenty-nine, and McGill, with only twelve; and these figures still put Queen's in first place in absolute terms over Western, which has had twenty-four championship seasons since joining the league in 1929.

As frequently noted, football has in many ways defined Queen's to itself and to the country at large. Countless examples from the record are possible,

---

* Others suggest that fortune may have been given a helping hand. Mike Lewis, a manager for the team in the 1960s, in personal correspondence with the author, told the following story: "I had returned to Kingston in the late eighties to watch my first game since 1965. Queen's was playing Ottawa U, the game was tied with less than a minute to play and Ottawa had the ball on Queen's twenty-five yard line. Instead of going for the one point that needed to win, they elected to kick a field goal. The kicker slipped, hooked the ball, and the Queen's return man ran it out to the ten-no point with Queen's then going on to win in overtime. Dr. Kerr, with whom I was standing on the sidelines, went back to the stands before the overtime started and asked Tindall, who was long-since retired, and sitting with Herb Hamilton, 'Why in hell would they do such a dumb thing, Frank?' Without hesitation Tindall replied, 'Because God goes to Queen's!' One draws from this the added information that Tindall was not unaware of whose influence was at work, for example, in ensuring that he won all those coin tosses over playoff venues during his many years of coaching."

but a few will suffice. The school song, known to all who have attended Queen's, developed out of football at the end of the century. Principals from the earliest to most recent times have associated themselves with the game to further their other agendas. Principal Grant, for example, with his strong nationalist and anglophile tendencies, saw football as the perfect representation of the qualities required of men, and he appeared with the team in photos, held receptions for championship sides, and otherwise supported and advanced the game. Principal Mackintosh was always aware of the contribution of the game to his efforts to raise funds from the alumni. And Principal Leggett recently observed, with tongue somewhat in cheek, "that one of the first things he realized when he arrived in Kingston was that the Principal reported directly to the head football coach, and it was his duty to build a university that the football team could be proud of."[1] Countless receptions have been held at City Hall in Kingston by mayors happy to be associated with championship teams, and on the occasion of the 1992 Vanier Cup triumph, the local member of Parliament, a loyal Queen's graduate and a strong football supporter, the Honourable Peter Milliken, placed recognition of the victory, and the pride of all Queen's and Kingston, into Hansard, the official record of the House of Commons.

Then, too, there have been literally hundreds of thousands who have attended the Gaels' games at Queen's and elsewhere, whether as students, staff, parents, alumni, townspeople, or just interested spectators. Millions more have listened to those same games on radio or watched them on television. For all these people, a major defining aspect of Queen's has been its football team, accompanied by the band, with its Scottish traditions, and the fanatical student and alumni supporters led by the cheerleaders.

In the introduction, I speculated about why this should be so. And I suggested that the need to prove something on the part of a tightly knit group in an out-of-the-way place meant that there was fertile ground for some institution to represent or give voice to the collective's sense of itself, and to do so with a special fervour that would make everyone take notice. I argued that football was far better suited to this role than the older game of soccer or the newer ones of hockey and baseball. For not only is it a spectator sport, but it is played out of doors in the fall when school is in session. And it requires "manliness," "collective endeavour," and "a host of other late-Victorian synonyms for an assertive, virile, male, activity which everyone accepts as the ideal."

In view of the historical record, it is worth looking at some of these themes in more detail, particularly the role that sport has played at the university and the nature of the institutional cohesiveness, especially among the players themselves.

THE PLAYERS THEMSELVES

Consider, for example, the nature of the student body as one of the forces that carried the game forward through time and established its importance. It will be recalled that the school was very small throughout much of its first one hundred years. Indeed, it almost disappeared on several occasions when enrolment virtually died away, and it had only about 2,500 students until the 1960s explosion in growth. The small size of the university meant that everyone could and for the most part did know everyone else. It also meant that those who went to Queen's had consciously chosen it, bypassing the larger schools in Montreal and Toronto. This may have been because of religious affiliation in the early days. Or it may have been because of social class, for the political and commercial elites of Montreal and Toronto more commonly went to McGill and Varsity, respectively. Or it may simply have been a matter of cost: Queen's was cheaper both for tuition and for living costs. For whatever reason, there was a sense of "differentness," of "small-ness and family," and thus of cohesiveness.

It is arguable whether this cohesiveness was accompanied by a need to prove oneself in relation to larger schools. Certainly, throughout much of Queen's first century, the university fathers were continually struggling to establish the "distinctiveness and worth" of Queen's to the government and others in order to justify its continued separate existence. These efforts were no doubt partly self-serving. But they must surely also have been a result of the sociology of the institution. Unlike the largely English and Anglican elites of Toronto and Montreal, many of the students at Queen's were Scottish Presbyterians, and a good many came from immigrant and working-class backgrounds. Had the elites been at Queen's, there would likely have been far less need to prove the worth of the place or establish its distinctiveness. Elites do not usually need to establish their self-worth or self-esteem.

An excellent example in support of this contention can be found in the football players themselves, their comments about what the game meant to them, and their subsequent activities in life. Since the players could arguably be said to have carried the hopes of Queen's on their collective shoulders, they would likely be one of the first groups that a social scientist would study when looking for the strongest manifestation of the underlying moti-vation that gave the university its overall character.

In this respect, the record shows three things: the players were almost exclusively from working-class or middle-class backgrounds, and many were immigrant or first-generation Canadians; those interviewed for the book almost unanimously said that one of the major personal benefits of having played for the university was a heightened sense of self-esteem; and,

Table 12
A comparison of the occupations of living male Queen's graduates: Football players vs alumni as a whole[1]

Occupation	Football players		Living male alumni	
	No.	%	No.	%
Accounting	12	2.2	11	2.0
Corporate/industrialist	105	20.2^2	222	41.0^2
Engineer/scientist	29	5.5^2	71	13.1^2
"Entrepreneur"	47	9.0	40	7.4
Government	12	2.2	13	2.5
Journalist	3	0.6	6	1.1
Lawyer/judge	73	14.0^2	35	6.4^2
Medical doctor/dentist	74	14.2^2	38	7.0^2
Minister of the cloth	4	0.6	5	0.9
Police/corrections/social	4	0.6	5	0.9
Professor	18	3.4^2	30	5.5^2
Retired	31	5.9^2	2	0.4^2
Sports administration	15	2.8^2	2	0.4^2
Teacher/principal	100	19.2^2	62	11.4^2
Total	517	100.0	542	100.0^2

Source: Data files of Queen's University Alumni Association

[1] In the case of football players, the sample represents virtually all living ex-players, *minus* those for whom there is no occupation data available (or those who do not fit in the occupation groups listed – a total of 121 in addition to the 517 reported). In the case of the living male alumni, the data represents a random sample of 1,000 from all living male alumni of the university, *including* the football players, *minus* those for whom there is no occupation data available (or those who do not fit in the occupation groups listed – a total of 444 in addition to the 542 reported). The samples reported are thus of roughly equal size (517 vs 542)

[2] Indicates significant difference at 0.05 level

time and again, there is evidence of success in the more "socially oriented" professions after graduation. The players' subsequent success in certain professions was apparent in all periods. Indeed, so many seem to have become doctors or lawyers that one might well wonder whether this was something peculiar to the football team or whether it was simply typical of Queen's graduates as a whole.

In order to examine the question further, information on the occupation of all living Queen's alumni, including football players, was gathered from the data files of the Alumni Association.[2] All living ex-football players were identified from the records of the Football Club (see appendix D). There were 517 for whom occupational designations were available, as well as a further 121 for whom no such data were available (the latter, for the most part, being the more recent graduates). The 517 were then classified into the occupational groups reported in table 12. A random sample of 1,000 living male alumni (including football players) was then drawn from the university data bank. It yielded a final sample of 542 when those for whom no occupational data were available were removed.[3] Thus, the samples were of roughly equal size.

A statistical test of the significance of the differences observed in individual occupation groups[4] is revealing: the ex-football player is significantly more likely to be a lawyer/judge, doctor/dentist, teacher/principal, or sports administrator (perhaps obviously) than the "typical" living male alumnus, and is significantly less likely to be an engineer or scientist, a professor, or a corporate executive or industrialist.[5] These results agree with the anecdotal evidence about the earlier periods from which no living ex-players are to be found. And they suggest that these working-class, immigrant, socially-thrusting young players were successful in their drive to be upwardly mobile and that, in effect, they ended up in arguably more socially oriented (one might even say "socially higher-ranked") occupations than the male alumni of the university as a whole.[6]

In this sense at least, they could be said to have been a truer if more "acute" representation of the aspirations of the university than the average graduate was. It is interesting to add that they themselves have become an important part of the new elite. For example, the twenty-fifth anniversary reunion of the 1968 College Bowl championship team contained its appropriate number of doctors, lawyers, principals, and so on. Moreover, players such as these have helped change the character of the university, which is now popularly alleged (and probably with justification) to have become a school for the elite.[7] In this respect, football through the years has more than fulfilled one of its major roles, not only at but for the university.*

It is possible, though, to make too much of this argument. One alternative reading of the historical record would suggest that the game was not so much a reflection of its time, but that it had a momentum all its own. That is, instead of playing a kind of Jungian archetypical role for the university as a whole, the players and the game were somehow separated from larger concerns. Although the players were, of course, affected by the two world wars, other major developments – whether economic depressions, cultural revolutions, oil shocks, or inflation – seemed to come and go, with football

---

* The same argument could be made, for example, about the importance of football to the evolution of the University of Western Ontario, whereas McMaster, which should perhaps have followed a similar course, was probably too identified with its Baptist/Methodist roots. Because of its injunction against public demonstrations, which sport surely is, McMaster was likely "held back" (or, perhaps, was "changed in the course of") its development as a university as compared to Queen's.

The new elite? The twenty-fifth reunion of the 1968 College Bowl champions
(Art Martin)

showing up each fall to be played as surely "as God made little green
apples." If this is true, then the game may have been addressing other needs
as well as the aspiration-driven ones suggested above; and it may have been
driven by other forces. To understand what these may have been, it is
necessary to reflect on the role of sport more generally and to consider how
it, and especially football, developed at Queen's over the years.

THE PHILOSOPHY OF SPORT AT QUEEN'S:
FOOTBALL'S PLACE

In the earliest times – the pre-football years before 1882 – sport at the
university consisted mainly of an annual "athletics day" (track and field)
and impromptu games of association football (soccer). As noted in earlier
chapters, once football started, it very quickly supplanted soccer as the main
competitive sport in which the students represented the university as a team
in competition.[8] Hockey, recently begun, soon became another. Track and
field, somewhat later gymnastics, and still later swimming (with the building
of the first indoor pool) were more "recreational" or "intramural" activities
for the students and were not the basis for intercollegiate competition. This

pattern of Queen's sport was apparently satisfactory, for it held from the mid-1880s all the way to the mid-1960s, a period of nearly seventy-five years. Certainly basketball, hockey, tennis, and other games existed. But for the most part, students exercised somewhat during the week (gymnastics, swimming, and so on) and went to the football game on the weekends in the fall. And that, by and large, was sport and recreation at Queen's.

However, it has to be observed that there were times when it looked as if this pattern might break down – times when football was in serious trouble. One thinks of the period following the First World War when, if it had not been for the strong action of Lindsay Malcolm in reorganizing the team and building a stadium, the game might arguably have disappeared;[9] or of Reeve, "the doctors," and Colonel McGinnis, who kept the game going during the Great Depression, finding summer jobs for players and raising money for travel and uniforms for both the team and the band. Certainly, Tindall and McCarney, along with Edwards and a different set of "doctors" – especially Melvin, Dunlop, and Kerr – were responsible for a fifties and sixties resurgence after the difficult years that followed the Second World War. And in recent times Hargreaves, with support from ex-players through the Football Club and with direct coaching help from Miklas and others, manfully kept the tradition and the quality of football alive at the university when once again it might have died away.

Except in Hargreaves's case, these periodic rejuvenations of football took place within the context of an acceptance of the traditional pattern of sport at the university. In other words, the difficulties with football were for the most part due to outside circumstances; they did not represent a loss of faith in the belief that football was unquestionably the primary avenue for intercollegiate competition – and that other sports were either distinctly minor by comparison or were for recreation purposes only. But as we have seen, this basic philosophy began to change during the late 1960s. Together with various factors not directly related to the definition and role of sport and competition, the change in philosophy fundamentally altered the traditional "profile" of sport at Queen's and football's pre-eminent place in it. I am referring, of course, to the move to "broaden" the number of sports in which the university competed, thus shifting the emphasis from "competition" to "participation and recreation"[10] – an attitude reflected in the Milliken Report of the late 1960s.

It was significant that Donald MacIntosh, the new head of the Department of Physical Education, was an outsider to Queen's and an early supporter of this change in philosophy. Moreover, he was able to implement it because of the explosion in enrolments and a commensurate jump in athletic fee revenues, which meant that the department no longer relied exclusively on football revenues. As a result of all this, the emphasis in sport at Queen's was gradually changed in the early 1970s. And one should not forget that football itself was facing several problems: the change in the stadium's location, which symbolically removed football from the heart of the campus and directly reduced revenues flowing from the program; the dilution of the acute competitive focus which the game represented to the school, since so many new schools wanted to compete in football, though at first they were not considered "worthy" to compete with the "old four"; and the relatively poor record in Tindall's last years (1972–75) when a good year or two might have brought strong fan support. In view of all these developments, it is easy to understand how this transformation in the role of football as part of sport at the university, and its importance to the institution, took root.

There were other factors as well, perhaps the most important being the arrival of women in sport in large and organized numbers. Bearing a justifiable claim, they helped increase the number of sports that wished to compete intercollegiately (for example, women's and men's basketball, men and women's hockey, women's and men's cross-country, and so on). Many of these new teams were in sports that required budgets but provided little if any revenues. This was not immediately a problem for the more traditional sports as long as the number of students (and hence the government funding) continued to grow. But in the early 1970s, when Queen's decided to cap its enrolment and government funding began to decrease, difficulties arose with the allocation of the budget for sports. During the eighties, the number of teams wishing to compete and thus needing funds continued to grow, exacerbating the problem.

Now, twenty-five years or so after this revolution began, Queen's competes in over forty interuniversity sports (more than any other university in the province), and it provides a very large intramural program which includes virtually all of these sports, for students who wish to participate but cannot (or choose not to) compete intercollegiately. The cost of these programs is, of course, in addition to those required to maintain the various sports facilities: the arena, gymnasia, tennis courts, weight and exercise rooms, playing fields, stadium, and those that are purely for more general recreational purposes. This is a heavy load for the "sports" budget to bear, especially in view of the draconian cuts in government spending in recent times. Inevitably, facilities and budget are simply not available or are severely constrained; and, of course, this had led to some acrimonious debates over which team or sport will get what portion of the shrinking pie.

During this period, football has naturally come under attack both at Queen's and more generally. The complaints, some more valid than others, have included the following: its cost, for equipment[11] and travel, and for a while there was also the cost of insurance (until U.S. civil suits against helmet manufacturers, which threatened to destroy the game, were no longer entertained by the courts); its potential for injury, an accusation made by chiropractors who had not done their homework on other sports;* its essential "maleness" and "political incorrectness" – for example, it was popularly reported, though later proved to have been a complete distortion of the statistics, that violence against women increased on Super Bowl Sunday;[12] the complaint that football has for too long had its due at the university and that it is time for other sports to come to the fore; that crowd support for football is down, especially among the students, and that other sports (such as track and field or rowing) now better reflect the nature of the student body; and that the team is no longer as competitive as some of the others (in an ironic twist of fate, the rugby club is often used as an example, having enjoyed considerable and well-deserved successes in recent times).[13]

Throughout all this, Hargreaves struggled to keep the program alive. He acknowledges that some of the complaints are valid but feels that the main problem has been the inability to attract competitive players to the university in the face of heavy recruiting efforts by universities across North America. This has been made even more difficult for Queen's because of its high grade requirements for admission and scholarships. Since athletic scholarships are not allowed, the football program has suffered, for it has been impossible to give an academic scholarship to any but the most brilliant scholar-athletes. And such people can easily get a scholarship at any university, or they could and often do go to Stanford or Harvard, for example, which do give athletic scholarships. Hargreaves summed up the problem succinctly:

The issue is not that Queen's lower its academic standards to those of some of the other schools in the country that we play to admit football players, although a "window" down say 5 per cent on the academic average for guys who have a lot of extracurricular stuff in high-school which might include football might be nice (we've had some success arguing this, by the way). But it's more the guy who has the average to get in, but not the 92 per cent or so necessary to get an academic

---

* Dave Ross, trainer for athletics at Queen's, estimates that based on his statistics for the various sports at the university, football might have a marginally higher rate of injury than other sports but that rugby and hockey are very close seconds. He confirms Dr Kerr's statement that there have only been two serious injuries in football at the university as far back as either of these two gentlemen can remember – both neck injuries and both successfully treated to complete recovery (Ross, personal interview).

scholarship, that I'm talking about. We lose almost all those guys to other schools like McGill, for example, or Yale, where they can both get in and get academic or athletic scholarship money. It's those guys that make the recruiting such a heart-breaking thing. And it's something the university really has to do something about if it wants to stay competitive, or in good conscience put a team on the field that isn't putting the players it has out there at considerable personal risk.[14]

For all these reasons, football at Queen's, and perhaps elsewhere, is a "game under seige," to use a phrase coined by Professor Hart Cantelon, a sociologist of sport in the School of Physical and Health Education at Queen's (and a longtime Gaels assistant coach). It is his opinion that if one studies the history of sport, it is possible to observe that there is a time when every sport comes under scrutiny. This time it happens to be football's turn.[15]

THE PHILOSOPHY OF SPORT MORE GENERALLY

It seems more likely, however, that the very nature of sport in all its mani-festations is being questioned. Not only has it been the subject of debate in academic circles, but the popular press has now begun to take notice, largely as a result of the baseball and hockey strikes of the past few years. Consider, for example, the following quotation from a very thoughtful article by Charles Pierce on the "Future of Sports" in the *Gentleman's Quarterly (GQ)*, a widely read men's magazine:

The country is as uncomfortable with its sport as it is with itself, riven by the same discontented joylessness that affects us more generally … There now thrives a school of thought that maintains that sports are about to be crushed between the upper millstone of heedless greed and the nether millstone of cultural anarchy … the modern athlete [being] so warped by money and fame that he has all but abandoned the idea of civilization, let alone teamwork and fair play …

There is a longing for the connection we used to feel with sports, for the sense we once had that our athletes represent what we truly are. But as the games go global, as Rupert Murdoch beams them to every corner of the world … and they grow and prosper, there is an unsettling feeling that they are moving ever further from us … A gap – racial, social, and cultural – yawns between the athlete and his audience.[16]

The article goes on to make the point that it is ultimately the public perfor-mance of sports that is the compelling aspect of the exercise, a point also made by Stephen Brunt in a *Globe and Mail* article commenting on the possible departure of the Winnipeg Jets hockey club from that city and the citizenry's response to that possibility: "In a world where there are fewer and fewer vestiges of community, fewer and fewer forms of consensus, the fact that a large number of people can gather together and care passionately together means something, even if it's an empty spectacle that brings them there. It is part of an identification process, a way of celebrating your home, your neighbours, yourself. It is a way of saying to the world, this is where I live, this is who I am."[17]

Even the American novelist John Updike is disturbed. In a 1995 newspaper column, he bemoaned the fate of baseball, which used to be "the working man's idyll" but is declining in popularity relative to golf. As Updike pointed out, although golf is more refined, peaceful, and genteel, it does not mimic life as baseball does.[18] Plato equated sport with music as being "important to the improvement of the soul," and in this context a community such as Kingston may well take as much pride in its symphony as in its Junior A hockey team or the Gaels.

Clearly, the globalization resulting from improved communications, computers, and so on, and the whole experience that constitutes what economists and others have called the Second Industrial Revolution is also having its impact on sport as surely as it is on every other area of human activity.[19] For example, Vladimir plays for the Jets, as does Timo; kids walk the streets of Jakarta wearing Blue Jay hats; Englishmen play soccer for Turin in the Italian League, Nigerians for Houston in the NBA; and a Tongan rugby player with the New Zealand All-Blacks is one of the heroes of the planet – or at least of Rumania, Japan, Western Samoa, Argentina, Wales, England, and everywhere else where rugby is played. This globalization is new to sport, and it is disconcerting – far more so than when focus and allegiance shifted merely from the local scene of, for example, Drumheller, Alberta, to the national scene of the Toronto Maple Leafs with the coming of the telegraph, telephone, radio, and Foster Hewitt.

That was manageable; this is not. The Anaheim Mighty Ducks' hockey club is too far removed, not only geographically but, as Pierce states, culturally, to say nothing of Wayne Gretzky in St Louis or a CFL team in Shreveport. Similar feelings must surely be felt by the citizens of Moscow as they see their countrymen leave to play in the NHL; or by the people of Manchester who must cheer for a German striker who is here today but gone tomorrow – gone to Marseilles for more money.

We have not yet understood what this revolution means for sport – or for many other areas of human activity. We do not know how it will affect the question of which sports will be played globally (for example, individual or team, soccer or tennis) and whether there will be any local variants. In "football" alone, there are at least six variants if one includes soccer; five if one does not: rugby union, rugby league, Aussie rules, Canadian football, and American football. The fact that there are so many questions to be addressed has caused the country, as Pierce says, to be "as uncomfortable with its sports as it is with itself."

So while it is certainly true that football at Queen's has its problems, this is only partly because of local considerations. The tectonic plates of global economics, politics, and culture are shifting and are taking all sport, including Queen's football, with them. Recognizing this makes it possible to understand that football has always addressed other needs at Queen's besides a localized need for institutional self-esteem. In essence, it has been pulled along by a more general commitment to a certain profile of sport throughout much of North America during the late-nineteenth and much of the twentieth centuries. It is for this general reason that Queen's played football each fall "as surely as God made little green apples." But football came to have special significance to Queen's over and above this, because of the nature of the school and its history, and because of the nature of those who attended the university and chose to represent it in one of the most important sports of the time.

THE WAY AHEAD

What is to be made of all this for the game and the university is another matter. We are certainly a long way from that beginning made by the Booth brothers and others in 1882 or by Curtis and his boys in that first Dominion championship season of 1893. It would seem, however, that although the future of football at Queen's is tied to the future of sport in general, the two are somewhat distinctive. Certainly, both require decisions to be made and revitalization of a sort to take place. At one level, it is all too easy to call for or hope to see a "saviour" appear. A separate article in the GQ issue cited above identified Mr Grant Hill, a professional basketball player late of Duke University, as supposedly possessing all the "saintly" properties required "to make sport right again" (both personally and as a role model). One should, perhaps, hope fervently for a local version of the same, for example, another Lindsay Malcolm.

More likely, though, it is a matter of needing a "Pogovian" realization: "I have seen the enemy and he is us." That is, the Rupert Murdochs of this world will assuredly continue their relentless drive to make tractor pulling a global sport. But if individuals or local communities want to be anything more than vicarious channel-surfing spectators, they will have to act individually, or locally in groups, to organize the sport they choose. They will have to behave as the Winnipeggers did when they rose up to demand that their NHL hockey club not be moved; or the way alumni did at the universities of Alberta and Toronto when the central administration threatened to close down the football programs at those two institutions.[20]

In all such cases some key questions will have to be answered; for example, whether all sport and sport programs will be purely recreational or whether there will be some subset in which "competition" takes place; whether they will all be individual sports, all team sports, or a mix of the two (and if so, which sports). These are all very different things. As well, if "competitiveness" is involved, to what level of competition will the individual or the team aspire (and by implication the collectivity that supports it): simply intramural (within the collectivity), with other neighbourhood collectives, with anybody else in the country, or with everyone in the world (as in the Olympics and World Cup)? To what extent will a philosophy of support for all "new" sports – the many that are being willingly entertained and added – be adopted as opposed to one that concentrates on a more selective group of older, more familiar and proven sports? How much can be accomplished given the resources available? Is there a clear understanding of what these resources actually are or could be? What are the true costs of each sport being considered? And which sports are most in keeping with the way the collective wishes to see itself and organize its affairs? Many other questions might be asked, but these seem the most important.

If one views sport at Queen's, and the place of football in it, in the light of these questions, a number of thoughts come to mind. In brief they are as follows:

1 The university has made various choices about the "recreational vs competitive" balance over its lifetime, starting with the purely recreational, roughly from 1840 to 1890; then, roughly from 1890 to 1970, some recreational (gymnastics, track, swimming, and soccer) and some competitive (principally football and to a lesser extent hockey and basketball); then, roughly from 1970 to the present, "a lot of recreational" and "a lot of competitive" (again principally football but now including a host of other sports).

2 For virtually all of the university's existence, recreation has been both individual and team-based, whereas when the university or members of its community have chosen to compete outside, they have done so in a team sport – again, most importantly, football.

3 The focus and level of the competitiveness has varied over time, beginning with any available opposition, which until the 1930s consisted of city teams in football and hockey, any other university in North America in hockey, and Varsity and McGill in football. Later, the opposition was

usually a subset of competitors consisting of other Canadian universities, though in recent times there have also been some notable competitors in individual sports who have reached all the way to the Olympics or the World Cup. And there have been times when the competition has come from far afield to play the rugby side, the volleyball and basketball clubs, and on one occasion even the football team, with its game in Britain.

4 For much of its existence, the university has adopted a "tried and true" philosophy in its choice of sports, concentrating on swimming, gymnastics, track and field, and skating as individual and recreational sports; an intramural program for all students at the university in those sports, and a selected number of team sports such as touch football, hockey, and basketball; and a competitive, external program oriented principally around football in the fall, with hockey and basketball featured as more minor sports played in the winter. As noted, beginning in the late 1960s and accelerating throughout the seventies and eighties, the university moved to a much more broadly based philosophy across the board (both recreationally and extramurally), welcoming new sports and teams at a very accelerated rate relative to the past.

5 For much of its history, the revenue sources for sport at the university and its costs were well known. To be sure, the balance shifted from time to time. On the revenue side it moved through several stages: purely self-funding until the 1880s; a small athletics fee plus self-funding until the first arena, pool, and gym were built; these sources plus rental revenue, particularly from the arena, until the stadium was built; primarily revenues from football from that time (1921) until roughly the late 1960s; finally, from the 1960s to the present, athletics fees have taken over as the major source of revenue, along with a direct grant from the university. The grant comes from a general subsidy of the university that largely supports the administrative overhead not only of sport but also of the teaching and research aspects of the School of Physical and Health Education. Football gate receipts and facilities rental fees are the other two noninconsequential sources of revenue.[21]

6 Sport in all its aspects has become more costly. This applies both to costs that have been incurred for a long time (facilities maintenance, football equipment, travel, food, and so on) and to new costs associated with the sports that have been added in recent years (rowing shells, squash rackets, video equipment, and so on). As noted in an earlier chapter, the university does not have a clear or consistent picture of what these costs are (whether in definition or in actual size), just as it has a very imperfect idea of the exact sources, or potential sources, of revenue from sport.[22] This is a decided contrast to the situation during the period from the late 1920s to the end of the 1960s, when revenues and costs flowed through the Athletic

Is the faith lost or not? (Art Martin)

Board of Control, whose financial reporting appeared as part of the overall university's audited financial statements each year.
7 As has been noted repeatedly throughout this book, during much of the university's history by far the most important of all its sports, in terms of how Queen's has seen itself, has been football. Arguably, this may have changed in very recent times. But one has to strain to make that argument if one recalls the response of the entire university community to the 1992 Vanier Cup experience or the continued attendance at the Homecoming game each year. Moreover, one has to make allowances for the university's draconian efforts to suppress all forms of student demonstrativeness and enthusiasm, a measure that has particularly touched football, though it has also cast a pall on nearly every activity around the campus.[23]

All of this suggests that if the university needs to make choices in sport, and clearly it does, football should and likely will remain at the core of any collection of sports the university continues to support.[24] It certainly can lay claim to being the longest-played competitive sport and the most successful (judged in terms of any number of criteria: number of championships, size of revenues, number of spectators, and so on). It continues to provide for student participation in competition, and it draws more spectators in total than any other sport in which the university competes, thus bringing in more outside revenues than any other sport. Finally, football is so clearly intertwined with the university's sense of its tradition that it is hard to separate the two in the minds of most alumni. These are strong claims to its continued pride of place.

It may well be true that football is in a period of crisis. But so is sport in general, and thus it is difficult to separate out the local situation with respect to football. In any event, the game is certainly not yet in the dinosaur class, despite what some people may believe. Indeed, its decline may simply be yet another manifestation of the ebb and flow in the fortunes of the game at Queen's. Such a phenomenon has been seen before, especially during the changeover to a new head coach. Certainly, because of the change in the fundamental character of the university – from small, working class, and isolated to large, elitist, and mainstream – football is not as close to characterizing Queen's as it was,[25] but there is still a need for collective expression and release.[26]

Football is still the sport best suited to this purpose: it is healthfully out-of-doors; it is played in the fall when the students are not yet fully committed academically; it offers a place to meet and be seen and especially to socialize, for unlike rugby and soccer, the game is watch-stop-watch-stop-watch and thus does not require continual attention; it is (or could be if properly controlled) one of the few places where young people could learn to drink in public; it is one of only a few sports at which the band can be present (this is not possible to the same extent, for example, indoors); and it is part of a traditional activity whose stories can be shared with parents, grandparents, and others who themselves went to the games in their time at Queen's. No other sport at the university has such a multitude of advantages for Queen's. Nor has any other brought as much positive publicity over the years. These are compelling arguments in support of continued pride of place and for action to find solutions to some of the current problems.

For example, hard choices have to be made about which sports to maintain and which to drop. There are too many claims and no real criteria to judge individual legitimacy. True, cost and revenues must be established, and all efforts made to reduce the former and increase the latter.[27] Judgments about what is acceptable student behaviour and what is not must be made more uniform. Condoning extensive hazing and other such activities around women's rugby, for example, but prosecuting it in connection with football is manifestly unfair. Awards originally intended for specific sports – for example, the Ted Reeve and Frank Tindall awards in football – should go to those sports and not to others, as has recently occurred.[28] Most important, efforts must be made to develop some way by which Queen's can compete for the scholar-athlete. Perhaps a series of leadership scholarships would be the answer, or scholarships tied to another university objective such as increased multicultural diversity. There is considerable evidence that if the university just had something to offer, "many would come."[29]

These decisions will not only require the input and action of those who lead the university, traditionally the principal, the trustees, and the university council. They will also need the opinions and involvement of all who have been associated with the game over the years, whether as players, coaches, doctors, bandspeople, cheerleaders, or spectators. Such decisions are too important to be left to an ad hoc committee, no matter how noble and well-intentioned its motives. As has nearly always been the case in the past, this type of broad-based approach will assuredly result in a continued appreciation of and renewed dedication to the special place that football has traditionally held in Queen's heart. In this way, the efforts of more than a century of seasons, over almost 115 years, will continue to be validated, and the contribution of all those who have been involved with the game, their hopes and their strivings, will not have been in vain or forgotten.[30]

TRULY THE END

Much of this conclusion may well have seemed more editorial in nature than is appropriate to a history. But it is clear that, at the moment of writing, there are a number of important questions facing sport at the university, especially football. Some have arrived from elsewhere, but others have grown out of the unique history of the game at Queen's. Not to have addressed them, however briefly, would have been to shirk a responsibility. But the picture is now complete;* that story has been told and the issues discussed.

It is to be hoped that the spirits of Guy Curtis, Pep Leadlay and Harry Batstone, Mike Rodden, Alfie Pierce, the "Moaner" and the "Mentor," and whatever other ghosts happen to be looking over one's shoulder will be pleased, as well as all living ex-Gaels and those who wear the colours at present. It is also to be hoped that for years to come, Queen's footballers

---

* Early in 1996, after a careful review of some excellent candidates, the university appointed Bob Howes as its new head football coach. Howes, who spans both the Tindall and Hargreaves eras, is well suited to carry forward the tradition of Queen's football. All those whose names bless this book, and those more generally who follow football at Queen's, wish him well.

and supporters will still gather to greet that time each succeeding year when the berries are heavy on the mountain ash and the sumac shows the first sign of its coming richness of orange and red. The nights will certainly grow longer, colder, clearer, and it will once again be time for football at Queen's.

No doubt some seasons will again go poorly, but if history is to be any judge, far more will be successes. Queen's will win more than it loses, it will bend but never break, and it will return each year to play once more. In this way, paraphrasing "the Moaner" of old, Coach Reeve, one can confidently say, "There will always be a lot of happy days at Queen's when the trees are turning gold and red against the background of the old stone buildings; the smell of burning leaves will hang in the autumn air, and the Gaels will be whooping it up at Richardson Stadium: coaching (and playing and watching) will be all right like that."

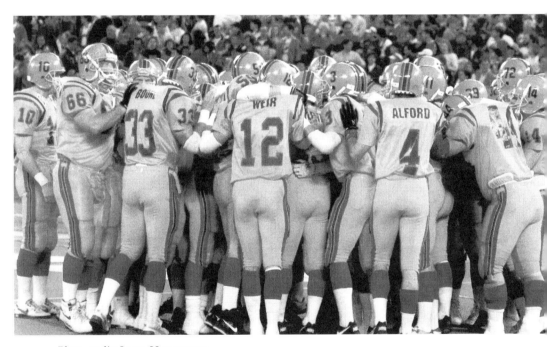

Photo credit: Lynn Hargreaves

Epilogue

Shakespeare may well have captured it best, as he so often did. One can almost imagine the following words being spoken in the middle of the gathering of the Gaels before that Vanier Cup game in 1992:

> We few, we happy few, we band of brothers;
> For he to-day that sheds his blood with me
> Shall be my brother: be he ne'er so vile
> This day shall gentle his condition:
> And gentlemen in England now a-bed
> Shall think themselves accursed they were not here,
> And hold their manhoods cheap whiles any speaks
> That fought with us upon Saint Crispin's Day.
>
> *Henry V,* 4.3

APPENDIX A

One Hundred Years of
Statistical History: A Summary

Table A1

Queen's University Football: Summary of games (league and playoff), 1893–1994

Year	Won	Lost	Tied	For	Against	Year	Won	Lost	Tied	For	Against
1893N[a]	6	2	0	182	76	1928N	2	2	0	29	24
1894N	2	1	0	40	20	1929CN	6	2	0	110	33
1895N	3	3	0	64	44	1930CN	5	2	0	42	20
1896	0	3	0	17	31	1931N	3	2	1	27	38
1897N	1	1	0	12	22	1932	1	3	2	45	69
1898	1	3	0	15	27	1933N	4	3	0	40	45
1899N	2	2	0	20	21	1934CN	5	2	0	37	31
1900c[b]N	2	1	1	43	26	1935CN	4	3	1	73	93
1901	1	3	0	30	43	1936N	4	3	0	32	37
1902	1	2	1	13	27	1937CN	5	2	0	42	28
1903	0	3	1	28	58	1938	0	6	0	30	70
1904CN	4	1	0	77	31	1939N	3	3	0	57	67
1905	1	4	1	75	105	1940–44	war years, no play				
1906	2	3	0	77	63	1945N	2	2	0	35	61
1907	2	3	1	53	71	1946	1	5	0	41	138
1908N	5	1	0	90	50	1947	0	5	1	33	146
1909N	3	3	0	84	63	1948	2	4	0	51	79
1910N	3	3	0	67	53	1949	2	3	1	75	73
1911	0	6	0	59	124	1950	2	4	0	53	99
1912	2	4	0	42	74	1951	0	6	0	43	118
1913	2	4	0	46	121	1952	2	5	0	54	105
1914	0	4	0	46	93	1953N	3	3	0	90	73
1915–18	war years, no play					1954N	4	3	0	132	80
1919	0	4	0	9	126	1955CN	6	1	0	114	59
1920	0	4	0	13	108	1956CN	5	1	1	106	55
1921N	2	2	0	28	46	1957	0	6	0	30	137
1922CN	6	1	0	85	66	1958	2	4	0	67	150
1923CN	6	0	0	137	19	1959	2	4	0	49	102
1924CN	6	0	0	73	31	1960N	4	3	0	129	102
1925CN	5	1	0	70	27	1961CN	6	1	0	178	48
1926	2	3	0	34	33	1962N	4	3	0	150	102
1927CN	3	2	0	42	43	1963CN	6	0	0	154	82

Table A1 (continued)

Year	Won	Lost	Tied	For	Against	Year	Won	Lost	Tied	For	Against
1964CN	7	0	0	215	85	1980N	5	4	0	178	141
1965N	3	3	0	87	66	1981CN	6	4	0	278	210
1966CN	6	1	0	207	75	1982	4	5	0	235	213
1967N	4	2	0	135	87	1983CN	7	2	2	316	192
1968CN	8	1	0	265	109	1984CN	7	3	0	368	205
1969N	5	2	0	133	96	1985N	6	2	0	207	143
1970CN	6	2	0	203	116	1986	3	5	0	222	195
1971N	6	3	0	310	162	1987	3	5	0	165	178
1972N	3	3	0	121	129	1988N	6	3	0	183	132
1973N	5	3	0	181	184	1989CN	9	1	0	294	148
1974	2	5	0	111	168	1990N	5	3	1	192	116
1975	2	6	0	121	177	1991CN	7	3	0	359	240
1976N	5	2	0	128	105	1992CN	10	1	0	334	145
1977CN	7	2	0	259	132	1993	2	5	0	122	168
1978CN	10	0	0	282	84	1994	1	6	0	136	188
1979N	7	2	0	202	101						

[a] N indicates non-losing season
[b] C indicates a championship of one kind or another

SUMMARY
Games played, 612
Games won, 335 (55%)
Games lost, 262 (43%)
Games tied, 15 (2%)
Points for, 10,366 (17/game)
Points against, 8,590 (14/game)
Non-losing seasons, 59 of 93 (63%)
Championships, 30 of 93 (32%)

Table A2
Individual years: Details, 1893–1994

1893					Queen's	7	Ottawa	8

1893

Queen's	13	Ottawa	23
Queen's	25	Ottawa	3
Queen's	27	Varsity	7
Queen's	6	Varsity	15
Queen's	27	Hamilton	13
Queen's	28	Varsity	3
Queen's	27	Varsity	1
Queen's	29	Montreal Athletic	11
for	182	against	76

(Queen's, Ontario and Dominion champions)

1894

| Queen's | 19 | Hamilton | 10 |
| Queen's | 14 | Hamilton | 2 |

| Queen's | 7 | Ottawa | 8 |
| for | 40 | against | 20 |

(Queen's, Ontario champions)

1895

Queen's	28	RMC	17
Queen's	22	RMC	1
Queen's vs Osgoode (loss, n.a.)			
Queen's vs Osgoode (loss, n.a.)			
Queen's	2	Varsity	19
Queen's	12	Varsity	7
for	64	against	44

(Varsity, champions)

1896

| Queen's | 16 | Varsity | 18 |
| Queen's | 1 | Varsity | 13 |

Queen's vs Montreal Athletic (loss, n.a.)
        for   17 against   31
(Varsity, champions)

1897

Queen's	2	Osgoode	17
Queen's	10	Varsity	5
for	12	against	22

(Osgoode, champions)

1898

8 Oct.	Queen's	2	McGill	3
22 Oct.	Queen's	8	Varsity	16
29 Oct.	Queen's	0	McGill	4
12 Nov.	Queen's	5	Varsity	4
	for	15	against	27

Won 1, lost 3, tied 0
(Varsity, champions)

1899

14 Oct.	Queen's	4	McGill	7
28 Oct.	Queen's	0	Varsity	8
4 Nov.	Queen's	8	McGill	4
18 Nov.	Queen's	8	Varsity	2
	for	20	against	21

Won 2, lost 2, tied 0
(Varsity, champions)

1900

20 Oct.	Queen's	6	McGill	7
27 Oct.	Queen's	11	Varsity	11
3 Nov.	Queen's	1	McGill	11
10 Nov.	Queen's	15	Varsity	2
	for	43	against	26

Won 2, lost 1, tied 1
(Queen's, champions)

1901

19 Oct.	Queen's	0	McGill	5
26 Oct.	Queen's	8	Varsity	23
2 Nov.	Queen's	11	Varsity	15
16 Nov.	Queen's	11	McGill	0
	for	30	against	43

Won 1, lost 3, tied 0
(Varsity, champions)

1902

19 Oct.	Queen's	6	McGill	6
1 Nov.	Queen's	5	Varsity	0
7 Nov.	Queen's	1	Varsity	11
14 Nov.	Queen's	1	McGill	10
	for	13	against	27

Won 1, lost 2, tied 0
(McGill, champions)

1903

24 Oct.	Queen's	1	McGill	11
31 Oct.	Queen's	7	Varsity	19
7 Nov.	Queen's	7	Varsity	7
14 Nov.	Queen's	13	McGill	21
	for	13	against	27

Won 0, lost 3, tied 1
(Varsity, champions)

1904

13 Oct.	Queen's	6	McGill	12
22 Oct.	Queen's	13	McGill	6
29 Oct.	Queen's	21	Varsity	10
12 Nov.	Queen's	31	Varsity	3
19 Nov.	Queen's	6	McGill	0
	for	77	against	31

Won 4, lost 1, tied 0
(Queen's, champions)

1905

14 Oct.	Queen's	5	Varsity	19
21 Oct.	Queen's	22	Ottawa	13
26 Oct.	Queen's	6	Varsity	20
5 Nov.	Queen's	15	Ottawa	19
11 Nov.	Queen's	11	McGill	11
18 Nov.	Queen's	16	McGill	23
	for	75	against	105

Won 1, lost 4, tied 1
(Varsity, champions)

1906

13 Oct.	Queen's	15	Ottawa	19
18 Oct.	Queen's	0	Varsity	12
27 Oct.	Queen's	20	McGill	23
10 Nov.	Queen's	31	Ottawa	0
17 Nov.	Queen's	11	Varsity	9
	for	77	against	63

Won 2, lost 3, tied 0
(McGill, champions)

1907

12 Oct.	Queen's	9	Ottawa	13
19 Oct.	Queen's	20	McGill	4
26 Oct.	Queen's	15	Ottawa	15
2 Nov.	Queen's	0	McGill	16
9 Nov.	Queen's	5	Varsity	20
16 Nov.	Queen's	4	Varsity	3
	for	53	against	71

Won 2, lost 3, tied 1
(Ottawa, champions)

1908

10 Oct.	Queen's	14	Ottawa	7
17 Oct.	Queen's	18	Varsity	3

24 Oct.	Queen's	12	McGill	5
31 Oct.	Queen's	22	McGill	4
7 Nov.	Queen's	16	Ottawa	11
14 Nov.	Queen's	8	Varsity	20
	for	90	against	50

Won 5, lost 1, tied 0
(Varsity, champions)

1909

9 Oct.	Queen's	1	Varsity	7
16 Oct.	Queen's	6	Ottawa	11
23 Oct.	Queen's	18	McGill	3
30 Oct.	Queen's	19	McGill	12
6 Nov.	Queen's	9	Varsity	21
13 Nov.	Queen's	31	Ottawa	9
	for	84	against	63

Won 3, lost 3, tied 0
(Varsity, champions)

1910

8 Oct.	Queen's	12	Ottawa	1
13 Oct.	Queen's	2	McGill	6
22 Oct.	Queen's	25	Ottawa	2
29 Oct.	Queen's	14	McGill	10
5 Nov.	Queen's	9	Varsity	25
12 Nov.	Queen's	5	Varsity	9
	for	67	against	53

Won 3, lost 3, tied 0
(Varsity, champions)

1911

7 Oct.	Queen's	6	Varsity	18
14 Oct.	Queen's	14	Ottawa	15
20 Oct.	Queen's	5	McGill	36
27 Oct.	Queen's	10	Ottawa	12
4 Nov.	Queen's	5	Varsity	23
11 Nov.	Queen's	19	McGill	20
	for	59	against	124

Won 0, lost 6, tied 0
(Varsity, champions)

1912

5 Oct.	Queen's	20	Ottawa	19
12 Oct.	Queen's	5	McGill	15
26 Oct.	Queen's	11	Varsity	17
2 Nov.	Queen's	3	McGill	14
9 Nov.	Queen's	3	Varsity	9
	for	42	against	74

Won 2 (1+1 Ottawa default), lost 4
(McGill, champions)

1913

11 Oct.	Queen's	2	McGill	49
18 Oct.	Queen's	6	RMC	15

25 Oct.	Queen's	3	Varsity	18
1 Nov.	Queen's	12	McGill	7
8 Nov.	Queen's	9	Varsity	29
14 Nov.	Queen's	14	RMC	3
	for	46	against	121

Won 2, lost 4, tied 0
(McGill, champions)

1914

17 Oct.	Queen's	14	Varsity	21
24 Oct.	Queen's	8	McGill	16
31 Oct.	Queen's	17	Varsity	25
14 Nov.	Queen's	7	McGill	31
	for	46	against	93

Won 0, lost 4, tied 0
(Varsity, champions)

1915–18, war years, no CIRFU played

1919

11 Oct.	Queen's	3	Varsity	41
18 Oct.	Queen's	2	McGill	32
25 Oct.	Queen's	2	Varsity	28
8 Nov.	Queen's	2	McGill	25
	for	9	against	126

Won 0, lost 4, tied 0
(McGill, champions)

1920

9 Oct.	Queen's	6	McGill	31
17 Oct.	Queen's	6	Varsity	27
30 Oct.	Queen's	0	McGill	16
13 Nov.	Queen's	1	Varsity	34
	for	13	against	108

Won 0, lost 4, tied 0
(Varsity, champions)

1921

8 Oct.	Queen's	9	Varsity	5
22 Oct.	Queen's	1	McGill	25
5 Nov.	Queen's	12	Varsity	13
12 Nov.	Queen's	6	McGill	3
	for	28	against	46

Won 2, lost 2, tied 0
(Varsity, champions)

1922

14 Oct.	Queen's	12	McGill	1
28 Oct.	Queen's	15	Varsity	13
4 Nov.	Queen's	20	McGill	10
11 Nov.	Queen's	1	Varsity	24
18 Nov.	Queen's[1]	12	Varsity	6
	for	60	against	54
25 Nov.	Queen's[2]	12	Argos	11 (PO)

2 Dec. Queen's[3] 13 Ed. Esk.   1 (PO)
          for   85 against   66
Won 6, lost 1, tied 0
(1. Queen's, Intercollegiate champions;
2. Eastern Canada champions;
3. Dominion champions)

1923

6 Oct.   Queen's   24 McGill   3
20 Oct. Queen's   9 Varsity   3
27 Oct. Queen's   19 McGill   3
3 Nov.   Queen's[1] 18 Varsity   5
          for   70 against   14
26 Nov. Queen's[2] 13 Ham. Tig. 5 (PO)
1 Dec. Queen's[3] 54 Regina   0 (PO)
          for 137 against   19
Won 6, lost 0, tied 0
(1. Queen's, Intercollegiate champions;
2. Eastern Canada champions;
3. Dominion champions)

1924

18 Oct. Queen's   8 Varsity   2
25 Oct. Queen's   13 McGill   8
1 Nov.   Queen's   16 McGill   4
8 Nov.   Queen's[1] 14 Varsity   13
          for   51 against   27
22 Nov. Queen's   11 Hamilton   1 (PO)
29 Nov. Queen's[2] 11 Balmy
                       Beach   3 (PO)
          for   73 against   31
Won 6, lost 0, tied 0
(1. Queen's, Intercollegiate champions;
2. Eastern Canada champions. Western
Canada champions did not come east;
therefore Queen's were Dominion
Champions. Undefeated season.)

1925

10 Oct. Queen's   8 Varsity   5
17 Oct. Queen's   14 McGill   0
24 Oct. Queen's   8 McGill   2
31 Oct. Queen's   17 Varsity   0
          for   47 against   7
21 Nov. Queen's   21 Balmy
                       Beach   9 (PO)
18 Nov. Queen's   2 Ottawa   11 (PO)
          for   70 against   27
Won 5, lost 1, tied 0
(Queen's, Intercollegiate champions;
Ottawa, Dominion champions)

1926

16 Oct. Queen's   5 Varsity   11
23 Oct. Queen's   14 McGill   0

6 Nov.   Queen's   12 McGill   13
13 Nov. Queen's   3 Varsity   1
27 Nov. Queen's   0 Varsity   8
          for   34 against   33
Won 2, lost 3, tied 0
(Varsity, Intercollegiate champions;
Ottawa, Dominion champions)

1927

15 Oct. Queen's   10 McGill   11
22 Oct. Queen's   3 Varsity   0
29 Oct. Queen's   12 Varsity   6
12 Nov. Queen's   11 McGill   5
          for   36 against   22
19 Nov. Queen's   6 Ham. Tig. 21 (PO)
          for   42 against   43
Won 3, lost 2, tied 0
(Queen's, Intercollegiate champions;
Hamilton Tigers, Dominion champions)

1928

6 Oct.   Queen's   7 Varsity   10
20 Oct. Queen's   4 McGill   2
27 Oct. Queen's   16 Varsity   4
3 Nov.   Queen's   2 McGill   8
          for   29 against   24
Won 2, lost 2, tied 0
(McGill, Intercollegiate champions)

1929

5 Oct.   Queen's   11 McGill   1
12 Oct. Queen's   11 Varsity   4
19 Oct. Queen's   25 Western   2
26 Oct. Queen's   25 McGill   0
2 Nov.   Queen's   14 Western   0
9 Nov.   Queen's   6 Varsity   7
16 Nov. Queen's   15 Varsity   5
          for 107 against   19
23 Nov. Queen's   3 Ham. Tig. 14 (PO)
          for 110 against   33
Won 6, lost 2, tied 0
(Queen's, Intercollegiate champions)

1930

11 Oct. Queen's   5 Western   1
18 Oct. Queen's   6 McGill   0
25 Oct. Queen's   1 Varsity   6
1 Nov.   Queen's   3 Western   0
8 Nov.   Queen's   12 Varsity   5
15 Nov. Queen's   12 McGill   0
22 Nov. Queen's   3 Hamilton   8
          for   42 against   20
Won 5, lost 2, tied 0
(Queen's, Intercollegiate champions)

1931

10 Oct.	Queen's	3	Varsity	2
17 Oct.	Queen's	8	Western	3
24 Oct.	Queen's	9	McGill	9
31 Oct.	Queen's	5	McGill	4
7 Nov.	Queen's	2	Western	3
14 Nov.	Queen's	0	Varsity	17
	for	27	against	38

Won 3, lost 2, tied 1
(Western, Intercollegiate champions)

1932

8 Oct.	Queen's	8	Varsity	23
15 Oct.	Queen's	7	Western	8
22 Oct.	Queen's	12	McGill	12
29 Oct.	Queen's	12	McGill	1
5 Nov.	Queen's	4	Western	4
12 Nov.	Queen's	2	Varsity	21
	for	45	against	69

Won 1, lost 3, tied 2
(Varsity, Intercollegiate champions)

1933

7 Oct.	Queen's	3	Western	5
14 Oct.	Queen's	3	McGill	2
21 Oct.	Queen's	8	Varsity	2
28 Oct.	Queen's	13	Varsity	6
4 Nov.	Queen's	1	McGill	17
11 Nov.	Queen's	9	Western	3
18 Nov.	Queen's	3	Varsity	10 (PO)
	for	40	against	45

Won 4, lost 3, tied 0
(Varsity, Intercollegiate champions)

1934

6 Oct.	Queen's	2	Western	1
13 Oct.	Queen's	5	McGill	4
20 Oct.	Queen's	4	Varsity	3
27 Oct.	Queen's	6	Varsity	7
3 Nov.	Queen's	8	McGill	4
10 Nov.	Queen's	4	Western	5
18 Nov.	Queen's	8	Varsity	7 (PO)
	for	37	against	31

Won 5, lost 2, tied 0
(Queen's, Intercollegiate champions)

1935

5 Oct.	Queen's	7	McGill	9
12 Oct.	Queen's	2	Varsity	2
19 Oct.	Queen's	4	Western	1
26 Oct.	Queen's	18	Western	10
2 Nov.	Queen's	14	Varsity	19
11 Nov.	Queen's	18	McGill	1
16 Nov.	Queen's	6	Varsity	4 (PO)

	for	69	against	49
23 Nov.	Queen's	4	Ham. Tig.	44
	for	73	against	93

Won 4, lost 3, tied 1
(Queen's, Intercollegiate champions)

1936

10 Oct.	Queen's	10	McGill	0
17 Oct.	Queen's	2	Varsity	13
24 Oct.	Queen's	3	Western	10
31 Oct.	Queen's	3	Western	1
7 Nov.	Queen's	6	Varsity	1
14 Nov.	Queen's	5	McGill	1
21 Nov.	Queen's	3	Varsity	11 (PO)
	for	32	against	37

Won 4, lost 3, tied 0
(Varsity, Intercollegiate champions)

1937

9 Oct.	Queen's	3	Varsity	5
16 Oct.	Queen's	4	Western	5
23 Oct.	Queen's	6	McGill	4
30 Oct.	Queen's	7	McGill	0
6 Nov.	Queen's	12	Western	8
13 Nov.	Queen's	3	Varsity	0
27 Nov.	Queen's	7	Varsity	6 (PO)
	for	42	against	28

Won 5, lost 2, tied 0
(Queen's, Intercollegiate champions)

1938

8 Oct.	Queen's	6	Varsity	13
15 Oct.	Queen's	7	Western	10
22 Oct.	Queen's	5	McGill	16
29 Oct.	Queen's	1	McGill	9
3 Nov.	Queen's	1	Western	10
12 Nov.	Queen's	10	Varsity	12
	for	30	against	70

Won 0, lost 6, tied 0
(McGill, Intercollegiate champions)

1939

7 Oct.	Queen's	17	Western	32
14 Oct.	Queen's	2	McGill	4
21 Oct.	Queen's	8	Varsity	6
28 Oct.	Queen's	11	Varsity	6
4 Nov.	Queen's	12	McGill	6
11 Nov.	Queen's	7	Western	13
	for	57	against	67

Won 3, lost 3, tied 0

1940–44 war years, no football played

1945

20 Oct.	Queen's	19	Toronto	15
27 Oct.	Queen's	6	Toronto	25
3 Nov.	Queen's	8	McGill	4
10 Nov.	Queen's	2	Western	17
	for	35	against	61

Won 2, lost 2, tied 0
(Western, Intercollegiate champions)

1946

5 Oct.	Queen's	12	McGill	18
12 Oct.	Queen's	0	Western	8
19 Oct.	Queen's	0	Toronto	21
26 Oct.	Queen's	7	Toronto	39
2 Nov.	Queen's	14	McGill	5
9 Nov.	Queen's	8	Western	47
	for	41	against	138

Won 1, lost 5, tied 0
(Western, Intercollegiate champions)

1947

11 Oct.	Queen's	13	McGill	13
18 Oct.	Queen's	6	Toronto	23
25 Oct.	Queen's	3	Western	52
1 Nov.	Queen's	0	Western	32
8 Nov.	Queen's	5	Toronto	15
15 Nov.	Queen's	6	McGill	11
	for	33	against	146

Won 0, lost 5, tied 1

1948

9 Oct.	Queen's	12	McGill	20
16 Oct.	Queen's	8	Toronto	6
23 Oct.	Queen's	12	Western	19
30 Oct.	Queen's	9	Western	23
6 Nov.	Queen's	0	Toronto	4
13 Nov.	Queen's	10	McGill	7
	for	51	against	79

Won 2, lost 4, tied 0
(Toronto, Intercollegiate champions)

1949

8 Oct.	Queen's	21	Toronto	22
15 Oct.	Queen's	11	Western	16
22 Oct.	Queen's	1	McGill	17
29 Oct.	Queen's	15	McGill	0
5 Nov.	Queen's	18	Western	18
12 Nov.	Queen's	9	Toronto	0
	for	75	against	73

Won 2, lost 3, tied 1
(Western, Intercollegiate champions)

1950

7 Oct.	Queen's	1	Toronto	7
14 Oct.	Queen's	13	Western	7
21 Oct.	Queen's	6	McGill	25
28 Oct.	Queen's	15	McGill	43
4 Nov.	Queen's	13	Western	10
11 Nov.	Queen's	5	Toronto	7
	for	53	against	99

Won 2, lost 4, tied 0
(Western, Intercollegiate champions)

1951

6 Oct.	Queen's	12	Western	24
13 Oct.	Queen's	7	McGill	14
20 Oct.	Queen's	2	Toronto	26
27 Oct.	Queen's	7	Toronto	15
3 Oct.	Queen's	2	McGill	19
10 Oct.	Queen's	13	Western	20
	for	43	against	118

Won 0, lost 6, tied 0
(Toronto, Intercollegiate champions)

1952

4 Oct.	Queen's	1	Western	33
11 Oct.	Queen's	20	McGill	7
18 Oct.	Queen's	1	Toronto	13
25 Oct.	Queen's	1	Toronto	9
1 Nov.	Queen's	5	Western	25
8 Nov.	Queen's	21	McMaster	9
15 Nov.	Queen's	5	McGill	9
	for	54	against	105

Won 2, lost 5, tied 0
(Western, Intercollegiate champions)

1953

3 Oct.	Queen's	7	Toronto	16
10 Oct.	Queen's	13	McGill	12
24 Oct.	Queen's	7	Western	19
31 Oct.	Queen's	34	McMaster	20
7 Nov.	Queen's	28	McMaster	0
14 Nov.	Queen's	1	Toronto	6
	for	90	against	73

Won 3, lost 3, tied 0
(Western, Intercollegiate champions)

1954

9 Oct.	Queen's	46	McGill	11
16 Oct.	Queen's	20	Toronto	0
23 Oct.	Queen's	1	Western	27
30 Oct.	Queen's	18	Western	11
7 Nov.	Queen's	20	McGill	0
13 Nov.	Queen's	9	Toronto	11

20 Nov. Queen's   18 Western   20 (PO)
              for 132 against   80
Won 4, lost 3, tied 0
(Toronto, Intercollegiate champions)

1955
1 Oct.   Queen's   30 McGill   10
8 Oct.   Queen's   6 Toronto   11
15 Oct. Queen's   12 Western   4
22 Oct. Queen's   25 Western   17
29 Oct. Queen's   11 Toronto   10
5 Nov.   Queen's   12 McGill   7
12 Nov. Queen's   18 Toronto   0 (PO)
              for 144 against   59
Won 6, lost 1, tied 0
(Queen's, Intercollegiate champions)

1956
6 Oct.   Queen's   7 Toronto   7
13 Oct. Queen's   35 Western   0
20 Oct. Queen's   1 McGill   6
27 Oct. Queen's   20 McGill   15
3 Nov.   Queen's   20 Western   13
10 Nov. Queen's   19 Toronto   12
17 Nov. Queen's   4 Toronto   2
              for 106 against   55
Won 5, lost 1, tied 1
(Queen's, Intercollegiate champions)

1957
5 Oct.   Queen's   8 Toronto   16
12 Oct. Queen's   6 Western   34
19 Oct. Queen's   6 McGill   33
26 Oct. Queen's   0 McGill   15
2 Nov.   Queen's   8 Western   21
9 Nov.   Queen's   2 Toronto   18
              for   30 against   137
Won 0, lost 6, tied 0
(Western, Intercollegiate champions)

1958
4 Oct.   Queen's   16 Western   48
11 Oct. Queen's   21 McGill   0
18 Oct. Queen's   0 Toronto   44
25 Oct. Queen's   3 Toronto   32
1 Nov.   Queen's   13 McGill   16
8 Nov.   Queen's   14 Western   12
              for   67 against   150
Won 2, lost 4, tied 0
(Toronto, Intercollegiate champions)

1959
3 Oct.   Queen's   8 Western   20
9 Oct.   Queen's   16 McGill   12
17 Oct. Queen's   0 Toronto   7

24 Oct. Queen's   6 Toronto   7
31 Oct. Queen's   6 McGill   1
7 Nov.   Queen's   13 Western   55
              for   49 against   102
Won 2, lost 4, tied 0
(Western, Intercollegiate champions)

1960
1 Oct.   Queen's   27 McGill   26
8 Oct.   Queen's   26 Toronto   13
15 Oct. Queen's   10 Western   21
22 Oct. Queen's   36 Western   0
29 Oct. Queen's   21 Toronto   6
5 Nov.   Queen's   9 McGill   15
12 Nov. Queen's   0 McGill   21 (PO)
              for 129 against   102
Won 4, lost 3, tied 0
(McGill, Intercollegiate champions)

1961
7 Oct.   Queen's   8 McGill   7
14 Oct. Queen's   29 Toronto   0
21 Oct. Queen's   38 Western   13
28 Oct. Queen's   27 Western   7
4 Nov.   Queen's   58 Toronto   6
11 Nov. Queen's   7 McGill   15
18 Nov. Queen's   11 McGill   0
              for 178 against   48
Won 6, lost 1, tied 0
(Queen's, Intercollegiate champions)

1962
6 Oct.   Queen's   32 Toronto   13
13 Oct. Queen's   26 Western   9
20 Oct. Queen's   24 McGill   38
27 Oct. Queen's   10 McGill   14
3 Nov.   Queen's   16 Western   13
10 Nov. Queen's   29 Toronto   0
17 Nov. Queen's   13 McGill   15 (PO)
              for 150 against   102
Won 4, lost 3, tied 0
(McGill, Intercollegiate champions)

1963
5 Oct.   Queen's   21 Toronto   14
12 Oct. Queen's   20 Western   18
19 Oct. Queen's   26 McGill   19
26 Oct. Queen's   17 McGill   7
2 Nov.   Queen's   51 Western   9
9 Nov.   Queen's   19 Toronto   15
              for 154 against   82
Won 6, lost 0, tied 0
(Queen's, Intercollegiate champions.
Queen's first undefeated season since
1924)

1964

3 Oct.	Queen's	11	Western	9
10 Oct.	Queen's	13	McGill	12
17 Oct.	Queen's	45	Toronto	24
24 Oct.	Queen's	34	Toronto	22
31 Oct.	Queen's	20	McGill	0
7 Nov.	Queen's	29	Western	12
14 Nov.	Queen's	63	McMaster	6 (PO)
	for	215	against	85

Won 7, lost 0, tied 0
(Queen's, Intercollegiate champions)

1965

2 Oct.	Queen's	20	Western	33
9 Oct.	Queen's	8	McGill	0
16 Oct.	Queen's	0	Toronto	1
23 Oct.	Queen's	31	Toronto	0
30 Oct.	Queen's	16	McGill	6
6 Nov.	Queen's	12	Western	26
	for	87	against	66

Won 3, lost 3, tied 0
(Toronto, Intercollegiate champions)

1966

1 Oct.	Queen's	28	McGill	16
8 Oct.	Queen's	19	Toronto	28
15 Oct.	Queen's	24	Western	9
22 Oct.	Queen's	33	Western	0
29 Oct.	Queen's	23	Toronto	15
5 Nov.	Queen's	30	McGill	0
12 Nov.	Queen's	50	Toronto	7
	for	207	against	75

Won 6, lost 1, tied 0
(Queen's, Intercollegiate champions)

1967

7 Oct.	Queen's	42	Western	14
15 Oct.	Queen's	41	McGill	23
21 Oct.	Queen's	14	Toronto	19
28 Oct.	Queen's	13	Toronto	16
4 Nov.	Queen's	15	McGill	10
11 Nov.	Queen's	10	Western	5
	for	135	against	87

Won 4, lost 2, tied 0
(Toronto, Intercollegiate champions)

1968

28 Sep.	Queen's	22	Western	17
5 Oct.	Queen's	35	Toronto	0
12 Oct.	Queen's	21	McGill	28
19 Oct.	Queen's	33	Waterloo	17
26 Oct.	Queen's	15	McGill	14
2 Nov.	Queen's	54	McMaster	7 (PO)
9 Nov.	Queen's[1]	14	Toronto	6 (PO)
	for	194	against	89

17 Nov.	Queen's[2]	29	Manitoba	6 (PO)
22 Nov.	Queen's[3]	42	Waterloo	
			Lutheran	14 (PO)
	for	265	against	109

Won 8, lost 1, tied 0
(1. Queen's, Intercollegiate champions;
2. Western Bowl champions; 3. College
Bowl champions [Vanier Cup])

1969

27 Sep.	Queen's	6	McGill	28
4 Oct.	Queen's	28	Waterloo	0
11 Oct.	Queen's	17	Western	6
18 Oct.	Queen's	24	Toronto	17
25 Oct.	Queen's	3	McGill	21
1 Nov.	Queen's	16	Toronto	14
8 Nov.	Queen's	39	McMaster	10
	for	133	against	96

Won 5, lost 2, tied 0
(McGill, Intercollegiate champions)

1970

26 Sep.	Queen's	18	Western	4
3 Oct.	Queen's	18	Toronto	27
10 Oct.	Queen's	44	McGill	11
17 Oct.	Queen's	29	Toronto	15
24 Oct.	Queen's	23	McGill	12
31 Oct.	Queen's	31	McMaster	17
7 Nov.	Queen's	20	Waterloo	6
	for	183	against	92
16 Nov.	Queen's	20	Manitoba	24 (PO)
	for	203	against	116

Won 6, lost 2, tied 0
(Queen's, Intercollegiate champions. The
Ontario-Quebec Athletics Association
terminates)

1971 The new OUAA begins

11 Sep.	Queen's	65	Laurntn	6
18 Sep.	Queen's	17	Ottawa	26
25 Sep.	Queen's	36	Waterloo	0
29 Sep.	Queen's	48	Carleton	25
2 Oct.	Queen's	22	Carleton	0
9 Oct.	Queen's	62	York	7
16 Oct.	Queen's	28	Toronto	25
23 Oct.	Queen's	29	Toronto	31
30 Oct.	Queen's	3	Western	42 (PO)
	for	310	against	162

Won 6, lost 3, tied 0
(Western, Intercollegiate champions)

1972

17 Sep.	Queen's	33	Carleton	0
23 Sep.	Queen's	16	Ottawa	13
30 Sep.	Queen's	18	Toronto	46

7 Sep. Queen's 23 Carleton   26
13 Oct. Queen's 18 Ottawa   17
21 Oct. Queen's 13 Toronto   27
         for 121 against   129
Won 3, lost 3, tied 0
(Waterloo-Lutheran, Intercollegiate
champions)

1973
15 Sep. Queen's 14 Ottawa   27
22 Sep. Queen's 27 Toronto   9
29 Sep. Queen's 33 Guelph   14
6 Oct.   Queen's 21 Carleton   13
13 Oct. Queen's 16 Ottawa   37
20 Oct. Queen's   6 Toronto   48
27 Oct. Queen's 34 McMaster   14
3 Nov.   Queen's 30 York   22
         for 181 against   184
Won 5, lost 3, tied 0
(Laurier, Intercollegiate champions)

1974
14 Sep. Queen's   7 Ottawa   27
21 Sep. Queen's 19 McGill   8
28 Sep. Queen's   9 Toronto   32
5 Oct.   Queen's 30 York   7
12 Oct. Queen's 16 Carleton   36
19 Oct. Queen's 20 Toronto   38
2 Nov.   Queen's 10 Guelph   20
         for 111 against   168
Won 2, lost 5, tied 0
(Toronto and Western, co-champions)

1975
13 Sep. Queen's 14 Concordia   17
20 Sep. Queen's   4 Carleton   1
27 Sep. Queen's   0 Toronto   26
4 Oct.   Queen's 10 Toronto   32
11 Oct. Queen's 14 Ottawa   35
18 Oct. Queen's 16 McMaster   3
25 Oct. Queen's 37 Bishop's   6
1 Nov.   Queen's 26 Ottawa   57
         for 121 against   177
Won 2, lost 6, tied 0
(Ottawa and Windsor, co-champions)

1976
11 Sep. Queen's 27 Bishop's   34
18 Sep. Queen's 15 Carleton   10
25 Sep. Queen's 28 Carleton   18
2 Oct.   Queen's   9 McGill   8
9 Oct.   Queen's   7 Ottawa   26
16 Oct. Queen's 23 Concordia   9

23 Oct. Queen's 19 Ottawa   0
         for 128 against   105
Won 5, lost 2, tied 0
(Western and Ottawa, co-champions)

1977
17 Sep. Queen's 44 Bishop's   25
24 Sep. Queen's 24 Ottawa   15
1 Oct.   Queen's   4 McGill   5
8 Oct.   Queen's 40 Carleton   1
15 Oct. Queen's 21 McGill   9
22 Oct. Queen's 45 UQTR   1
29 Oct. Queen's 27 Ottawa   14 (PO)
5 Nov.   Queen's 45 Bishop's   27 (PO)
12 Nov. Queen's 22 Acadia   35 (PO)
         for 259 against   132
Won 7, lost 2, tied 0
(Queen's, co-winner of OQIFC East
championship with national champion
Western)

1978
16 Sep. Queen's 46 UQTR   7
23 Sep. Queen's 52 Concordia   0
30 Sep. Queen's 27 McGill   17
6 Oct.   Queen's 28 Ottawa   16
14 Oct. Queen's 26 Carleton   3
21 Oct. Queen's 15 Bishop's   14
28 Oct. Queen's 17 Carleton   13
4 Nov.   Queen's[1] 23 McGill   1 (PO)
11 Nov. Queen's[2] 32 StFX   10 (PO)
18 Nov. Queen's[3] 16 UBC   3 (PO)
         for 282 against   84
Won 10, lost 0, tied 0
(1. Queen's, Intercollegiate champions; 2.
Atlantic Bowl champions; 3. College Bowl
champions [Vanier Cup]. Queen's first
undefeated season since 1964)

1979
8 Sep.   Queen's 42 UQTR   7
22 Sep. Queen's 20 Ottawa   21
29 Sep. Queen's 16 Concordia   10
6 Oct.   Queen's 23 Carleton   7
13 Oct. Queen's 23 Bishop's   8
20 Oct. Queen's 17 McGill   6
27 Oct. Queen's 25 Carleton   5 (PO)
3 Nov.   Queen's 22 McGill   5 (PO)
10 Nov. Queen's 14 Western   32 (PO)
         for 202 against   101
Won 7, lost 2, tied 0
(Queen's, OQIFC East champions)

1980

13 Sep.	Queen's	11	Ottawa	21
20 Sep.	Queen's	34	Concordia	30
27 Sep.	Queen's	12	McGill	22
4 Oct.	Queen's	16	Carleton	3
11 Oct.	Queen's	9	Ottawa	10
18 Oct.	Queen's	30	Bishop's	17
25 Oct.	Queen's	31	Carleton	4
1 Nov.	Queen's	23	McGill	21 (PO)
8 Nov.	Queen's	12	Ottawa	13 (PO)
	for	170	against	141

Won 5, lost 4, tied 0
(Western, Intercollegiate champions)

1981

19 Sep.	Queen's	17	Concordia	27
26 Sep.	Queen's	7	McGill	18
3 Oct.	Queen's	38	Carleton	19
10 Oct.	Queen's	29	Ottawa	28
17 Oct.	Queen's	52	Carleton	10
24 Oct.	Queen's	46	Bishop's	14
31 Oct.	Queen's	10	Ottawa	24
7 Nov.	Queen's	39	Concordia	11 (PO)
14 Nov.	Queen's	26	McGill	19 (PO)
21 Nov.	Queen's	14	Acadia	40 (PO)
	for	278	against	210

Won 6, lost 4, tied 0
(Queen's, OQIFC East champions)

1982

11 Sep.	Queen's	20	Ottawa	22
18 Sep.	Queen's	32	Carleton	34
25 Sep.	Queen's	30	McGill	1
2 Oct.	Queen's	32	Ottawa	35
9 Oct.	Queen's	27	Carleton	21
16 Oct.	Queen's	44	Bishop's	27
23 Oct.	Queen's	4	Concordia	18
30 Oct.	Queen's	31	Ottawa	30 (PO)
6 Nov.	Queen's	15	Concordia	25 (PO)
	for	235	against	213

Won 4, lost 5, tied 0
(Concordia, OQIFC East champions)

1983

10 Sep.	Queen's	36	Carleton	4
17 Sep.	Queen's	38	Carleton	11
24 Sep.	Queen's	26	Condrdia	23
1 Oct.	Queen's	38	Bishop's	25
7 Oct.	Queen's	18	Ottawa	18
15 Oct.	Queen's	16	Ottawa	16
22 Oct.	Queen's	33	McGill	34
29 Oct.	Queen's	32	Carleton	18 (PO)
5 Nov.	Queen's[1]	36	McGill	5 (PO)
12 Nov.	Queen's[2]	22	U of T	7 (PO)

19 Nov.	Queen's[3]	21	Calgary	31 (PO)
	for	316	against	192

Won 7, lost 2, tied 2
(1. Queen's, OQIFC champions; 2. Central
Bowl champions; 3. Vanier Cup finalists)

1984

15 Sep.	Queen's	36	Bishop's	39
22 Sep.	Queen's	59	McGill	30
29 Sep.	Queen's	9	Carleton	10
5 Oct.	Queen's	39	Ottawa	13
13 Oct.	Queen's	52	Ottawa	1
20 Oct.	Queen's	27	Concordia	25
27 Oct.	Queen's	27	Carleton	24
3 Nov.	Queen's	65	McGill	29 (PO)
10 Nov.	Queen's[1]	37	Bishop's	35 (PO)
17 Nov.	Queen's[2]	17	Mt Allison	28 (PO)
	for	368	against	205

Won 7, lost 3, tied 0
(1. Queen's, OQIFC champions; 2. Atlantic
Bowl finalists)

1985

21 Sep.	Queen's	26	Concordia	23
28 Sep.	Queen's	34	Ottawa	13
5 Oct.	Queen's	26	Bishop's	19
12 Oct.	Queen's	28	Carleton	27
19 Oct.	Queen's	41	McGill	7
25 Oct.	Queen's	17	Ottawa	20
2 Nov.	Queen's	21	Carleton	19
9 Nov.	Queen's	14	Concordia	15 (PO)
	for	207	against	143

Won 6, lost 2, tied 0

1986

13 Sep.	Queen's	15	Bishop's	28
20 Sep.	Queen's	8	McGill	11
27 Sep.	Queen's	18	Carleton	39
4 Oct.	Queen's	23	Ottawa	17
10 Oct.	Queen's	32	Ottawa	15
18 Oct.	Queen's	69	Concordia	16
25 Oct.	Queen's	32	Carleton	37
1 Nov.	Queen's	25	Bishop's	31 (PO)
	for	222	against	194

Won 3, lost 5, tied 0

1987

12 Sep.	Queen's	20	Concordia	27
19 Sep.	Queen's	36	Ottawa	29
26 Sep.	Queen's	29	Carleton	6
3 Oct.	Queen's	22	Ottawa	13
10 Oct.	Queen's	14	Carleton	16
17 Oct.	Queen's	10	McGill	21
24 Oct.	Queen's	10	Bishop's	39

31 Oct. Queen's   24 McGill   27 (PO)
          for 165 against   178
Won 3, lost 5, tied 0

1988
10 Sep. Queen's   23 Ottawa   10
17 Sep. Queen's   15 Bishop's   18
24 Sep. Queen's   31 McGill   28
1 Oct.   Queen's   9 Ottawa   4
8 Oct.   Queen's   15 Concordia   29
15 Oct. Queen's   35 Carleton   14
22 Oct. Queen's   32 Carleton   0
29 Oct. Queen's   16 Ottawa   13 (PO)
5 Nov.   Queen's   7 Bishop's   16 (PO)
          for 183 against   132
Won 6, lost 3, tied 0

1989
9 Sep.   Queen's   13 Ottawa   9
16 Sep. Queen's   28 Bishop's   17
23 Sep. Queen's   51 Carleton   7
29 Sep. Queen's   28 Ottawa   24
7 Oct.   Queen's   25 Concordia   5
14 Oct. Queen's   38 Carleton   11
21 Oct. Queen's   29 McGill   0
28 Oct. Queen's   33 McGill   17 (PO)
4 Nov.   Queen's[1] 39 Ottawa   18 (PO)
11 Nov. Queen's[2] 10 Sask.   40 (PO)
          for 294 against   148
Won 9, lost 1, tied 0
(1. Queen's, OQIFC champions; 2.
Churchill Bowl finalists)

1990
16 Sep. Queen's   11 Concordia   20
22 Sep. Queen's   30 Ottawa   2
29 Sep. Queen's   19 McGill   14
6 Oct.   Queen's   36 Carleton   6
13 Oct. Queen's   20 Bishop's   20
19 Oct. Queen's   1 Ottawa   6
27 Oct. Queen's   29 Carleton   13
3 Nov.   Queen's   37 Concordia   15 (PO)
10 Nov. Queen's   9 Bishop's   20 (PO)
          for 192 against   116
Won 5, lost 3, tied 1

1991
14 Sep. Queen's   44 McGill   30
21 Sep. Queen's   34 Carleton   19
28 Sep. Queen's   49 Concordia   22
4 Oct.   Queen's   15 Ottawa   19
12 Oct. Queen's   58 Carleton   10
19 Oct. Queen's   52 Ottawa   13
26 Oct. Queen's   26 Bishop's   29

2 Nov.   Queen's   25 Concordia   23 (PO)
9 Nov.   Queen's[1] 34 Bishop's   31 (PO)
16 Nov. Queen's[2] 22 Laurier   42 (PO)
          for 359 Against   240
Won 7, lost 3, tied 0
(1. Queen's, OQIFC champions;
2. Churchill Bowl finalists)

1992
12 Sep. Queen's   13 Concordia   8
19 Sep. Queen's   14 Bishop's   49
26 Sep. Queen's   43 Carleton   3
3 Oct.   Queen's   27 McGill   17
10 Oct. Queen's   44 Carleton   10
17 Oct. Queen's   35 Ottawa   0
23 Oct. Queen's   49 Ottawa   15
31 Oct. Queen's   24 McGill   21 (PO)
7 Nov.   Queen's   31 Bishop's   6 (PO)
14 Nov. Queen's   23 Guelph   16
21 Nov. Queen's   31 St Mary's   0
          for 334 against   145
Won 10, lost 1, tied 0
(Queen's, Dunsmore Cup, Churchill Bowl,
and Vanier Cup champions)

1993
11 Sep. Queen's   17 Ottawa   11
18 Sep. Queen's   7 Bishop's   24
25 Sep. Queen's   20 Carleton   25
2 Oct.   Queen's   16 Concordia   19
9 Oct.   Queen's   26 Carleton   8
16 Oct. Queen's   12 Ottawa   34
23 Oct. Queen's   24 McGill   37
          for 122 against   168
Won 2, lost 5, tied 0

1994
10 Sep. Queen's   16 McGill   33
17 Sep. Queen's   20 Ottawa   45
24 Sep. Queen's   19 Carleton   21
1 Oct.   Queen's   7 Concordia   34
8 Oct.   Queen's   44 Carleton   7
15 Oct. Queen's   14 Bishop's   19
22 Oct. Queen's   16 Ottawa   29
          for 136 against   198
Won 1, lost 6, tied 0

APPENDIX B
Some Individual Records and Awards

Jamie Galloway (1988–92)	369	Bill Barrable (1982–83)	152
Blaine Shore (1975–79)	254	Larry Mohr (1980–85)	146
Connie Mandala (1983–87)	236	Keith Eaman (1968–70)	137
Brad Elberg (1990–93)	216	Jock Climie (1986–89)	137
Doug Cozac (1968–72)	204	Jim Young (1962–64)	121
Frank "Pep" Leadlay (1921–25)	187	Brian Warrender (1968–72)	108
Bob O'Doherty (1974–78)	174	Robin Ritchie (1958–62)	106
Heino Lilles (1963–69)	168	Bill Edwards (1961–63)	95
Ron Stewart (1953–57)	162	Tom Macartney (1978–82)	90
Scott Bissessar (1981–84)	156	Bayne Norrie (1962–67)	86
Dave Marinucci (1976–79)	156	Kelly Kinahan (1981–82, 1985–86)	85

B2   HEAD COACHES AT QUEEN'S, 1919–1994

1919	Jack Williams	1933–38	Ted Reeve
1920	Lindsay Malcolm	1939	Frank Tindall
1921	George Awrey/	1940–44	no play
	W.P. (Bill) Hughes	1945	Bob Elliott
1922–26	W.P. (Bill) Hughes	1946	Doug Munsson
1927–28	Orrin Carson	1947	Bob Elliott
1929–31	Harry Batstone	1948–75	Frank Tindall
1932	Milton Burt	1976–94	Doug Hargreaves

B3   THE JOHNNY EVANS MEMORIAL TROPHY (MVP) WINNERS

After the untimely death of John Evans in 1930, his former teammates dedicated a trophy to the memory of this great Queen's star who captained the 1921 team and so inspired his teammates from his quarterback position that he is regarded as one of the greatest players ever to wear the Tricolour.

This trophy is awarded annually to the member of the senior intercollegiate team who, in the opinion of his teammates, is the most valuable player (MVP) on the team that year. The following are the names of the players so selected.

1932	Howard Carter	1968	Keith Eaman
1933	Howard Hamlin	1969	Keith Eaman
1934	Ed Barnabe	1970	Heino Lilles
1935	Clayton Krug	1971	Brian Warrender and
1936	Harry Sonshine		Mike Lambros
1937	Bernie Thornton	1972	Doug Cozac
1938	George Sprague	1973	Dave Hadden
1939	Nick Paithouski	1974	Darrell Penner
1945	Peter King	1975	Darrell Penner
1946	Jim Crothers	1976	Darrell Penner
1947	Bob Stevens	1977	Jim Rutka and
1948	Peter Salari		Dave Marinucci
1949	Dick Harrison	1978	Bob Mullen and
1950	Peter Salari		Jim D'Andrea
1951	Ross McKelvey	1979	Ed Andrew and
1952	Stu Kennedy		Tom Macartney
1953	Gary Lewis	1980	Ross Francis
1954	Ron Stewart	1981	Tom Macartney
1955	Gus Braccia	1982	Tom Macartney
1956	Ron Stewart	1983	Ross O'Doherty
1957	Ron Stewart	1984	Peter Harrison
1958	Ron Delisle	1985	Harry Mohr
1959	Terry Porter	1986	Steve Porter
1960	Dave Skene	1987	Vince Pinetta
1961	Gary Strickler	1988	Jock Climie
1962	Peter Thompson	1989	Jock Climie
1963	Bob Latham	1990	Paul Beresford
1964	Jim Young	1991	Tim Pendergast
1965	Larry Ferguson	1992	Brad Elberg
1966	Bayne Norrie	1993	Paul Kozan
1967	Bayne Norrie	1994	Jonathan Taylor

B4 CAPTAINS AT QUEEN'S, FROM 1921

1921	Johnny Evans	1964	John Erickson and Bob Latham
1922	Red McKelvey	1965	Merv Daub and Cal Connor
1923	Bill Campbell	1966	Larry Ferguson and Frank Arment
1924	Pep Leadlay	1967	Don Bayne and Bayne Norrie
1925	Harry Batstone	1968	Bob Climie and Ron Brooks
1926	Liz Walker	1969	Cam Innes and Jim Tait
1927	Cliff Howard	1970	Cam Innes and Jim McKeen
1928	Bubs Britton	1971	Brian Warrender and Mike Lambros
1929	Ike Sutton	1972	Brian Warrender and Gord Squires
1930	Ian Gourley	1973	Dave Whiteside
1931	Gib McKelvey	1974	Dave Hadden and John Waddell
1932	Howard Carter	1975	Darrell Penner and Darryl Craig
1933	Howard Hamlin	1976	Maurice St Martin and Norm Haggarty
1934	John Kostuik	1977	Larry Small, Randy Edgeworth, and Jim D'Andrea
1935	Johnny Wing	1978	Jim D'Andrea and Randy Edgeworth
1936	Ed Barnabe	1979	Jim D'Andrea and Pat Plishka
1937	George Sprague	1980	Ed Andrew and John Wilson
1938	Art Stollery	1981	Rob Ball, Tom Macartney, and Tony McDowell
1939	Doug Annan	1982	Tom Macartney, Tony McDowell, and Phil Marsland
1940	George Carson	1983	Tony McDowell and Phil Marsland
1945	Jack Milliken	1984	John Larsen, Larry Mohr, Jeff Kyle, and Ian Deakin
1946	Bob Stevens	1985	Tom Langford and Larry Mohr
1947	Al Lenard	1986	Tom Langford, Charlie Galunic, and John Flannery
1948	Al Lenard	1987	Tom Langford and Charlie Galunic
1949	Ross McKelvey		
1950	Jim Charters		
1951	Harry Lampman		
1952	Jack Roberts		
1953	Gary Lewis		
1954	Jack Cook		
1955	Gary Lewis		
1956	Gary Lewis		
1957	Karl Quinn and Dave Wilson		
1958	Jocko Thompson		
1959	Kent Plumley and Gary Strickler		
1960	Don Robb and Gary Strickler		
1961	Dave Skene		
1962	Dave Skene and Terry Porter		
1963	Don Rasmussen		

1988   Randy Zarichny and
       Paul Senyshyn
1989   Matt Clifford and Doug
       Corbett
1990   Tim Pendergast and
       Mike Boone
1991   Mike Boone and
       Paul Beresford

1992   Mike Boone, Brad Elberg,
       and Don Rorwick
1993   Joel Dagnone, Brad Elberg,
       and Don Rorwick
1994   Mark Robinson and Tim Ware

APPENDIX C
List of Interviewees

John Albinson, professor, School of Physical and Health Education, Queen's (Kingston)

John Ashley, player 1952–55; retired high school teacher (Kingston)

Don Bayne, player 1963–68; lawyer (Ottawa)

Wally Berry, photographer, late 1940s to the present (Kingston)

Mike Boone, player 1988–92; chartered accountant (Toronto)

Hart Cantelon, coach and professor, School of Physical and Health Education, Queen's (Kingston)

George Carson, player 1935–39; retired physician (Kingston)

Bob Climie, player 1964–69, coach 1973; physician (Ottawa)

Jock Climie, player 1986–89; professional football player and lawyer (Ottawa)

Randy Edgeworth, player 1974–78, coach 1981–86; educator (Kingston)

Jake Edwards, player 1934–36, coach and athletic director 1938–77; retired professor (Kingston)

Brad Elberg, player 1989–93; professional football player

Ross Francis, player 1976–80; lawyer (Toronto)

Dave Hadden, player 1971–74; educator (Lakefield)

Doug Hargreaves, player 1953–57, head coach 1976–94; retired (Kingston)

Tom Hopkins, equipment manager 1977– (Kingston)

Bob Howes, player 1965, professor and coach 1982–94, head coach 1996– (Kingston)

Jack Kerr, team physician 1958–76; retired (Kingston)

Fred Lehman, fan and insurer 1938– ; insurance executive (Kingston)

Al Lenard, player 1946–49, coach 1950–71, athletic director 1962–82; retired professor (Kingston)

Rolf Lund, professor and head of athletics, Queen's (Kingston)

Hal McCarney, player 1948–50, coach 1959–75; entrepreneur (Gananoque)

Alex Melvin, player 1967, 1971–72; entrepreneur (Ajax)

Bill Miklas, player 1959–64, coach 1965–66, 1979–94; professor (Kingston)

Harv Milne, fan and equipment/grounds keeper 1939–72; entrepreneur (Kingston)

Bob Mullen, player 1976–80, coach 1982–84; educator and coach (Kingston)

Johnny Munro, player 1934–37; retired executive, died early 1996 (Toronto)
Terry Porter, player 1957–62, team physician/trainer 1969–70; physician (Barrie)
Mark Robinson, player 1990–94; graduate student (Kingston)
Dave Ross, trainer 1980– (Kingston)
Mike Schad, player 1982–85; professional football player, entrepreneur (Ottawa)
Gary Schreider, player 1953–55; master, Ontario Court of Justice (Ottawa)
Ron Stewart, player 1953–57; federal ombudsman for corrections (Ottawa)
Jocko Thompson, player 1955–59; physician (Barrie)
Chuck Tindall, photographer and entrepreneur (Kingston)

APPENDIX D
Queen's Old Boys, 1919–1995

Queen's Football Hall of Fame members are marked with an asterisk; also noted are team captains and winners of the most valuable player (MVP) award. The players in this and the following list are identified by their familiar (rather than formal) names.

While every effort has been made to ensure that the following lists are complete, the author will be grateful for any information that will allow the correction of any omissions or errors.

"Tiny" Adams, 1923–25
Chuck Agnew, 1926–28
Bert Airth, 1921–24
Arnold Anglin, 1923
Doug Annan, 1937–39 (capt. 1939)

Noellie Baird, 1927
"Baldy" Baldwin, 1923
Reg Barker,* 1934–36
Ed Barnabe,* 1934–36 (MVP 1934, capt. 1936)
Bob Basserman, 1926–30
Harry Batstone,* 1922–27 (capt. 1925)
Erwin Bean, 1939
Malcom Bews, 1934–36
Ted Bishop, 1938
Jack Bond, 1922–23
C. Jackson Booth,* 1882–84
W.D. Cy Bracken, 1921

Bill Brass, 1939
John Brewster, 1937–38
Bubs Britton,* 1925–29 (capt. 1928)
Hank Brown,* 1923–25
Jack Brown, 1938–39
Frank Buckmaster, 1939
M.A. Milt Buell, 1930–32
R.P. Flip Burns, 1921
Wimpy Byen, 1937–38
Jerry Taft Byrne, 1932–33

George Caldwell, 1928–31
Bill Campbell,* 1919–23 (capt. 1923)
Bill Carr, 1932
George Carson, 1936–40 (capt. 1940)
Orrin Carson, 1922–26
H.W. Howie Carter,* 1927–31 (MVP & capt. 1932)
Ken Carty, 1938–39

Maurice Cheepwick, 1938

Al Clarke, 1938

Jerry Conlin, 1936–39

Howie Conquergood, 1932

Guy Curtis,* 1887–98

Colin Dafoe, 1933–35

Jack Dargavel, 1932–33

Hugh Davidson, 1931

Bob Davis, 1937–39

Jim Davis, 1930–33

Paul Davoud, 1932

R.C. Weenie Day, 1931–32

A.J. Art DeDiana, 1929–31

John Delahaye, 1921–23

Grover Dennis, 1935–37

Herb Dickey, 1929

Bill Dobson,* 1906–09

Tom Doherty, 1935

Ed Dolan, 1922

Robert L. Dunsmore, 1913–14

Frank Earle, 1933–35

Bus Edwards, 1938–39

Jake Edwards,* 1934–36

Bob Elliott,* 1929–34

Ed Elliott,* 1906–09, 1922

Teddy Etherington,* 1898–1901

Johnny Evans,* 1919–23

Fitton, 1931

W.D. "Red" Gilmour, 1928–31

Bill Glass, 1930–34

Bud Gorman, 1928–33

Ian Gourley, 1928–30 (capt. 1930)

Roly Graham, 1921

V.T. Tuffy Griffiths, 1937

Babe Grondin, 1922–24

Ted Hallett, 1931

Hammy Hamilton, 1926

How Hamlin,* 1929–34 (MVP & capt. 1933)

Ed Handford, 1926–28

Dave Harding, 1921–22

Murray Hastings, 1929–30

Jack Hazlett,* 1911–14

Earl Hendershot, 1931

Joe Hoba, 1938–39

Henry Hosking, 1931–32

Cliff Howard, 1925–27 (capt. 1927)

Ralph Jack, 1937–38

Jakey Jamieson, 1928

Bud Johnston, 1938–39

Coley Johnston, 1920–22

Harry Jones, 1938–39

Marty Jones, 1933–37

Jud Kennedy, 1932

Archie Kerr, 1937–38

Jim Kilgour, 1927–29

Arch Kirkland, 1934–36

John Kostuik,* 1931–34 (capt. 1934)

Curly Krug,* 1933–35 (MVP 1935)

Lackey, 1932

Jack Latimer, 1936–37

"Pep" Leadlay,* 1921–25 (capt. 1924)

Norman "Tout" Leckie,* 1908–10

Art Lewis,* 1921–25

Jack Lewis, 1934–36

Ford Loucks, 1939

C. Ludgate, 1921

Don McCrimmon, 1925

Tupper McDonald,* 1902–03

Hugh Macdonnell,* 1906–09

Ivan McDonough, 1939

Ding McGill, 1938–39

Dunc McIntosh, 1933

Ross McKay, 1921

Gib McKelvey, 1930–31 (capt. 1931)

John "Red" McKelvey,* 1921–25 (capt. 1922)

Chuck McLean, 1935–37

Pres McLeod, 1921–24

Gord McMahon, 1934

Joe McManus, 1934–35

Ken McNeil, 1923

Jack McNichol, 1931–35

Mucher Macpherson, 1936

Joe Madden, 1912–13

Pete Malachowski, 1938–39

Peter Marshall, 1939

Ab Miller, 1933–37

Ralph Miller, 1937

Irish Monaghan, 1925–27

Ben Morris, 1930

Bill Muirhead, 1922–25

Lou Mulvihill, 1938–39

"Chick" Mundell, 1922–25

Ga Mungovan, 1927–30

Johnny Munro,* 1934–37

Armour Munroe, 1928–29

Spud Murphy, 1931

Earl Nagel, 1926–28

Don Nickle, 1920–22

Eric "Red" Nicol, 1929–30

H.C. Hal Norman, 1938

Bozo Norrie, 1925

Nick Paithouski,* 1937–39 (MVP 1939)

Bob Paterson,* 1902–05

Chuck Peck, 1935–38

Merve Peever, 1932–33

Ken Preston, 1938–39

Bill Purvis, 1930–32

Bob Ralph, 1929–33

Barry Reist, 1930–31

Honey Reynolds, 1926–27

Roy Reynolds, 1922–24

George T. Richardson,* 1900–05

Mike Rodden,* 1910–13

Arthur Ross,* 1888–98

Ed Ryan, 1920–21

Hugh Sampson, 1937–38

Jim Saylor, 1921–22

Jim Scott, 1934–35

Sprout Shaw, 1926

D.S. Buff Simmons, 1931

Bob Simpson, 1938–39

D. Skelton, 1924–25

H. Skelton, 1938

Ernie Sliter,* 1910–12

Cog Smith, 1930

Harry Sonshine,* 1934–36 (MVP 1936)

George Sprague, 1936–38 (capt. 1937, MVP 1938)

Stan Stanyar, 1930–31

Jack Stevenson, 1927

Art Stollery,* 1935–38 (capt. 1938)

Dick Storms, 1932

E.A. "Blurp" Stuart, 1930–31

Ike Sutton, 1927–29 (capt. 1929)

Ted Teskey, 1930–32

Russ Thoman, 1932

Bud Thomas,* 1924–26

Mel Thompson, 1934–37

Bernie Thornton,* 1937 (MVP)

Art Turner,* 1905–08

Jesse Turner, 1937

Joe Turner, 1938

Smut Veale, 1920–22

Carl Voss, 1925–26

Art Walker, 1939

Bert Walker, 1930–31

"Liz" Walker,* 1921–27 (capt. 1926)

Fred Warren, 1927–28

Casey Waugh, 1934

Doug Waugh, 1933–34

F. Waugh, 1931–33   Jim Wright, 1924–26, 1928
Bob Weir, 1933–35
Jack Williams,* 1904–05, 1908   Howie Young, 1926
Ken Williams,* 1906, 1909   Ted Young, 1934, 1936–37
Johnny Wing,* 1933–35 (capt. 1935)
Beano Wright, 1926   Abe Zvonkin,* 1934–35

QUEEN'S OLD BOYS (AFTER SECOND WORLD WAR)

Queen's Football Hall of Fame members are marked with an asterisk; also noted
are team captains and winners of the most valuable player (MVP) award.

Jack Abraham, 1954–55   Leo Bandiers, 1943–45
Geoff Adair, 1965   Roger Banting, 1979–80
Brian Alford, 1990–92   Sheridan Baptiste, 1985–88
Bob Anderson, 1986–87   Pete Barker, 1966
Greg Anderson, 1972–75   Joe Barnabe, 1962
Ian Anderson, 1972–74   Bill Barrable, 1982–83
Joel Andersen, 1964–68   Paul Barsanti, 1988–90
John Andreoli, 1965–67   Greg Baun, 1979, 1984–87
Ed Andrew,* 1976–80 (MVP 1979,   Don Bayne,* 1964–68 (co-capt. 1967)
   co-capt. 1980)   Mike Beatty, 1979–80
Matt Angus, 1988–89   Paul Beck, 1955–56
Ross Arber, 1957–59   Pete Beck, 1951–53
Russ Arbuckle, 1971   Bill Bell, 1948, 1950
Frank Arment, 1964–66 (co-capt. 1966) Doug Bell, 1952–53
Tony Arnoldi, 1951–52   Jeffrey Bell, 1985
Floyd Ashley, 1981–82   Ted Bellinger, 1977
Sam Ashton, 1981–85   Paul Beresford, 1988–90
Johnathan Aston, 1989   Ted Bergeron, 1983–87
Ken Atwood, 1951–52   Dave Best, 1976–80
                                       Steve Best, 1982–83
Don Bahner, 1948–52   George Bethune, 1959–61
Floyd Baijaly, 1953–55   Tom Beynon, 1962–64
Dave Baines, 1968   John Biggs, 1971–72
Dick Bakker,* 1974–79   Alex Binkley, 1966–67
Brad Ball, 1988   Robert Bird, 1988–90
Don Ball, 1949–52   Scott Bissessar, 1981–84
Rob Ball, 1977–81 (co-capt. 1981)   Tom Black, 1989–92
Bob Ballantyne, 1986–87   Gerry Blacker, 1973
Bruce Balson, 1974–78   Dave Blair, 1971
Dino Bandiera, 1948   Rick Blake, 1974

Steve Bodnar, 1982–85

Mike Boone, 1988–92 (co-capt. 1991–92, MVP, all-Cdn)

John Booth, 1971–72

Joe Bourdon, 1983

Keith Boyd, 1989–90

Gus Braccia, 1955 (MVP)

Ian Brady, 1961–63

Mike Brady, 1965

Chris Brennan, 1967–68

Pete Broadhurst, 1962–64

Bob Bronk, 1980–81

Ron Brooks, 1964–68 (co-capt. 1968)

John Brown, 1963

Dirk Brubacker, 1987–90

Lou Bruce,* 1952–55

Dave Bryane (Rozumulak), 1946–49

Greg Bryk, 1990–92

Murray Buchanan, 1974–76

Murray Bulger, 1947–50

Bill Burgess, 1945–50

Bob Burleigh, 1957–58

David Burleigh, 1985–89

Mark Burleigh, 1983–87

Mike Burleigh, 1989–90

Larry Burridge, 1961

Paul Callahan, 1985

Archie Campbell, 1945

Aron Campbell, 1991–93

Bob Campbell, 1956

Dave Campbell, 1969–73

Kelly Campbell, 1980

Mike Cant, 1989

Bruno Caranci, 1966

Bill Carlyle, 1961–62

Dan Carmichael, 1963–66

John Carrick, 1962

Mel Carson, 1947

Chris Carty, 1981

Brian Casey, 1968, 1971

Lorne Chapman, 1961

Jim Charters,* 1946–51 (capt. 1950)

Moe Chochinor, 1945

Tom Chown, 1966–70

Joe Churchill, 1968

Bev Clark, 1963, 1965

Dave Clark, 1984–86

John Clark, 1978–81

Ron Clark, 1965–69

Steve Clark, 1985

Dale Clarke, 1983

Henry Clarke, 1956

Des Clements, 1950

Matthew Clifford, 1985–89 (co-capt. 1989)

Bob Climie,* 1964–69 (co-capt. 1968)

Jock Climie, 1986–89

Scott Clouston, 1985

Bob Cole, 1949–50

Cal Connor,* 1958–65 (co-capt. 1965)

Jack Cook, 1951–54 (capt. 1954)

Don Cooper, 1969–70

Doug Corbett, 1986–89 (co-capt. 1989)

John Corrigan, 1980–83

Doug Cowan, 1964–67

Doug Cozac,* 1968–72

Darryl Craig, 1975–76 (co-capt. 1976)

Theron Craig, 1965–68

Pete Cranston, 1952–53

Bruce Cronk, 1945

Jim Crothers, 1945–46 (MVP 1946)

John Crouchman, 1961–66

Jim Crozier, 1967

Jim Cruickshank, 1954–55

Doug Cunningham, 1966

Ron Cunningham, 1971

Shawn Cymbalisty, 1982–85

Stu Dafoe, 1991–95

Joel Dagnone, 1989–93 (co-capt. 1993)

Dave Dakers, 1981–83

Jim Daley, 1974–75

Jim D'Andrea,* 1975–79 (co-capt.
    1978–79)
Merv Daub,* 1962–65 (co-capt. 1965)
Steve Davis, 1967–68
Don Dawdy, 1953
Andy Day, 1987–90
Ian Deakin, 1981–84 (co-capt. 1984)
Don Delahaye, 1945–47
John De La Vergne, 1960–62
Ron Delisle, 1957–58 (MVP 1958)
Eric Dell, 1989–92, 1994
Peter Demontigny, 1973
Braden Dent, 1992–94
Dave Devonshire, 1971–73
Harry Dick, 1948–49
Tom Dickinson, 1971–73
Carl Di Giacoma, 1966–67
Terry Dolan, 1956–58
Larry Dolecki, 1960–61
Ben Doliazny, 1951
Brian Donnelly, 1966–68
Devin Donovan, 1978
Bodie Dorrance, 1987–88
Gord Dougall, 1959
Al Dresser, 1966, 1971
Jim Duncan, 1975–77
Norm Dunstan, 1959–61
Norm Dyson, 1951, 1954

Keith Eaman,* 1968–70 (MVP 1968)
Randy Edgeworth,* 1974–78 (co-capt.
    1977–78)
Bill Edwards, 1961–63
Chris Edwards, 1989
Terry Edwards, 1984–87
Brad Elberg, 1990–93 (co-capt.
    1992–93)
John Elford, 1951
Don Endleman, 1946
Fred Endley, 1961–62
John Erickson,* 1960–64 (co-capt. 1964)
Bruce Evans, 1981

Roy Fardell, 1945–49
Ron Faulker, 1968–70
John Faulkner, 1947–49
Paul Fedor, 1956–57
Bill Ferguson, 1964–65
John Ferguson, 1985–87
Larry Ferguson,* 1963–66 (MVP 1965,
    co-capt. 1966)
John Flannery, 1985–86 (co-capt. 1986)
Dennis Fleming, 1950–51
Brian Fordyce, 1968–69
Ian Forster, 1975
Ross Francis,* 1976–80
Terry Fraser-Reid, 1988
Bob Freeman, 1975
Bob Fuller, 1945
John Futa, 1961–62

Hugh Gallagher, 1978
Jamie Galloway, 1988–92
Charlie Galunic, 1984–87 (co-capt.
    1987)
Tim Gardiner, 1980
Wess Garrod, 1974
Bill Gatfield, 1948
Ian Gavaghan, 1979
Frank Geard, 1953–55
Brian Gibbo, 1951
Bill Gladu, 1981
Russ Glithero, 1984–88
Jeff Gnehi, 1987
Bob Good, 1961
Donald Gordon, 1971–72
John Gordon,* 1963–68
Paul Gordon, 1967–69
Richard Gorman, 1967
George Gorrie, 1978
Gordon Graham, 1985–86
Phil Grandjean, 1939
Scott Gray, 1989–93
Jay Graydon, 1971
Andrew Green, 1990

Jim Greenwood, 1963, 1965

Ted Gregory, 1965

Don Griffin, 1950–52

Robert Grimm, 1972

John Haag, 1961–62

Dave Hadden,* 1971–74 (co-capt. 1974)

Eric Hafemann, 1962–65

Richard Haggar, 1984

Norm Haggarty, 1972–76 (co-capt. 1976)

Terry Haggerty, 1967–68

Trevor Hains, 1985–88

Gord Hall, 1962

Mike Halliday, 1947

Bill Halvorson, 1956–57

Geoff Hamlin, 1972

Al Hammond, 1945

Paul Hand, 1969–72

Julian Hanlon, 1978

Chris Harber, 1973

Doug Hargreaves,* 1953, 1959

Gerry Harness, 1968

Dick Harrison, 1948–49, 1951 (MVP 1949)

Graydon Harrison, 1956–57

Peter Harrison,* 1981–85

Dave Harshaw, 1955–57

Stuart Harshaw, 1986–87

Mike Hartley, 1965–67

Frank Hawkins, 1958–60

Paul Hazlet, 1976–80

Geoff Heinricks, 1980–82

Elton Hemingway, 1946

James Hendry, 1985–86

Ron Herman, 1987–91

Gavin Higgs, 1986–89

Roy Hiscock, 1956

John Hollingsworth, 1968–72

Sherm Hood, 1952–54

Bill Hoose, 1945–47

Andrew Horembala, 1987–88

Chris Houston, 1981

Pete Howe, 1956

Bob Howes, 1963–64

Tony Howie, 1985–88

Mike Hrishevich, 1947

Steve Hudson, 1982–85

Jim Hughes,* 1954–56

Bill Huntley, 1948

Cam Innes, 1968–70 (co-capt. 1970)

John Irvine, 1963

Art Jackson, 1948

George Jackson, 1981–84

Dick James, 1953–54

Norm Jamieson, 1962–64

Mike Jefferies, 1985, 1987–88

Mario Jelic, 1988–89

Al Jette, 1976–77

Bill Johnson, 1958–59

Dave Johnson, 1964

Gord Johnson, 1959

Jamie Johnston, 1964–68

Pete Johnston, 1951

Jerry Kaczmarek, 1975

Frank Kakouros, 1984–87

Steve Kelman, 1977

Joe Kennedy, 1964

Rob Kennedy, 1989–90

Stu Kennedy, 1951–52 (MVP 1952)

Will Kennedy, 1972, 1974–75

Ed Kidd, 1989–93

Kelly Kinahan, 1982, 1985–86

Geoff Kindle, 1965

Peter King, 1945 (MVP)

Ken Kirkwood, 1990–93

Don Kitchen, 1974–77

Andy Kniewasser, 1945–46

Brian Knox, 1978–81

Al Kocman, 1953–56

Kees Kort, 1967–68

Bill Koski, 1953

Roderic Koski, 1972

Paul Kostvik, 1958–60

Nick Koutroubouasism, 1988–89

Paul Kozan, 1989–93

Harald Kreps, 1982–83

Robert Krog, 1990

John Kustec, 1980

Jeff Kyle, 1980–84 (co-capt. 1984)

Gary Kynoch, 1981–85

Gil Labine, 1970–73

Mike Lambros,* 1969–71 (co-capt. 1971)

Garry Lamourie, 1968–70

Harry Lampman, 1949–51 (capt. 1951)

Ron Lane, 1952, 1954–55

Stu Lang,* 1969–73

Paul Langevin, 1976–80

Tom Langford, 1984–87 (co-capt. 1985–87)

Jerry Langlois, 1965–67

Ike Lanier, 1951

Geoff LaPlante, 1990

John Larsen, 1982–85

Bob Latham, 1961–65 (MVP 1963, co-capt. 1964)

Doug Latham, 1973–76

John Latham, 1963–66

Scott Lattimer, 1955

Brent Lavictore, 1975

Mike Law, 1961, 1963

Herbert Lawler, 1943–45

Carl Leeati, 1968–70

Al Lenard,* 1946–49 (1947–48)

Jay Lepp, 1981–82

Jamie Lewin, 1990–93

Charlie Lewis, 1956

Gary Lewis,* 1950, 1953–55 (MVP 1953, capt. 1953, 1955–56)

Heino Lilles,* 1963–70 (MVP 1970)

Paul Lindros, 1967–68

John Lindsay, 1963, 1965–66

Steve Livingstone, 1988

Jack Logan,* 1948–50

Doug Lowry, 1973–77

Gary Lucenti, 1959–61

John Lynch, 1976, 1978

Bob McAleese, 1956, 1958–60

Tom Macartney,* 1978–82 (MVP 1979, co-capt. 1981–82)

Terry Macaulay, 1968–69

Peter McCallum, 1962, 1964

Hal McCarney,* 1948–51

Bill McCarthy, 1963–67

Dan McCarthy, 1967–70

John McCombe, 1952–53

Lorne McConnery, 1967–70

Chris McCormick, 1988–92

John McCrossan, 1981

Dan McCullough, 1988–92

Don McCullough, 1989–90

Al MacDonald, 1963

Bernie MacDonald, 1986–90

Dave MacDonald, 1980–81

Ian MacDonald, 1946

Ken MacDonald, 1945–46

Tony McDowell, 1979–83 (co-capt. 1981–83)

Scott McElhearn, 1968

Bob McFarlane, 1980–81

Jack McGee, 1952

Wayne McGill, 1959–61

Reid McGruer, 1988–90

James McGuire, 1947

Eric McIlveen, 1950–51

Don McIntyre, 1965, 1967–70

Frank Macintyre, 1946–48

Bill McIver, 1973–75

Don McKay, 1957

Jim McKeen,* 1966–70 (co-capt. 1970)

Ross McKelvey,* 1947–51 (capt. 1949, MVP 1951)

George McKenzie, 1967–68

Derek Mackesy, 1961, 1963

Jamie McKinnon, 1983–85

Tony McLean, 1985

Gord McLellan, 1971–72

Scott McLellan, 1981–82

Jay McMahan,* 1954–56

Peter McNabb, 1973–74

Gregory McNamara, 1972–76

Don McNay, 1959

Bill McNeill, 1966–71

Peter MacPhail, 1967–70

Burns McPherson, 1969–70

Bob McRae, 1953

Darrell Majdell, 1985

Kevin Malone, 1979–80

Jim Manake, 1971

Tony Manastersky, 1975–79

Connie Mandala, 1984–87

Dave Marinucci,* 1976–79

Phil Marsland, 1980–83 (co-capt. 1982–83)

Don Marston, 1953–54

Rick Mellor, 1979

Wally Mellor, 1951, 1953–54

Alex Melvin, 1966, 1968, 1971–73

Stacey Merritt, 1974

Bill Miklas,* 1960–64

Rob Miller, 1978–80

Bud Milliken, 1946

Jack Milliken, 1945 (capt.)

John Milliken, 1955

Jason Moeller, 1990–92

Larry Mohr,* 1981–85 (co-capt. 1985)

Eric Monkman, 1977

Rod Montrose, 1949–50

Alex Morris, 1971–74

Ike Morris, 1947

Mark Morrison, 1990–94

Don Morton, 1981

John Moshelle, 1956

Bob Mullen, 1977–80 (MVP 1978)

Greg Mullen, 1978–79

Jim Muller,* 1976–79

Scott Munnoch, 1981

Jim Murphy, 1968–71, 1974

Ken Naples, 1961

Marsh Nicholishen, 1961, 1963–64

Pete Nicholson, 1953–55

Colin Nickerson, 1975

Mike Nihmey, 1967–68

Bayne Norrie,* 1962–67 (MVP 1966–67, co-capt. 1967)

Chris Nowakoski, 1957

Mark Oakley, 1980–84

Joe O'Brien, 1953

Mike O'Connor, 1976

Bob O'Doherty,* 1974–78

Ross O'Doherty, 1980–82

Bud Ohike, 1946

Al Orr, 1947

Derek Orr, 1967–68

Mike O'Shaughnessy, 1973–74

Peter Ostrom, 1974

Peter Pain, 1989–92

Joe Pal, 1969–73

Vince Panetta, 1985–88

Kevin Parker, 1991–95

Ken Parkinson, 1947–48

Brian Parnega,* 1963–66, 1968–69

Jack Parry, 1945

Dick Pasloski, 1959

James Paterson, 1990–93

Mike Patterson, 1982–85

Dan Pawliw, 1988–91

Russ Payson, 1964–66

Stu Pearce, 1945, 1947

Jeff Peat, 1946

Jim Pendergast, 1980–83

Tim Pendergast, 1988–92 (co-capt. 1990)

Bo-Bo Penner, 1949–51

Darrell Penner,* 1972–76 (co-capt. 1975)

Glen Penwarden, 1965–68

John Perry, 1955

Mike Pettit, 1956, 1960–61

Norm Pfenning, 1981, 1983–84

Dick Pierce, 1958

Pierre Pinard, 1968–70

Larry Plancke, 1965–67

Pat Plishka, 1975–79 (co-capt. 1979)

Don Plumley, 1958–62

Kent Plumley, 1958–62 (co-capt. 1959)

Sam Poaps, 1957–60

Frank Poce, 1964–66

Bruce Pollock, 1973–74

Steve Porter, 1982–86

Ted Porter, 1945–47

Terry Porter,* 1958–62 (MVP 1959,
    co-capt. 1962)

Bruce Potter, 1971–73

Guy Potvin, 1963–67

Al Poutanen, 1953

Bob Pow, 1956

Kerry Powell, 1974–76

Wayne Powell, 1969–70

Ian Press, 1986

Hal Pringle, 1947

Fred Prinzen, 1978–80

Rick Prinzen, 1981–84

Merv Pritchard, 1945

Myles Pritchard, 1979–80

John Quinn, 1960–62

Karl Quinn, 1955–57 (co-capt. 1957)

Peter Quinn, 1960–62

Rusty Radchuk, 1955–56

Chuck Ramaden, 1951

Don Rasmussen, 1960–63 (capt. 1963)

Laird Rasmussen, 1960–63

Peter Raudzena, 1962

John Redfern, 1956–57

Mark Redfern, 1975

Pete Redfern, 1955

Joe Reeve, 1958

Dave Richards, 1956, 1958–59

Moe Richardson, 1948–50

Chris Rick, 1985–87

Robin Ritchie, 1958–62

Don Robb,* 1958–60 (co-capt. 1960)

Dave Roberts, 1980–81

Jack Roberts,* 1949–53 (capt. 1952)

Glen Robinson, 1963–65

Mark Robinson, 1990–94 (co-capt.
    1994)

Arthur Rochette, 1969–70

Mark Roe, 1978

Claude Root, 1955

Don Rorwick, 1989–93 (co-capt. 1992–
    93)

Brian Rose, 1970–71

Harold Rose, 1961–63

Mike Ross, 1987–90

Rob Rowe, 1990

Ron Roy, 1953–56

John Rudan, 1974–75

Chris Ruskay, 1985–88

Jim Rutka,* 1977–78

Peter Sabiston, 1973–74

Pete Saegert, 1959

Chuck Safrance, 1955–57

Barry St George, 1973

Moe St Martin, 1973–76, 1979 (co-capt.
    1976)

Andy Sakell, 1972–73

Pete Salari, 1948–50 (MVP 1948, 1950)

Bruce Salder, 1949

Rod Sanderson, 1966

Hank Sandlos, 1951–52

Doug Sapsford, 1968–69

Sam Sawchuck, 1953

Mike Schad,* 1982–85

Ron Schmidt, 1980–82

Gary Schreider,* 1953–55

Gary Schreider, Jr, 1978–81

Clair Sellens, 1953–55

Paul Senyshyn, 1985–88 (co-capt. 1988)

Raold Serebrin, 1971–73

Dennis Sharp, 1958–59

Mike Sharp, 1969–70

Andy Shaw, 1961–63

Dave Shaw, 1986

Jim Shea, 1966, 1969–70

Jim Shearn, 1958–59

Francis Sheridan, 1978–79

Sam Sheridan, 1949–50

Jim Sherritt, 1967–71

Greg Sherwin, 1977

Blaine Shore,* 1975–79

Paul Shugart, 1975–79

Tom Shultz, 1969–70

Gord Simester, 1960–62

Hank Simola, 1948–50

Jack Simous, 1953

John Simpson, 1953

Peter Sirko, 1981–82

Bill Sirman, 1961–62

Jack Sisson, 1949–50, 1952

Dave Skene,* 1958–62 (MVP 1960,
   capt. 1961, co-capt. 1962)

Ken Skeoch, 1968–69

Larry Small, 1974–77 (co-capt. 1976)

Bob Smiciklas, 1987–88

Don Smith, 1971–72

Lorne Smith, 1946

Rob Smith, 1981

Rod Smith, 1979

Dave Sonshine, 1960

John Sopinka, 1952

Peter Sops, 1976–78

Jim Southey, 1945–46

Bob Spencer, 1989–90

Nick Speropoulos, 1947, 1949

Gord Squires, 1968–72 (co-capt. 1972)

Sam Stankovic, 1989–90

B. Starr, 1967

Gary Steen, 1964

Chris Stefopulos, 1985–88

Tom Stefopulos, 1980–84

Jerry Steinberg, 1957

Rob Steller, 1986–89

Bob Stevens,* 1945–48 (capt. 1946,
   MVP 1947)

Ross Steves, 1947

Bruce Stewart, 1963–64

Ron Stewart,* 1953–57 (MVP 1954,
   1956–57)

Stephen Stewart, 1985–86

John D. Stirling, 1966–68

Scott Stirling, 1980, 1983

Mike Stoneham, 1969–70

Al Strader, 1966–69

Al Stretton, 1973–74

Gary Strickler,* 1959–61 (co-capt. 1959–
   60, MVP 1961)

Andy Stubbert, 1984–85

Ron Suksi, 1950–51

Steve Surman, 1964–66

Bill Surphlis, 1954–56

Robert Sutherland, 1942–44

Joel Swenor, 1989

Owen Switzer, 1946

Keith Taggart, 1972–76

Jim Tait, 1966–69 (co-capt. 1969)

Mike Tait,* 1990

Ken Takasaki, 1957–58

Mark Tayles, 1979–80

Johathan Taylor, 1993–95

Tom Taylor, 1970–74

Jim Telford, 1955

Rusty Thoman, 1954–56

Bill Thompson, 1971–72

Brad Thompson, 1978

Jocko Thompson,* 1954–58 (capt. 1958)

John Thompson, 1983–86

Kevin Thompson, 1975–76

Peter Thompson,* 1959–64 (MVP 1962)

Scott Thompson, 1985–86

Steve Thompson, 1974

Brian Timmis, 1952

Rob Timpson, 1984

Frank Tindall, Jr, 1960–61

Brian Titley, 1974–75

Brian Todd, 1959, 1961

John Tovee, 1972–75

Courtney Treleavan, 1987–90

Richard Trenker, 1981

Bill Truelove, 1957–58

Noel Trumpour, 1979

Stan Trzop, 1955, 1957

Mike Tureski, 1956

Jim Turnbull, 1967–69

Ted Tyczka, 1975–79

Emil Uhrynuk, 1952

Vic Uzbalis, 1952, 1955

Joe Valente, 1980–84

Rick Van Buskirk, 1966–69

Bob Vanderwater, 1974–77

John Varcoe, 1950–51

John Vernon, 1977–78

Mike Vickers, 1957

Joe Visocchi, 1971

Todd Vokes, 1993

John Waddell, 1971–74 (co-capt. 1974)

Walt Waddell, 1950–52

George Wade, 1968

Jerry Wagar, 1946–47

Rob Walcot, 1983

John Walcott, 1948

Doug Walker, 1967–70

Lee Wallace, 1964–66

Kyle Wanzel, 1990–93

Tim Wardrop, 1976–79

Jim Ware, 1962–64

John Ware, 1958–60

Mike Warren, 1977

Brian Warrender, 1968–72 (co-capt. 1971–72)

Mitch Wasik, 1956–58

Bob Watson, 1960

Graham Weatherby, 1986

John Welton, 1949

Garry West, 1961–62

Brian Wherrett, 1954–56

Gary White, 1964

Dave Whiteside, 1968–73 (capt. 1973)

Mike Wicklum, 1958–60

Dean Wilcox, 1984–85

Bruce Williams, 1946

Dave Wilson, 1955–59 (co-capt. 1957)

John Wilson, 1976–80 (co-capt. 1980)

Bert Winnett, 1964

John Wintermeyer, 1973

Pete Wityk, 1958, 1960–61

Dave Wood, 1945

Jeff Wood, 1976

Lloyd Woods, 1947–48

Peter Woolhouse, 1964–65

Doug Woolley, 1949–50

Bob Wright,* 1979–83

Dan Wright, 1989–92

Fred Wright, 1951

Terry Wright, 1976–77

Jeff Yach, 1989–92

John Yach, 1984–85

Don Young, 1985–86

Jim Young,* 1962–64 (MVP 1964)

Ron Young, 1956–57

Steve Yovetich, 1988–92

Ken Zagrodney, 1983

Randy Zarichny, 1986–90 (co-capt. 1988)

Pete Zarry, 1952–53

Don Zondag, 1986, 1988

Hank Zuzek, 1953–54

Jack Zwirewich, 1951, 1953

Notes

INTRODUCTION

1 I am very much indebted in what follows to three graduating essays written for the bachelor's program at the School of Physical and Health Education at Queen's: Bally, "Developmental Changes in Rugby Football," Harvey-Kean, "Ontario Rugby," and Lougheed, "Rugby at Queen's." All traced the history of the game as part of their additional interests in "rugger" as it is called, especially in North America (elsewhere, it is mostly still "rugby"). These essays were invaluable. Regrettably, like the bachelor theses in most other faculties, such essays are no longer being written, a sacrifice to increased enrolments, reductions in professors' pay and time, and a general disinclination on the part of students to want to write.

2 Wakefield and Marshall, *Rugger*.

3 There is also evidence that the Micmac and certain other North American tribes had a similar game (Jenness, *The Indians of Canada*).

4 Owen, *History of Rugby Football Union*.

5 Ibid., and Herbert, *Rugby*.

6 Marples, *History of Football*.

7 Bally, "Developmental Changes in Rugby Football."

8 Wymar, *Sport in England*, and others.

9 Harvey-McKean, "Ontario Rugby."

10 Danzig, *Oh How They Played the Game*.

11 Harvard played McGill in 1874 in the first recorded intercollegiate game involving a Canadian university. (Some sources suggest that this was the first normal rugby game in North America, not the Princeton-Rutgers game of 1869.) McGill, of course, had played before this, as early as 1865 on the record (Cosentino, *Canadian Football*).

12 Calvin, *Queen's University, 1841–1941*; Neatby, *And Not to Yield, 1841–1917*; Gibson, *To Serve and Yet Be Free, 1917–1961*.

13 One that particularly interested the author was what football players "became" after they left the university. Did they, as a group, go on to be "doctors, lawyers, and kings," or did they settle into "less socially valued" occupations? Were they better, worse, or about the same as a representative group of other graduates from their time? An attempt will be made to assess this in the conclusion.

14 See, for example, C. Scilley, "A Not-So-Warm Homecoming," Kingston *Whig-Standard*, 23 October, 1993, 23.

15 See appendix A for a complete statistical summary of the game for the years 1893–1994.

16 Chapter 1 will, of course, have a great deal to say about these first years, but not in a statistical way.

17 The word "senior" is needed because, in certain periods during these years, there were intermediate and/or junior teams representing Queen's (e.g., the Comets during the 1950s who played RMC, Balmy Beach, and others). Their record is not included here, though they are mentioned in the narrative where appropriate.

18 The leagues that Queen's played in vary somewhat over the period in question. Also, nationally, it played for the Dominion championship, then the Grey Cup, and later still the Vanier Cup. If it won *any* league championship and/or any national championship, that is counted as a championship season.

19 While Queen's has marginally the best record on an absolute basis, the University of Western Ontario, which started much later (in 1929), has the best percentage record of all, having had 24 championship seasons since then to Queen's 16 and Varsity's 12.

20 A perusal of appendix C will show that these interviewees include many of the better-known living ex-players of the Gaels. An effort was made to choose as representative a sample of them as possible, i.e., to reflect all eras of the team, a variety of positions (backs, line, offence, defence), and as varied a group of personalities as could be obtained (extroverts and introverts, big guys and little guys, touch guys and punters).

CHAPTER ONE

1 *Queen's Journal*, 25 October 1882, 9–11.
2 Ibid., 8 November 1882, 16.
3 Ibid., 22.
4 Garvock, "How Rugby Began."
5 *Queen's Journal*, 5 March 1884, 106–7.
6 Ibid., 110.
7 Garvock, "How Rugby Began," 165.
8 Neatby, *And Not to Yield*, 131. Much of the discussion here follows Neatby's treatment of the period.

9 Garvock, "How Rugby Began," 167.

10 Indeed, by 1888, with the culmination of the Jubilee Campaign (linked both to Queen Victoria's golden jubilee and to the upcoming fiftieth anniversary of the university), Queen's was on a much better financial footing, having doubled in size since 1880 to about four hundred students, and it was starting another building, Carruthers Hall.

11 *Queen's Journal*, 5 November 1881, 2.

12 Cosentino, *Canadian Football*, 13–14.

13 Garvock, "How Rugby Began," 164.

14 Ibid.

15 Ibid., 164–7.

16 There is, in fact, a good deal more of the modern "rugger" (i.e., rugby union) in the description.

17 See Lester, *Stagg's University.*

18 The fact that Strange was not a student – and that this was allowed – indicates that "town and gown" were actively involved in fielding a good team. This practice of a mixed team would was to continue until the formation of the Intercollegiate Union in 1898, when only students were permitted to play. Obviously, the contribution of the town in support of the team has continued down to modern times, albeit in a different form.

19 Garvock, "How Rugby Began," 164.

20 Hamilton, *Queen's, Queen's, Queen's.*

21 Calvin, *Queen's University at Kingston*, 282.

22 See, for example, the Kingston *Daily British Whig* for Friday, Saturday, and Monday, 24–7 November, 1893, under the front-page headlines "Great Football Score: Queen's Wins Championship of Canada" and "The Champions at Home," and references in the text such as: "News of the Queen's victory in Montreal received with delight and clamouring in Kingston" and "Arrangements were speedily made, almost every piece of material of red, yellow and blue shade was captured, hacks hired, omnibus' rented and the freedom of the city taken for granted." It was reported that "the boys were good specimens of the manly integrity, honour and muscle of Queen's." Guy Curtis, the captain, spoke at City Hall, as did Principal Grant, the mayor, a senator, and others. And Rev. MacGillivray gave a sermon on the lessons to be learned from the Queen's victory. It was front-page news, in detail, in the Monday evening edition of the *Daily British Whig.* Oriard, in his book on the influence of newspapers on the development of football in the United States, argues that this type of concentration on the achievements of a college football team by the press was typical of journalism in this period. The "yellow press" of Joseph Pulitzer and William Randolph Hearst combined naturally with the mayhem of football to produce heroic myth, parallels to war, and numerous other metaphors that we understand today. See Oriard, *Reading Football.*

23 See *Queen's Review*, October 1930, 325.

24 Malcolm ("19th Century Bo Jackson") reports that by the time Curtis "played his last game for Queen's in 1901, he had led the university to at least a dozen major titles, as well as to three unsuccessful appearances in the Stanley Cup final."

25 *Queen's Review*, October 1930, 251.

26 Malcolm, "19th Century Bo Jackson," 12.

27 *Queen's Review*, October 1930, 251.

28 He died in 1930 at the age of sixty-one and is buried in Delta, where he was an innkeeper from the time he left Queen's until his death.

29 *Queen's Journal*, 7 November 1896, 5.

30 Ibid., 1 December 1894.

31 There will be more about the evolution of the game itself during this period at the beginning of chapter 2. What is worth noting is that an attempt to maintain the old English rugby game (or even the game as it was evolving there) in the face of the new North American game proved difficult. Rugby, "English style," vanished for a while in the 1890s, reappeared in several places up to the First World war, stopped during the war, and then reappeared in only token form at the universities (McGill and University of Toronto). Queen's joined the Intercollegiate *English* Rugby Union in 1932. The game was also played in several city leagues in the interwar period, but all play again stopped with the Second World War. It was resumed after the war, once more at the universities of McGill and Toronto, and it slowly began to diffuse out into the city leagues and private prep schools (for example, Upper Canada College). Queen's began to play it again in the fall of 1960 and has enjoyed considerable success in recent times, winning the intercollegiate championships with monotonous regularity since 1985 (Harvey-McKean, "Ontario Rugby," and Lougheed, "Rugby at Queen's").

32 The trophy for the CIRFU championship, the Yates Cup (donated by Dr H.B. Yates of McGill) is the oldest annually awarded football trophy in Canada (Cosentino, *Canadian Football*).

33 Bumsted, *The Peoples of Canada*.

34 Ibid., 52.

35 One of the questions that will be considered later concerns the economics of football at Queen's over the years – the revenues vs. expenses. A careful review of the "Annual Reports of the Principal," the minutes of the Board of Trustees, and the actual daily journal financial entries over the entire period 1882–1914 yielded no explicit references to any revenues or expenses associated directly with the football team. Athletic fees were levied for all students to support the gym and other activities. Some of this probably found its way to the football team but was either not recorded or the records were made at a lower level of accounting and then thrown out. Alternatively, some money

may have flowed directly through the principal's office (Principal Grant himself paid the gas bills of the university over a certain period!) but again there is no record as such, only pure conjecture given his evident interest in football. That some money other than the players' covered expenses is clear from Curtis's letter (regarding expenses being covered by the Canadian Union). But it was likely little more than travelling expenses (if at all) and the provision of a uniform. Revenues from spectators only began after the war with the erection of Richardson Stadium in 1921 and the ability thereafter to control admission to the games.

36 The *Journal* was considerably exercised, as were others struggling with the important question of amateurism versus professionalism in the sport in the 1906–08 period:

> We are surprised to learn from outside sources that at Queen's the students are clamouring for the services of a professional coach … For the edification of those whom it may concern, we render the assurance that the desire for anything but an amateur coach does not exist in the minds of the students … On the question of professional coaching it is almost impossible to generalize. To pay a man to teach rugby men the art of disabling opponents and other forms of roughness is utterly bad. A man who will earn a living by this means is moreover unfit to be the preceptor of college men in any regard.

The *Journal* does go on to allow that if the coach is also the athletic director or "has other means of support" (Camp at Yale and the Harvard coach are given as examples), or "is a young man whose life has been clean and pure" (apparently a characteristic of the McGill coach in those days!), it was prepared to make an exception. But it is clear that there were few worse names than "professional" that could be used in respect of an athlete at the time.

37 Neatby, *And Not to Yield*, 291. Much of what follows is also based on Neatby, 291 ff.

CHAPTER TWO

1 Bumsted (*The People of Canada*, 175) reports that Stephen Leacock, writing as the McGill economist he was, for the *New York Times*, in the fall of 1919, estimated that "some seven million lives were sacrificed; eight million tons of shipping were sunk beneath the sea; some fifty million adult males were drawn from productive labour to the line of battle."

2 Ibid., 170. Bumsted goes on to remark: "Serving as the shock troops of the Empire, Canadians rapidly achieved a reputation for bravery and fierceness. They were continually thrown into the most difficult situations and performed well. The list of battles at which they fought heroically was a long one beginning at Ypres in 1915 and continuing through to the Belgium town

of Mons, where fighting ended for the Canadians at 11 a.m. on 11 November 1918."

3 Neatby, *And Not to Yield*, 299. Neatby notes that most of those in attendance were women and it is from this period that the strong presence of women in Queen's activities dates. For example, Charlotte Whitton, who became mayor of Ottawa, was the first woman editor of the *Journal* in 1917; the first two women professors were appointed (in the classics department), and so on.

4 Gibson, *To Serve and Yet Be Free*, 18.

5 This was due to a number of factors: a desire for social justice on the part of returning veterans, who would not easily settle into the docile labour role of the prewar period; a strong intention to share in the gains everyone knew would develop from the pent-up demand for output; and a new philosophy in the air, that of communism (the Bolsheviks had taken over in Russia in the last stages of the war), and more benignly, socialism (as seen, for example, in the efforts during the 1920s to unionize large segments of American labour).

6 McLeod, "Reminiscences," 13. McLeod, who was for years a professor of obstetrics and gynaecology at Queen's, played during the early 1920s and later wrote this article on football in the 1920s.

7 Ibid.

8 Cosentino, "Football," 151–2.

9 Ibid., 152. A short film clip of Queen's playing in the early twenties confirms the "Eastern Style" of play described by Cosentino. It was to dominate the Western approach until the official introduction of the forward pass in 1931, at which time the two distinct styles merged for the last time.

10 The University of Toronto was one of the earliest to field such a band. They wore no particular uniform. The first "Queen's" band (as opposed to bands who played the odd time at Queen's games) appeared in 1924. It was a pipe band with six or so members led by W.A. Watson (Meds '29). There had been a brass band at Queen's as early as 1905, whose members wore no uniform and marched to the games in a somewhat haphazard way. They became some-what more formalized during the 1920s but were still without uniforms, and they looked like poor cousins to the pipe band whose members supplied their own pipes and uniforms. See Queen's University, *Queen's Bands*.

11 The case of Professor Malcolm is an interesting one, for there is little doubt from the record that it was his considerable efforts that led to the renaissance of Queen's football in this period. Lindsay Malcolm (from Mitchell, Ontario) was a Queen's master's grad in math (in which he won the medal) who also took a degree in civil engineering at the university (and played briefly for the football team). He joined the faculty in that department in 1907. Overseas during the war, he rose to the rank of lieutenant-colonel commanding engineers. After the war he returned as professor of municipal and civil engineering. It was during this period that he designed and helped build the new

stadium (as well as the original hockey rink and the sanitary engineering building, helped with the new library, and otherwise occupied himself). That he was an avid football fan is reflected in the fact that he approached Principal Taylor in late 1919 to do something about the football situation (see *Queen's Journal*, 5 March 1920, 1); helped organize the alumni and students' support; coached the 1920 season until a full-time coach could be found; and brought the first full-time trainer to Queen's in 1920.

Once his job was done, he moved on to other things, teaching, acting as a town planner for Guelph, Stratford, and other places, and being very active in professional engineering circles on both sides of the border. In 1937 he finished his PHD in civil engineering at Cornell University. The following year they appointed him director of the School of Civil Engineering there. He died in Ithaca, N.Y., in February 1948. To say that Lindsay Malcolm was a force in his lifetime is to understate the record dramatically.

12 McLeod, "Reminiscences," 14. As in later years (until the intermediate team was abolished in the early 1960s), players did not usually play for the senior team in their first year. When there was a particularly good crop of rookies, the intermediates could sometimes beat the seniors. It also meant, as it did in the fall of 1920, better times for the senior team in succeeding years.

13 His Hamilton links also opened the way to the arrival of several Hamilton-area players such as Batstone and Leadlay.

14 McLeod, "Reminiscences."

15 "Editorial," *Queen's Journal*, 10 October 1922, 2. It has been some time since "fans crowded the stand and bleachers every afternoon to watch the practices."

16 McLeod, "Reminiscences," 14.

17 There is an interesting and ironic tale here, for Awrey was not present at the end of the season having fallen seriously ill (he had been sick all season but the condition worsened noticeably) just before the last regular game against Varsity (which Queen's lost 25–1). Queen's was desperate and tried to hire Shaughnessy for the remainder of the season. McGill said no, so Shaughnessy recommended W.P. (Bill) Hughes, who had coached the Montreal entry in the city league that year (the famous Montreal Amateur Athletic Association's "Winged Wheelers" were by that time out of the contest). Hughes lost "the shocker" with only two days' preparation, but over the next week, within the secrecy of the Jock Hardy Arena, he put in a whole new offence (in effect the Winged Wheeler system), got the university to buy new cleats for the team, and then went to the playoff against Varsity on neutral ground in Montreal. Varsity never knew what hit them. As a result, Awrey never did get his job back. Bill Hughes stayed on until the mid-1920s and established a Queen's record which has never been matched. There is a wonderful account of this aspect of the 1922 season in McGowan's column in the *Montreal Star*, 15 September 1951.

18 McLeod rightly points out that of the eighteen players regularly permitted to dress for a game (everyone played both ways, and six substitutes were designated), nine were originally from Kingston, quite an impressive concentration of football talent in so small a city as Kingston at that time; also, nine were in medicine (eleven in 1923, ten in 1924).

19 The next longest is thirteen in a row set by the 1963 and 1964 teams, which were undefeated over two seasons in regular and playoff games.

20 Queen's substituted liberally at the end of the Regina game, and McLeod recorded in his "Reminiscences" that "a telegram was sent to their [Regina's] home club congratulating them on the type of players they had and remarking that the score did not give full credit to their play." By now it should be clear that McLeod is capable of considerable understatement.

21 As well, the Queen's intermediates won the intermediate championship of Canada that year. The season of 1924 was of note for two other reasons: Bill Hughes, of Queen's, first used films of games to analyse past results and prepare future strategy; and it would be the last Grey Cup a university team ever won.

22 Queen's had 1,200 students, of whom 900 were men, in 1924.

23 Clark: "Where Is the Secret of Queen's Success?" 1.

24 Ibid.

25 The new constitution of the Athletic Board of Control gave it the right "to receive and disburse all monies ... for athletic purposes at the university" (section 36), and gave the director of athletics administrative control of the board (section 4). Thus all accounting was done at the level of the Athletic Board of Control (which was to report to the Alma Mater Society [AMS]) and no entries appear anywhere either in the university's daily journal or in the audited university statements for athletics (except for one entry each year in the 1920s – for football trophies, $300). Unfortunately (or fortunately ...), there are no Athletic Board of Control records for this period. A report was made to the AMS each year, but the AMS minutes just note the fact and the general content (e.g., how each team had done, etc.). As mentioned in the text, this was also true of the principal's report and the Board of Trustees' minutes during the early 1920s.

  In early 1926, the *Queen's Journal* (5 February 1926) reported that the "finances were in a hazardous state" with every sport, including football – "the one which had always been profitable" – losing money. (It had finally received a financial report from the Athletic Board of Control.) Steps were taken to ensure proper public accounting, and by the next year the *Journal* was able to report: "The financial side of Queen's athletics is in a better state than it has been for many years ... A profit of sixteen thousand dollars was made on the activities of the fall term ... Football is responsible for practically all the profit shown, and of this, ten thousand dollars was derived from the Senior Intercollegiate

Play-off. Most of the other sports do not pay for themselves" (*Queen's Journal*, 28 January 1927). This $10,000 in 1927 would be about $95,000 in 1995 dollars – a healthy gate. Cosentino reports that Queen's cut from the record attendance at the Eastern final against Hamilton in Varsity Stadium in 1924 was $7,250 (or about $69,000 in 1995 dollars). Fortunately, as we shall see, better records are available in the archives from the 1930s, so that a judgment can be made on the exact details of the football operation. The figures that are available, though, suggest that it was very remunerative to the university.

26 See Danzig, *Oh How They Played the Game*. The *Queen's Journal* (27 November 1928) reported that the famous Heisman (of Heisman Trophy fame), in a speech given at Queen's, actually "ripped aside the curtain of secrecy about professionalism in college football" to reveal that this was common practice. Indeed, athletic scholarships developed as a way of curbing the worst excesses of this earlier system.

27 Certain big American college teams did decide to do this (e.g., the University of Chicago which was a Big Ten power in the 1920s) but not until the 1930s. See Lester, *Stagg's University*.

28 Gibson, *To Serve and Yet Be Free*, 71–2.

29 See n25 above.

30 Throughout this period of the late 1920s, several "old boys" games were played (graduates against the senior team for that year). The old boys always won, principally because of Leadlay, but also because Campbell and the other non-pros from the early 1920s could be counted on for good games.

31 *Queen's Journal*, November 1929, 6.

32 Gibson, *To Serve and Yet Be Free*.

33 Football players were elected to many of the most important student government posts in the 1920s, e.g., McKelvey and Carson were also AMS presidents, Batsone was athletic stick and a member of the Athletic Board of Control, and Douglas Skelton of the mid-20s won a Rhodes Scholarship (1926).

CHAPTER THREE

1 Bumsted, *The Peoples of Canada*, 186.

2 Recall that this is in a period before UI, welfare, old age security, CPP and the various other federal "social security" programs we now enjoy.

3 Internationally, the Depression led, of course, to the rise of the fascists, Mussolini in Italy and Hitler in Germany, whose solution to the crisis was based on military expenditures and social cohesiveness.

4 Gibson (*To Serve and Yet Be Free*, 93–6) estimates that the University lost one-seventh of its 1929–30 income due to endowment and the grant reductions by 1935 and could not make up the difference in fees, despite the fee increases and the fact that enrolments held up better than expected.

5 Much as it continues to be today: it is said that Queen's seldom if ever runs a deficit and that when it does, the deficit is never large, nor is it there the following year.

6 Also of note in 1930 was the fact that the first Eastern game was played under the lights (29 October 1930).

7 Cosentino, *Canadian Football*, 93.

8 Shaughnessy (back at McGill in 1931) felt that it would eventually "open up the game as a whole and bear down on the mass formations we have had in the past" (Cosentino, *Canadian Football*, 94).

9 Stevens went on to lead the Montreal Amateur Athletic Association to the Grey Cup with his passing (defeating Western along the way 22–0) causing an uproar about the presence of imports in the Canadian game. It was to be the start of a long debate, which continues down to the present in connection with the professional game. The *Journal* agitated early in the season for an American assistant to Batstone "to teach the boys the American game," but the movement died out as it became clear that the pass was having little influence on the university game even at McGill.

10 It is not clear why Burt was replaced after only one season, though the *Journal* in a late March 1933 editorial makes oblique reference to "poor coaching" being a problem during the 1932 season. There is no doubt that Reeve was much more suited by personality to Queen's than Burt was – Reeve being a bon vivant of the first order while Burt was a rather humourless disciplinarian.

11 There would also be the few who saw that he was not as good a student of the game as he might or should have been, or who did not take to him personally. But they respected his ability both to play the game himself and to win as a coach in spite of his philosophy about football, which stressed defence and was probably more limited than it need have been (especially as regards offence and the role of the forward pass). But they were the few. Most saw him as a kind of 1930s arch-hero, an anchor in very troubled times, and honoured him for it during the rest of their lives. There is, for example, the Ted Reeve Memorial Fund at Queen's, which was organized by Johnny Munro and to which many well-known Canadian sports personalities have contributed (including Conn Smythe, Jack Kent Cooke, and John Bassett). It is currently under the direction of Jimmy Hughes, a 1950s Gael.

12 Edwards, "The Fearless Fourteen," 7.

13 Gibson, in his official history of the university, notes that freshman enrolments held up because young men unable to find employment were sent to university (actually an observation of Hilda Laird, the dean of Women) but that the number of seniors declined as the Depression worsened because their money ran out or because they took a job if they saw one (Gibson, *To Serve and Yet Be Free*, 103). These were desperate times and any chance to trade football skills for a living maintenance and a university degree was jumped at if it was at all competitive with what the city teams were offering (Sarnia, for

example, was supported by the chemical companies, which provided players jobs).

14 Or at least part of it did! There can be no doubt that Fyfe, the outsider, either understood little about this or chose to ignore it as a minor aggravation compared to his bigger problems during the Depression. But it was clearly the Athletic Board of Control's policy that football would once again flourish. McGinnis, for example, bought the band its first uniforms during this period.

15 Hamilton, *Queen's, Queen's, Queen's*, 148.

16 Gibson, *To Serve and Yet Be Free*, 106.

17 Canadian sportswriters that year voted it the most thrilling sports event of the year in Canada (Hamilton, *Queen's, Queen's, Queen's*), and the Board of Trustees voted Reeve a present of $100 for the purchase of furniture for his new home "because he was so good-humoured and loyal when the ban deprived him of four useful players" (Gibson, *To Serve and Yet Be Free*).

18 Edwards, "The Fearless Fourteen," 8.

19 There were several others who worked out with the team, but these were the fourteen who played.

20 Edwards and Munro, personal interviews (see appendix C).

21 Edwards, personal interview.

22 This happened often in Reeve's time, so much so that he came to take credit for it in his column, writing of how "the goalpost play – the flower of McGuffey's genius" (McGuffey being one of Reeve's sobriquets for himself) was put in to block a McGill placement (Hamilton, *Queen's, Queen's, Queen's*, 154).

23 Gibson, *To Serve and Yet Be Free*, 145.

24 Ibid.

25 The 1936–37 academic year saw, for example, the first presence of AMS "constables" to keep order at events. It was also the first year for Colour Night, an event that at first recognized not only sporting but also non-athletic achievements (and would lead shortly to the Tricolour Society Awards for important student contributions to campus life).

26 Edwards (personal interview) reports that Jimmy Bews had given some classes in physical training (he also helped the football team in this respect – today he would be called the fitness coach) but that he was a mason by trade. Edwards was the first full-time, trained, named, and paid director of physical education at a Canadian university. In that respect, Wallace was very forward-looking in his approach to athletics. He just didn't like football all that much.

27 Reeve, "The 1937 Football Team." This little piece is a nice example of Reeve's literary style.

28 "Athletics," *Queen's Review*, December 1937, 289.

29 Ibid.

30 Thus in the five consecutive yearly playoffs between Queen's and Varsity over the years 1933–37, Queen's won three (8–7, 6–4, 7–6) and Varsity two, the total points for and against being 38–27 in Varsity's favour.

31 It is clear from other sources that Roosevelt, like the leaders of all the democracies, was by this time very worried about Hitler's actions in Europe, the brutal-
ities of the Spanish Civil War, Japanese expansionism, and other evidence that
a large war might be at hand. Indeed, thirteen months after Roosevelt's convo-
cation address at Queen's, Germany invaded Poland to start the Second World
War.

32 Gibson, *To Serve and Yet Be Free*, 180.

33 As is well known, it came sooner. The famous French Maginot Line collapsed
before the German blitzkrieg in a few short weeks in 1940, leaving Britain
alone by mid-June and very much in need of its Canadian friends.

34 While with the Argos, Tindall had helped his friend Warren Stevens coach
Varsity. He was also well liked by Reeve. As noted above, they were in many
ways similar personalities. Both recommended him to Queen's. Wallace liked
Tindall straight off. After interviewing him for the position, he remarked, "I
don't know anything about football, but I know a man when I see one"
(Hamilton, *Queen's, Queen's, Queen's*, 165).

35 This would leave George Carson, elected captain of the 1940 team in the
spring, the only undefeated, unscored-on captain in Queen's history (as he
pointed out in his interview).

36 If one thinks of the interwar years as a whole, the team won 73 games, losing
50 (with 4 ties); it won 10 championships in 21 years; and it had only 5 losing
seasons during that time. That is quite a record.

37 Gibson, *To Serve and Yet Be Free*, 180.

CHAPTER FOUR

1 Gibson, *To Serve and Yet Be Free*, 188. Gibson remarks that it was "a grey and
forbidding world" by 1942. Failures, for example, were not tolerated; all those
who failed were expelled or reported to the military authorities under an
agreement which allowed university students to keep studying during the war
(due to the "complex technological nature and needs of modern war") but
required them to take military training while there, and certainly not to "hide
behind the university shield" (as it were) to avoid one's military obligations.
Failing but continuing to enrol and simply repeating years for the duration was
thus not tolerated by society. It must be remembered that all of this was in the
absence of conscription (until very late in the war); it is a comment on the
cohesiveness of Canadian society in these years around one's social obligations in times of war.

2 Bumstead, *The Peoples of Canada*, 201. Gibson reports that "more than 3000
Queen's graduates and students enlisted … Of this number, 168 had been
killed or died on active service. They had won 268 honours and decorations
including the Victoria Cross awarded to Major John Weir Foote, Arts '36" (*To
Serve and Yet Be Free*, 256).

3 Such legislation was much in favour at the time, for example, in Britain following on the work of Beveridge and others.

4 Gibson, *To Serve and Yet Be Free*, 250.

5 Ibid., 253.

6 Ibid.

7 Al Lenard (in a personal interview) recalled Munsson arriving at his house in Toronto in a limousine with a box of chocolates for Lenard's wife. Lenard had played Big Four football in Hamilton in 1940–42 and again in 1945 after service in the navy. He decided to return to university rather than play in Winnipeg (to which he had been traded after the 1945 season) and chose Queen's over the University of Toronto for reasons only partly related to that box of chocolates. He remained at the university, in various athletic-related capacities, until his retirement in the 1980s.

8 Edwards, personal interview.

9 C. Tindall, personal interview.

10 Gibson, *To Serve and Yet Be Free*, 252.

11 As before in Queen's history, "incentives" other than boxes of chocolates came into play. Tuition and rent would on occasion be paid by local alumni (e.g., "the doctors"), especially to veterans with families to support who might otherwise find it difficult to cope (or more advantageous to go elsewhere). But the sense was that it was always highly selective and never for large amounts of money (with one exception in 1955, as we shall see below).

12 It is also puzzling in that the intermediate team (and on occasion the junior team, for Queen's sometimes fielded three teams in these years) called the Comets and coached by Edwards (of 1930s fame) often won its championship, as it did, for example, in 1949. Indeed, as in the 1920s, the intermediate team occasionally beat the senior team. Unlike the 1920s, however, these good results did not seem to carry up into the senior team in subsequent years until into the 1950s.

13 McCarney, personal interview.

14 A good friend of Tabby Gow, the man who would become the trainer of the team in the late 1960s, Leaman made it a part of his routine to visit the stadium every day, to see all the games home and away, and eventually to do yeoman service for the team doctors, water boys, Tabby himself, and any players who might on the occasion need the services of a "shepherd" who was a proven teetotaller.

15 For many of those same years, this was all done at Berry's personal expense and as a contribution to Queen's by Novish's company in Montreal.

16 Gibson, *To Serve and Yet be Free*, 300.

17 This crew included other well-known Kingston characters, such as Stan Smallridge, Azel Plane, Tommy Partis, and later Harv Milne and Bill Duncan.

18 Indeed, inasmuch as Doug Hargreaves played a season in 1951 and would become the head coach from 1976 to 1994, it could well be said that the seeds

of Queen's success in football from that point down to the present were all
planted in the early 1950s.

19 Hamilton, *Queen's, Queen's, Queen's*, 122.

20 Ibid.

21 Hamilton uses the terms "mascot" and "good-luck charm" to describe Pierce,
but he was more than that. He was a symbol of both the continuity of the
Queen's tradition and its different nature from that of the big-city schools like
Varsity and McGill. Words such as "idiosyncratic," "jaunty," "self-assured,"
"tightly knit," "capable of any tomfoolery," "wild-eyed" come to mind as
descriptors of that "different nature."

22 Hamilton, *Queen's, Queen's, Queen's*, 124–5.

23 Ibid, 127.

24 The intermediates under Edwards as coach also won their championship that
year, as they had the previous year, and were finally beginning to contribute
in important ways to the senior club. Ashley (personal interview) reports that
the life of an intermediate player in this period (Ashley played only intermediate ball during his four years at Queen's) was also an enjoyable experience.
Edwards was a tough taskmaster but trained the clubs well. Tindall naturally
had first choice of players, so it was not always easy. By the time the fifties
were done, it was clear that so was intermediate ball. Platooning required
more players; the cost of equipment and travel was rising rapidly. Ultimately
(in 1961), the teams were combined into one large club, where those who did
not dress for the games were carried along throughout the season, called the
"Hamburg Squad," and practised with the team but did not play their own
independent schedule. It should be noted that Ashley graduated in honours
history, taught high school in St Catharines much of his career, coached football at that level, and is now retired and living in Kingston. He retains an
active interest in Queen's football and a passionate commitment to the option
as the only possible offensive system.

25 *Ottawa Business News*, July 1986, 10. They would become known as the Pony
Backfield (because of their size) or the Go-Go Gaels and were capable of
breaking games open with long touchdown runs from scrimmage or on kick
returns.

26 It will be recalled that a touchdown was worth five points in those times, the
convert one, as now.

27 *Queen's Review*, November 1955, 225.

28 Ibid., 226.

29 Ibid.

30 Hamilton, *Queen's, Queen's, Queen's*, 150.

31 The story of the principal actors in arranging this little escapade are well
known among an older circle of Queen's football supporters, some of whom
are still living. There were some murmurs of complaint from others in the

league at the time (an enterprising *London Free Press* reporter claimed to have found that Braccia was still registered at Temple, but Queen's was able to refute this), but Braccia clearly qualified as a student, and the practice of "payments under the table" (Braccia reportedly received about $3,000) was sufficiently widespread that "kettles could not risk calling pots black." It was done that one time only and not repeated – at least on that scale. As already noted, smaller "side payments" to players (at Queen's and elsewhere) was a fact of life in the league until the middle sixties.

32 Braccia returned to Philadelphia, was visited by Stewart, Schreider, and several others at various occasions over the years, and died very young of a heart attack while coaching basketball, a game at which he was also very good.

33 Moshelle was no Braccia. Found by Tindall, and a legitimate transfer student, he would last only the one season for academic reasons. During that season, Stewart would actually call the plays much of the time.

34 *Queen's Journal*, 20 November 1956, 4.

35 Gibson, *To Serve and Yet Be Free*, 413.

36 The surplus would have been considerably greater had the $2,500 charge for new lights in the stadium not been completely expensed in that year but instead been depreciated over a number of seasons.

37 The figures in appendix B, calculated later using more statistically comparable methods, indicate that the gap between the two was larger than realized at the time. That said, if Stewart had scored in 1957 at anything like his frequency of the previous four seasons, he would easily have surpassed Leadley.

38 *Queen's Review*, November 1957, 203.

39 Stewart was blessed with a "God-given physique." He invariably left his preseason training until very late, yet when he showed up he would be in better shape than anyone else. "It has to be genetic" (unnamed source!). Stewart retains that appearance to this day. Approaching sixty, he still looks capable of playing. No doubt, genes and also attitude are factors: Stewart was always known as a "nasty, tough character." Luck plays a role too.

CHAPTER FIVE

1 There are several points to be made. The first is that decades may not be the best basis of comparison. Another time frame one might adopt would be "the most successful run of years." On these grounds, a careful examination of appendix A also points to the sixties in that the period 1960–73 jumps out: the team went fourteen years in a row without a losing season and won six championships. Using a much shorter horizon such as five years, the best five-year record would be 1921–25 (all non-losing years, four of the five being championships) followed by a series of others (all non-losing, three of five being championships) including 1927–31, 1933–37, 1960–64, 1964–68, 1966–70, 1977–

81, and 1988–92. On many of these comparisons, the sixties again stand out. The second point to note is that one can take issue with the variables used to form the judgment or the weight given to them in an overall conclusion. Thus, it is likely best to put it this way: the bulk of the statistical evidence points to the sixties as being perhaps the most successful decade in Queen's football history, the twenties being a close second.

2 This is not to suggest that the Queen's coaching staff were not the best, or among the best. They clearly were. Rather, it is to indicate that they were not the main reason, for the coaching staff was essentially the same in the sixties as it had been in the fifties, when Queen's had won far less frequently.

3 Bumsted, *The Peoples of Canada*, 397.

4 McGill had changed coaches and had recruited strongly, especially for entry into its dentistry program (which was five years in length and promised longevity in its own special way). It had been particularly successful in finding a quarterback of considerable note, an American named Tom Skypeck, who was to cause Queen's no end of trouble over the three years 1960–62.

5 *Queen's Review*, November–December 1961, 160. This season of 1961 witnessed one of the more serious injuries that ever occurred in Queen's football history (Kerr, personal interview). Ironically, it involved Tindall's son, Frank junior, who essentially broke his neck. Fortunately, no damage was done to the spinal cord, but the accident ended a promising career. It is perhaps not surprising to learn that he went on to be an orthopaedic surgeon.

6 Terry Porter, who had played virtually every position for the team over his time at Queen's (which reached back to 1957), remembers with particular disgust this last game of his career. He and Skene (both subsequently medical doctors) were the only two left by this time playing both ways. "Dead tired, with all those seasons behind us, and to lose it that way at the end. It wasn't so good" (Porter, personal interview).

7 The tarnishing quality of the claim to back-to-back undefeated seasons brought about by the loss to the University of Alberta in an exhibition game at the end of the 1963 season is discussed at some length below.

8 *Queen's Review*, November–December 1963, 156.

9 There is an irony here: the father played for the last team to go undefeated (in the twenties), his son for the next one, forty years later.

10 *Queen's Review*, November–December 1963, 156.

11 Ibid.

12 Thus, part of the explanation was the calibre of the Western club. They were also well coached (by Gino Fracas, he of Western and 1954 Queen's nemesis fame); and the Gaels failed to make the necessary adjustments, especially on offence, perhaps because the field phones on the Gaels' side linking the bench with the spotter's booth failed to work throughout the game.

13 It is interesting to note that in a game a week later, between Toronto and St Francis Xavier (undefeated in the Maritime Conference that year), Toronto lost 19–13. This, coupled with the Queen's loss, indicated that college play elsewhere was beginning to reach the Intercollegiate standard. It also likely explains the formal beginning of nationwide post-season competition two years later with the Vanier Cup.

14 *Queen's Review*, November–December 1964, 151–3. Five Gaels were named to the all-Canadian team, Young was voted the league MVP, others were made all-star, and so on.

15 Arguably, they were also superior in this respect to almost all of the ones that followed, though this is always a matter of conjecture.

16 Hamilton, *Queen's, Queen's, Queen's*, 234. Hamilton reports that "Queen's, which had an agreement with the Government of Ontario to have 5,000 undergraduates and 600 graduate students by 1970–71 had already overrun this target"; and that the budget for running the university had tripled over the same period (from $5.7 million in 1961–62 to $17 million in 1967–68). He also observes, in a somewhat understated manner: "With the growth in numbers came a changing and even turbulent climate" (ibid.).

17 Ferguson and Arment, co-captains of the 1966 team, are difficult to characterize. "Free spirits," they were both old and new, Ferguson having done an undergraduate degree at Western (where he starred especially at basketball) before studying medicine at Queen's, while Arment, an American, had played some U.S. college ball and served in the military. Perhaps it is best simply to conclude that their leaving after the 1966 season completed the transition from the old to the new.

18 McCarney (personal interview) reports that the coaching staff regularly attended clinics in the United States (at Atlantic City, for example) over these years, as well as maintaining contact with Canadian professional clubs, especially Ottawa and Edmonton, all in an effort to remain current. They were also open to suggestions from players – as the author can attest, having encouraged McCarney in 1963 to try a four-man defensive front with a middle linebacker, an alignment then new in the NFL. It was adopted with considerable success and became part of the Queen's defensive package in the following years.

19 McCarney was driven to invent a new rain cleat (the "moose hoofs") which was marketed to professional clubs in Canada and the United States. It did not, however, make a difference to the team's fortunes in 1967.

20 The Ontario government had been systematically opening new universities and upgrading the status and facilities of older "near universities" to help relieve the pressure on the existing older Ontario universities, especially Toronto, Western, and Queen's (Bumsted, *The Peoples of Canada*, 366). Thus, for example, Brock, Waterloo, Trent, and others came into being, while McMaster,

Waterloo College, the Ontario Agricultural College at Guelph, and others found themselves elevated to university status. By the 1968 season, some of these new universities were quite large and were eager to play football and other sports against the older schools. McMaster, it will be recalled, had been particularly persistent since at least 1964.

21 *Queen's University Alumni Review*, November–December 1968, 149.

22 Ibid.

23 Ibid.

24 Feelings in Winnipeg against the team ran quite high. Climie and Bayne (personal interviews) reported several incidents of players and coaches being physically attacked in hotel lobbies and after the game.

25 However, both Climie and Bayne (personal interviews) stressed the overall balance of the team and its ability to make adjustments during the game, especially along the line where it was almost always outweighed but seldom outplayed. They also remarked on a certain sense of inevitability that began to develop in the team about winning, something others associated with championship teams have also noted: "It's almost as if we knew we were going to win."

26 *Queen's University Alumni Review*, November–December 1968, 149.

27 Kingston *Whig-Standard*, 18 February 1969.

28 Bayne, Climie, McCarney, and others, personal interviews.

29 Like Young of the early sixties, to whom he was often compared because of his ability to break open games with long runs or kick returns (Stewart is another point of comparison), Eamon remained at Queen's for only three seasons and thus would eventually be outdistanced in the all-time scoring derby by others with records based on more years of play (see appendix B).

30 *Queen's University Alumni Review*, November–December 1969, 149.

31 *Maclean's Reviews*, 1 November 1965, 70. The article goes on to suggest that "half the team works at Alcan or Fort Henry during the summer," implying that these "high-paying part-time jobs" were found by the school for the players; and it made similar allegations about jobs which must have been news to most of the players at Queen's at the time.

32 For an extremely interesting and personal account of Metras's time at Western, see the book written by his wife, *The Metras Years*. Metras came to Western in the 1930s when it was "three buildings and a stadium," coached the early Mustang football (and basketball) teams, and stayed, as noted, until 1969, much of the time as head football and basketball coach but also serving as director of athletics for a while. As has been noted, he was the very antithesis of Tindall – outspoken, stubborn, profane. But as his wife's book makes clear, this hid a deep inner concern for his players about which Tindall no doubt knew, for the men were good friends.

33 Lenard would be the only other one to mention, besides of course Braccia, and he did not play long enough or consistently enough at quarterback to challenge seriously this judgment of Connor's position.

34 See Young, *Dirty 30*.

35 Both Bayne and Lilles actually began their careers in the first half of the decade, namely in 1963. And while Lilles played from the start, it was not really until he was switched to offence in the 1964 season that he began to make his mark. Bayne did not really play until 1965 (and then as a flanker), and it was only when he came to quarterback in 1966 that his star began to rise.

36 Bayne, personal interview.

37 Ibid. Bayne is a most reflective and articulate individual, as the author can attest, having first met up with him as a fellow student in an advanced philosophy seminar on ethics in 1964. Bayne commented: "It sounds maudlin, goofy even, but it's true! I also enjoyed the intellectual aspects of the game especially studying films." He credits Tindall, but especially McCarney ("one of my very few personal heroes") for showing him the way in the need to return the good fortune one has had so that others who follow may also benefit.

38 McCarney (in a personal interview) stated: "Watching Heino Lilles cut up through a hole off-tackle was one of the prettiest things I can remember about all of my years at Queen's" (the author would agree). "He was also one of the bravest, or the maddest depending on your view, players we ever had. At the end, after all those operations, he really had no knees left at all, and still he played. The knee brace [Dr] Melvin made for him, probably the first in Canada, helped. But still, he had a lot of guts" (ibid.).

CHAPTER SIX

1 *Queen's University Alumni Review*, November 1970, 150.

2 Ibid., 153.

3 Ibid., 154.

4 As we shall see, during the 1970s there was much coming and going of universities wanting to play football. These will be noted only as they impinge on Queen's directly.

5 *Queen's University Alumni Review* noted: "It was a long afternoon at the end of a very uneven session" (November–December 1971, 154).

6 For those interested in pursuing the details, the appropriate sources are as follows: Queen's University Archives (QUA), "Minutes of the Building Committee of the Board of Trustees," January 1964 – December 1965; "Minutes of the Board of Trustees," collection 1227, vol. 21–6, October 1966 – April 1972; and

"Minutes of the Principal's Advisory Committee on Athletics and the Athletic Board of Control," file 1254, box 16.

7 Today's Mackintosh Corry Hall.

8 QUA, "Minutes of the Board of Trustees" (motion no. 67-145), 17 and 18 November 1967, 5 (in collection 1227, vol. 22, 116). Originally, phase one of the new arts and social science complex was to go on the existing playing field (Tindall Field) west of the stadium; thus, the stadium would stay. But by the following March, the Building Committee had decided to construct the ASSC on the site of the existing stadium (retaining the playing field for the use of students) and to put the new stadium on the new West Campus or, possibly, up Highway 15 on the university's Vivarium property (QUA, "Minutes of Building Committee of the Board of Trustees," 17 March 1968, 3).

9 See QUA, "Minutes of Principal's Advisory Committee on Athletics and the Athletic Board of Control," file 1254, box 16.

10 Ibid., memo of October 1969.

11 Ibid., letter of Peter C. Thompson, 10 February 1970.

12 It is worth noting that McCarney, Bayne, Lilles, and others who valued intercollegiate sports, and football in particular, reacted to the Milliken Report and the political climate of the times by starting the Queen's Football Club (as mentioned above, an association of former players) to help protect and further football's interests. They also established the Queen's Football Hall of Fame to remind everyone of the important history of the game at Queen's and the achievements of many of its players in later life.

13 There is a whole other story here, which involves the university finding itself overcommitted to construction in the face of government cutbacks and needing to raise capital in a hurry. Suffice it to say that the funds for the new ASSC were in place by early 1970, so everyone knew that the 1970 season would be the last for the old stadium.

14 Donald MacIntosh, a strong supporter of the Milliken Report's philosophy, realized by this time that the new stadium would in fact live up (down?) to Harrower's conception, and he wrote several hurried memos to Deutsch pointing that the new stadium had no covered portion, that the seating was poor, and that it had a number of other major faults which required correction. He managed to obtain an extra $50,000 or so worth of changes (on a budget of $750,000), but that was it. The stadium thus finally cost the university $808,000 ($3.4 million in 1995 dollars) as opened in the fall of 1971 (QUA, "Minutes of the Building Committee of the Trustees," 29 February 1972, 4).

15 Hadden and Melvin, personal interviews.

16 In addition, of course, to the uncertainties around intercollegiate sports at Queen's stemming from the Milliken Report and the impact of the new stadium. Both were undoubtedly part of the explanation.

17 The *Queen's University Alumni Review* claimed that his retirement was marked by "more farewell appearances than Sarah Bernhardt!" (November–December 1973), 169.

18 Hargreaves (personal interview): "Besides it was too good an offer to turn down. I'd always loved Queen's, thought there were a lot of things I could do to improve on the program, and just had to take a run at it."

19 Edgeworth (personal interview) refers to 1976 as a watershed in his time at Queen's, which began with the 1974 season and ended with the 1978 season. "Suddenly there were new guys, lots of positive things."

20 All of those interviewed who played on the 1977 and 1978 teams (i.e., Mullen, Francis, Edgeworth) particularly noted the sour taste the Acadia loss left in their mouths and the motivational focus it provided for the 1978 team. Acadia went on to the College Bowl, to be beaten by Western 35–22.

21 Edgeworth (personal interview): "We just had this idea that we were not gonna lose! Period. Then, too, it has to be said that there was unbelievable luck thrown in on several occasions." See also the comments above about this peculiar psychology around winning teams.

22 Kingston *Whig-Standard*, 20 October 1978.

23 Ibid., 13 November 1978.

24 O'Doherty had won the Eastern league MVP award, but only Bakker was named an all-Canadian. Carleton and McGill on the other hand, which Queen's had beaten, placed two players each on the all-Canadian team.

25 A similar outpouring of student support at the time of a big game was forthcoming in the 1992 Vanier Cup season. But it should be noted that the attendance in Kingston at the earlier games running up to the College Bowl in Toronto had been nowhere near the 1968 totals in the old stadium. For example, the *Whig-Standard* reported that the Carleton and Bishop's playoff games drew about 3,500 people each, a far cry from the 10,000 in earlier times.

26 Kingston *Whig-Standard*, 20 November 1978.

27 Ibid., 21 November 1978.

28 His medical studies would not permit him to practise often during the week, and since he felt that this was unfair both to the team and his backup, he honourably chose not to play.

29 Many of these players had had outstanding careers. Two in particular figure high on the Queen's all-time scoring list, namely O'Doherty and Shore (see appendix B). As a back, O'Doherty had outscored both Lilles and Stewart, again narrowly missing Leadlay because of his lack of a kicking game. Shore, on the other hand, went quietly but dramatically to the head of the all-time scoring rankings on the strength of his kicking. Like Leadlay, he also scored touchdowns (from the flanker position), which helped him to accumulate points. He remained at the top until overtaken in the early 1990s by another kicker, Jamie Galloway.

30 *Globe and Mail*, November 1979. It is worth noting again that this fan and alumni enthusiasm for the big games did not seem to extend to regular home games. For example, the *Whig-Standard* reported that attendance for several of the games averaged about 2,500 people. While this was still large in comparison with any other Queen's sporting (or other) event, it was a far cry from the numbers regularly drawn in the old stadium.

31 University of Western Ontario officials report that it was the largest crowd ever to attend a Western athletics event to that point and that it was one of the two or three largest of all time (Hargreaves, personal interview).

32 *Queen's Journal*, 13 November 1979. This is as good and succinct a description as one could find of what it is like to be in a losing team's room after a big game.

33 Albinson (personal interview). As we shall see, this situation was remedied at the level of the physical education department in the mid-1980s so that by 1992 more detailed, program-specific expenses and revenues were available (albeit with some very changed accounting conventions in place). However, it must be noted that even at present, there is no system of financial reporting and validation by program in place to match that of the earlier Athletic Board (see table 8, for example), which gave a much clearer and audited picture of the revenues earned and the expenses of each of the individual intercollegiate sports programs at Queen's.

34 This would be a good MA thesis topic for someone in the Department – to attempt to reconstruct a sample of the 1970s and early 1980s financial statements by program from some of the old journal books that do exist. There is evidence, for example, that the budget for football in the 1978 Vanier Cup season, not including any playoff expenses, was to be about $20,000. This figure is essentially meaningless when compared with the earlier ones (e.g., table 8) because it does not include, for example, coaching salaries (which by the 1970s were covered out of general departmental funds and not by the programs themselves). As well, there are, of course, no direct football revenue figures available.

35 Hadden, personal interview.

36 This was an affair that pitted a Canadian college all-star team against an American one in post-season play. Begun in this period, it lasted only a few years (in one of which O'Doherty also played and starred – see below) before folding for lack of fan and financial support.

37 Harrison became Hargreaves's special teams coach after he retired from teaching in the late 1980s.

38 Edgeworth, personal interview.

CHAPTER SEVEN

1 I have been consistently amazed that each time, in coming to a new decade or era, the background history of events in the larger community and at the

university more generally has proved to be far richer and more complex than I remembered it to be. Perhaps the reader will have had the same reaction.

2 The year had been eventful, not only because the team had done better than expected, thereby raising fan spirit and hopes, but because a definitive stand on athletic scholarships had been taken when the issue was finally raised for discussion. In June 1980 the Canadian Intercollegiate Athletic Union (CIAU) had voted to grant athletic scholarships, but implementation was delayed for one year because of the "adamant opposition of the OUAA (Ontario Universities Athletic Association) who threatened to withdraw from the CIAU [over the issue]" (*Queen's Journal*, 18 September 1981).

In September 1981 a compromise was voted down at a special CIAU meeting. But the OUAA and Queen's both agreed to compete for one more year before a definitive decision to withdraw was taken or the CIAU changed its position. Queen's was opposed to athletic scholarships down the line, partly because of its position on academic admission standards and partly because intercollegiate competition was a small part of its total athletic programming and it did not want to bias its whole athletic program in favour of these sports (something it felt would be inevitable if athletic scholarships were permitted). So the 1981 season was played.

Over the next few years, the situation gradually resolved itself into the present arrangement, in which the OUAA has remained in the CIAU but gives no academic admissions scholarships to freshmen with any athletic aspects attached. But it does permit scholarships to be given in upper years which have a capped athletic component to them whereas elsewhere in the CIAU, freshmen scholarships with an athletic component (but requiring minimum academic requirements) can be given (as well as capped upper-year awards). It is a classic Canadian compromise which, based on the recent record of, for example, Vanier Cup play in football, permits an acceptable balance of competitiveness across the entire country.

3 Thus in the four seasons, including 1979, Queen's played Ottawa nine times losing seven times; five of the games were decided by one point, two more by three points or less, the remaining two by two touchdowns or less: in 1983 the teams played to two back-to-back ties in season play. It would be 1984 and following before the Gaels finally turned the won-lost record back in their favour with some large-point-spread victories.

4 This policy of capping the size of the university has been gradually changing, beginning in the late 1980s, so that by the 1994–95 academic year the university had some 15,000 students in total.

5 This situation is explained in greater detail in the conclusion, as is the one following – the issue of "acceptable" student behaviour at games.

6 The second of these games, at home, was the first of the new annual Hall of Fame games, in which the first group to enter Queen's Football Hall of Fame

were at last inducted after almost a decade of reflection by the selection committee over who deserved the honour. It was also the game in which the Gaels set a modern-day (to that point) CIAU record of 667 yards in total offence to serve notice of what they had.

7 There was continuing speculation, indeed suspicion, that some of the Concordia players had used steroids. However, no such belief was ever substantiated.

8 Trent Frayne, *Globe and Mail*, 12 November 1983. This is a vintage Frayne column, which I have chosen to reproduce in its entirety because of its priceless pieces of important historical observation. It was a treasure to uncover.

9 It is a little-noted fact, but one that appendix A confirms, that this supposedly "no-name" club scored more points than any other team in Queen's history to that point. This record lasted only one year, for the 1984 club put up even more points. Indeed, their 368 points are second only to the 397 amassed by the 1992 Vanier Cup team.

10 In this same week, Pep Leadlay, at eighty-four, and Bubs Britton at eighty – two greats of Queen's and Canadian football – died. Hargreaves remarked to the media in connection with Leadlay's passing, "If this were the U.S., the flags would be at half mast for a guy of that stature" (*Whig-Standard*, 11 September 1984).

11 The Atlantic Conference schools were back after a one-year's self-imposed exile from post-season play. The previous year, they had wanted to protest a CIAU ruling on transfer eligibility which they felt hurt their competitiveness. It was a time of considerable agitation about rules, conference alignments, and so on. For example, throughout much of the 1984 season, there was much discussion about realigning the Ontario-Quebec Conference because the "old four," McGill, Queen's, Toronto, and Western, were talking of going their own way and forming a league of their own. Ultimately it failed to come to pass because of a lack of student support in several of these places, especially Western, and because of strong and continuing protests from everyone else in the league, who stood to lose a great deal if such a realignment went ahead.

12 Kingston *Whig-Standard*, 19 November 1984.

13 *Globe and Mail*, 5 October 1985.

14 Others had earlier been nominated (e.g., Mohr), but Galunic finally did the trick.

15 Kingston *Whig-Standard*, 23 August 1989.

16 Several of those interviewed for this book who played in the game remember the cold, the size of the Huskies, the turnovers, and the enormous letdown and shock of it all after winning nine straight games and then being beaten so badly.

17 Elberg and Boone, personal interviews. Both were captains for the 1992 season, and in actions reminiscent of Edgeworth and D'Andrea before the 1978 season (coming off a similar loss, to Acadia, in the 1977 post-season), they

organized those meetings and with some of the other vets (such as Pendergast) generally led the way.

18 For a considerable number of years, Hargreaves had been hard at work through Football Canada, taking the message of Canadian football to the Europeans. He had made several visits to Holland and elsewhere on the Continent to hold clinics on the game, and had had some Dutch players in camp. Later, a German would also spend a season with the Gaels, as part of his academic exchange program, but he never dressed.

19 The trip also had the unintended consequence of giving Pendergast an opportunity to play for the summer in the English league. One of the teams recruited him after the game, and once he had been assured that his status and his ability to play in the fall were not at risk, he stayed to play. It is generally concluded that he came back a better quarterback for the experience.

20 Elberg, personal interview.

21 Kingston *Whig-Standard*, 23 November 1992.

22 *Sunday Sun*, 22 November 1992.

23 Ibid. Regrettably, the column is less charitable in its characterization of Saint Mary's, an approach that was probably not necessary to help the columnist make his point.

24 See the following chapter for a continuing discussion of this issue.

25 Kingston *Whig-Standard*, 10 April 1995. It is interesting to note that three of his present and former assistant coaches have won national awards for coaching in recent years: Miklas, who, counting his playing days and excepting the years when he was away at graduate school or on academic sabbatical, has given thirty-one years to Queen's football and is the longest-serving of all Queen's coaches by a considerable amount; Doug Smith (from Toronto); and Mullen.

26 Ibid., 15 November 1989. It notes, for example, that "unlike in the U.S. where a school can realize up to $2 million for appearing in a game like the Rose Bowl, though Saturday's game was telecast nationwide on TSN, Queen's gets no money for it."

27 Mr Tom Hopkins, the Gaels' equipment manager since 1977, worries that in fact the reverse is true – that equipment is getting so expensive that there is a severe danger that this cost alone could destroy the game at Queen's (Hopkins, personal interview). However, the figures suggest that he is getting considerably less money than his predecessors. Clearly, the problem is one of revenue, not expenses. (For more on the cost of suiting up a player see the concluding chapter.)

28 Schad, personal interview.

29 Hargreaves, personal interview.

30 Climie, personal interview.

31 Kingston *Whig-Standard*, 22 October 1988.

CONCLUSION

1 Kingston *Whig-Standard*, 10 April 1995.

2 I am grateful for the cooperation of the association in providing this sample.

3 A relatively small number in each sample had occupations that did not fit into the chosen categories. Rather than use a "miscellaneous" category, I simply dropped them from the sample.

4 For the statisticians, chi-square using a 0.05 significance level.

5 These results may change somewhat because the first degree of a certain number of the lawyers is in engineering or sciences. The general point, however, still stands.

6 An alternative explanation is that football somehow attracted the most "socially aspiring" (and less "intellectually aspiring") group of students, who would have ended up with this particular form of achievement in life independent of whether they had played football or not. This is possible but unlikely. That is, it is more likely that they had a special reason to want to "prove themselves" to others, that they did so by competing in the "socially valued" game at the "socially valued" highest level of education, namely university, and went on to become "socially valued" lawyers, doctors, teachers, and so on. In this sense, their personal drive for self-esteem coincided with a similar collective desire of the university, and helped establish the latter as well.

7 They have more directly contributed to this process as well in that anecdotal evidence suggests that many of the sons and daughters of the players attended the university after completing private schooling at lower levels.

8 There is some evidence in the historical record of occasional interuniversity competition in track and field. But it was an irregular thing and not particularly noteworthy.

9 One says "arguably" because the game clearly took off elsewhere in the 1920s, especially in American colleges. Also, given Queen's traditional role in the game (nearly fifty years to that point), it is likely that if Malcolm had not acted to keep the game going and bring it into the modern era, others eventually would have done so.

10 Both can be seen as a direct result of the more extensive sociophilosophical revolution that was the sixties' "cultural revolution" with its emphasis on individualism, noncompetitiveness, concern for the environment, and "one's place as another animal in the natural order or things."

11 Tom Hopkins, the equipment manager for the Gaels, has estimated that in 1995 it cost about $600 to suit up an individual player in game dress ($100 for a sweater, $75 for pants, $200 for the helmet, $150 for shoulder pads, $50 for thigh, kidney, and other pads, and $25 for mouth guards, gloves, and so on). If forty or so players dress for each game, that comes to $24,000. However,

the equipment is expected to last for two to three years. Thus, on a per game basis, the cost would be about $1,600 in total, or about $40 per player. It should be pointed out that helmets can be reconditioned and are not always purchased new, that all equipment except the game uniforms are also used for practices, and that many of the older game sweaters are sold off to the players after their useful life has expired. All in all, the cost of equipment on a "per session of football" basis would likely drop to less than $5 per player per year.

12 A better but still flawed (in the author's opinion) case in this respect is made in the book by Burton Nelson, aptly titled for present purposes, *The Stronger Women Get, the More Men Love Football* (New York: Avon, 1994). It is strongly recommended reading for a better understanding of the feminist critique of "Sexism and the American Culture of Sports" (the book's subtitle).

13 Some of these arguments were made in the discussion paper on "Queen's University's University Council on Athletics' Move to the 21st Century," April 1995, prepared by an ad hoc committee on fiscal responsibility (of the QUCA). It clearly recognizes that the present situation cannot continue, that choices will have to be made. It courageously points to a certain philosophy, and certain sports, that should be the focus of the program and invites comment. Football suffers from their treatment of it, and as a result, the paper has drawn considerable criticism (from the author among others; see *Queen's Alumni Review*, July–August 1995, 32).

14 Hargreaves, personal interview.

15 Cantelon, personal interview. As we have seen, there have been other periods when the game went through a downturn, but Cantelon is of the opinion that this time the very place of the game is being called into question, as opposed to the more circumstantial aspects of these earlier difficulties.

16 *Gentlemen's Quarterly* (GQ), April 1995, 167–9. *Sports Illustrated*, another popular magazine of long standing, in this case devoted to sport more specifically, carried a similar series of articles on the future of sport in a January 1995 issue.

17 *Globe and Mail*, 1 May 1995.

18 *International Herald Tribune*, 22 June 1995.

19 Mark Robinson, one of the co-captains of the Gaels in 1994 and a very reflective 300-lb. offensive tackle doing graduate work in engineering, stressed this point as well as several others that are noted below (Robinson, personal interview).

20 Regrettably, these situations always seem to be reactive in nature, perhaps because that is somehow human nature. Better that they should be proactive – seen ahead of time and rationally (if possible!) considered. For this reason, the attempt made by the committee of the Queen's University Council on Athletics (QUCA) to start the debate, in the Queen's context, is to be applauded.

21 CIAU support of certain competitions, research grants (of a certain type), support for certain carded athletes by Sport Canada, individual alumni booster clubs related to certain sports (e.g., the Football Club), and miscellaneous gate receipts (principally from basketball and hockey) are among the other sources of revenue.

22 As noted, Professor Albinson and the QUCA also are struggling to refine these estimates.

23 This remark should be identified as even more "editorial" in nature than many of the others in this chapter!

24 Indeed, the CIAU has reached a similar decision about the core importance of football to the support of its other programs (Lund, personal interview).

25 One can detect this theme as a subtext of, for example, the QUCA ad hoc committee's discussion paper.

26 Hargreaves and Howes, among others, have remarked on the fundamentally unhealthy situation of university students working at their academics full-time, exercising individually, and moving through the university without a real sense of the larger institutional family of which they are a part (Hargreaves and Howes, personal interviews).

27 One possible solution that has been suggested would be to take football off the budget, let it set its own ticket prices, and let it advertise, and otherwise promote the game through tailgate parties and other activities; i.e., generally permit football to pay its way (including facilities fees to the university). Any excess would be retained and used by the football program much as is done, for example, by the various executive programs that are run by the School of Business.

28 If this practice continues, no donor will give money to support individual sports of any kind, for the donor coult not be sure that it would remain there. Worse yet, donors might withdraw support already given. One such case, at McGill and involving football, has recently come to light. An award originally intended and traditionally given to football was given to an individual in another sport. A committee of the donors visited the principal and stated that the money would be withdrawn the next year if written assurances were not given that the monies would go where originally intended. Those assurances were given.

29 Cantelon (personal interview): "My growing experience with recruiting strongly indicates to me that there are a lot of kids out there who want to come to Queen's if we could just offer them something, anything really. In amongst them, we'd get a hell of a lot of football players as well." Alternatively, the federal and/or provincial governments might well consider developing particular scholarship or bursary aid of this form as a way of furthering their multicultural goals.

30 In the 1995 season, the Gaels, under interim head coach Bob Howes, went
    five and three. After forfeiting a first-game victory against Concordia for (of
    all things, at Queen's!) using an academically ineligible player, the team put
    together an impressive season, led once again by a league-leading defence
    and with the offensive contributions of some excellent rookies, especially
    Howes's son Beau at quarterback and Paul Correale, a fine running back pros-
    pect. They lost the OQIFC championship game to Ottawa in the last minute of
    play when a 115-yard punt return for a touchdown by Paul Greenhow was
    called back for an illegal block at midfield. However, the team had played
    well, earning it the title "those pesky Gaels" from one *Globe and Mail* reporter
    who liked their style.

Bibliography

ARCHIVAL SOURCES

Queen's University Archives
   Athletic Board of Control, minutes
   Board of Trustees, minutes
   Building Committee, minutes
   Frank Tindall, personal papers and films
   Principal's Advisory Committee on Athletics, minutes
   Wally Berry Photo Collection

OTHER SOURCES

"Athletics." *Queen's Review* 2, no. 7 (December 1937): 289–90.

Bally, D. "A Brief History on the Developmental Changes in Rugby Football in England Between 1800 and 1940." Bachelor's essay, School of Physical and Health Education, Queen's University, 1973.

Bumsted, J.M. *The Peoples of Canada: A Post-Confederation History.* Toronto: Oxford University Press, 1992.

Burton Nelson, M. *The Stronger Women Get, the More Men Love Football.* New York: Avon, 1994.

Calvin, D. *Queen's University at Kingston: The First Century of a Scottish Canadian Foundation, 1841–1941.* Kingston: Queen's University, 1941.

Clark, G. "Where Is the Secret of Queen's Success?" *Toronto Star Weekly Magazine*, 1 November 1924.

Cosentino, F., *Canadian Football.* Toronto: Musson, 1969.

– "Football." In *A Concise History of Sport in Canada*, ed. D. Morrow and M. Keyes. Toronto: Oxford University Press, 1989.

Danzig, A. *Oh How They Played the Game.* New York: Macmillan, 1971.

Edwards, J. "The Fearless Fourteen." Kingston *Whig-Standard Magazine*, 6 October 1984, 7.

Frayne, Trent. "Only Residue of Fierce Rivalry Remains." *Globe and Mail*, 12 November 1983.

Garvock, W. "How Rugby Began at Queen's." *Queen's Review* 11, no. 6 (August 1937): 164 8.

Gibson, Frederick. *Queen's University*, vol. 2, 1917–1961, *To Serve and Yet Be Free*. Montreal: McGill-Queen's University Press, 1983.

Globe and Mail, 1979.

Hamilton, H. *Queen's, Queen's, Queen's*. Revd. ed. Kingston: Queen's University, 1977.

Harvey-McKean, G. "Ontario Rugby: The Past and Future." Bachelor's essay, School of Physical and Health Education, Queen's University, 1990.

Herbert, J. *Rugby*. Weidenfeld and Nicolson, 1969.

Jenness, D. *The Indians of Canada*. Ottawa: National Museum, 1955.

Keegan, J. *The Face of Battle*. New York: Viking Press, 1976.

Leacy, F., ed. *Historical Statistics of Canada*. 2nd ed. Government of Canada, 1990.

Lester, R. *Stagg's University*. Bloomington: University of Illinois Press, 1995.

Lougheed, D. "Rugby at Queen's: A Sociological Investigation." Bachelor's essay, School of Physical and Health Education, Queen's University, 1990.

McLeod, P. "Reminiscences." Queen's University *Medical Bulletin*, 1966, 13–16.

Malcolm, I. "19th Century Bo Jackson Struck Out in the Classroom." *Queen's Gazette*, 25 November 1991, 12.

Marples, M. *A History of Football*. London: Secker and Warburg, 1954.

Metras, S. *The Metras Years*. London: Selby Young, 1983.

Morrow, D., and M. Keyes, eds. *A Concise History of Sport in Canada*. Toronto: Oxford University Press, 1989.

Neatby, Hilda. *Queen's University*, vol. 1, 1841–1917, *To Strive, to Seek, to Find, and Not to Yield*. Montreal: McGill-Queen's University Press, 1978.

Oriard, M. *Reading Football: How the Popular Press Created an American Spectacle*. Chapel Hill: University of North Carolina Press, 1993.

Owen, O. *The History of the Rugby Football Union*. London: Playfair, 1955.

Pierce, C. "The Future of Sport." *Gentleman's Quarterly* (GQ), April 1995, 167–9.

Queen's Alumni Review, 1927–95 (entitled *Queen's Review*, 1927–67; *Queen's University Alumni Review*, 1967–74).

Queen's Journal, 1881–1995.

Queen's University. *Queen's Bands: 75th Anniversary 1905–1980*. Kingston: Alumni Association/Alma Mater Society, Queen's University, 1983.

– "Queen's University's University Council on Athletics Move to the 21st Century." Discussion Paper, Ad Hoc Committee on Fiscal Viability of the QUCA, March 1995.

– *75 Years of Football + 10*. Kingston: Queen's University, 1983.

Reeve, T. "The 1937 Football Team." *Queen's Review* 2, no. 6 (August 1937): 181–3.

Reyburn, W. *A History of Rugby*. London: Barker, 1971.

Wakefield, W., and H. Marshall. *Rugger*. London: Longman, 1930.

Whig-Standard (Kingston), 1930–95.

Wymar, N. *Sport in England*. London: Harrap, 1949.

Young, J. *Dirty 30*. Toronto: Methuen, 1974.

Index of Names

Simurda, Dr, 107
Sirman, Bill, 113, 118, 130, 134
Skelton, D., 175, 253
Skene, Dave, 104, 113, 130, 134, 260
Skypeck, Tom, 112–13, 260
Sliter, Ernie, 37–8
Smith, David, 165, 172
Smith, Doug, 269
Snodgrass, William, 20
Sonshine, Harry, 70, 79
Sops, Peter, 160
Sprague, George, 72
Squires, Gord, 138
Stagg, Amos Alonzo, 24
Stefopulos, Tom, 166, 171
Stevens, Bob, 86
Stevens, Warren, 65, 73, 256
Stewart, Bruce, 118
Stewart, Ron, 93–9, 105, 123–5, 107, 116, 119, 124, 132–3, 146, 159, 193, 259, 262, 265
Stewart, Steve, 174
Stirling, Scott, 167
Stollery, Art, 81
Stoneham, Mike, 138
Strange, Fred, 18, 24, 247
Surphlis, Bill, 95–9
Sutton, Ike, 56

Taylor, Bryce, 121
Taylor, Jonathan, 183

Taylor, Robert B., 41, 44, 50, 52, 54–5, 59, 60, 251
Taylor, Tom, 140
Thomas, Bud, 48
Thompson, Jocko, 95–6, 99–100, 104, 106, 190, 193
Thompson, Peter, 114, 118, 131, 134, 142–3
Thomson, John, 147, 166
Thornton, Bernie, 72, 74–5, 79–80, 81
Tindall, Frank, 13, 67, 75, 80, 84–5, 90, 93, 95, 99, 103–4, 107, 109, 113–14, 116, 117, 119–21, 123–5, 129, 133, 138, 141, 143–8, 151, 170, 183–4, 194, 200–1, 209–10, 256, 259–60, 262–3
Tindall, Frank, Jr, 260
Turnbull, Jim, 123
Turner, Art, 39
Tyczka, Ted, 149, 153, 156, 160

Van Buskirk, Rick, 123, 125, 131
Vernon, John, 148–9
Voss, Carl, 49, 255

Waddell, John, 144
Walker, Doug, 123
Walker, Liz, 47, 48, 54
Wallace, Robert, 72–3, 90, 145, 255–6

Wardrop, Tim, 150
Ware, Jim, 114, 133
Warren, Freddy, 55
Warrender, Brian, 139–40, 156
Watson, W.A., 250
Watts, Ronald, 145, 147, 164–5
Waugh, Doug, 69
Webster, C.R., 29
Weir, Bob, 69
Whiteside, Dave, 144
Wicklum, Mike, 104, 112
Williams, Jack, 33, 34, 35, 39, 42
Wilson, Dave, 104
Wilson, John, 148, 163
Wing, Johnny, 70
Wintermeyer, John, 144
Wright, Bill, 152
Wright, Bob, 152–3, 161, 164, 166, 171, 186, 191
Wright, Dan, 175, 178, 180

Yates, H.B. (Yates Cup), 248
Young, Fred, 18
Young, Jim, 34, 113–14, 116, 118, 130–3, 261–2
Young, J.M., 33, 34
Yost, M., 24
Yovetich, Steve, 177, 180

Zarichny, Randy, 174, 176
Zvonkin, Abe, 66, 69, 79